ILLUSION
OF
JUSTICE

ILLUSION
OF
JUSTICE

Inside

MAKING A MURDERER

and America's Broken System

JEROME F. BUTING

HARPER

An Imprint of HarperCollinsPublishers

HarperCollins books may be purchased for educational, business, or sales pro-
motional use. For information, please e-mail the Special Markets Department at
SPsales@harpercollins.com.

FIRST EDITION

Designed by William Ruoto

Courtroom image © tlegend/Shutterstock

Library of Congress Cataloging-in-Publication Data has been applied for.

ISBN 978-0-06-256931-8

17 18 19 20 21   LSC   10 9 8 7 6 5 4 3 2 1

To my loving wife and law partner, Kathy Stilling,
and my children, Stephen and Grace

"If you judge people, you have no time to love them."

—ST. TERESA OF CALCUTTA

Contents

Preface

As a teenage boy, I was the gawky kid who dribbled a basketball off his leg, which is bad enough anywhere when you're fourteen years old. I happened to grow up in Indiana, one of the most basketball-crazy places in the world. So in freshman year of high school, I went out for the cross-country team. Through the farmlands and developing suburbs on the northwest side of Indianapolis, we would run five-mile loops along the flat ground around the school. At home I would pound across the rolling hills of my neighborhood. I could run and run. The challenge for me was starting on those hot, muggy mornings that are built into the Indiana summers. Once I got going, and found the right pace, I kept moving. Competitive sports were not for me, so I quit the team. But for years, I ran long distances. They are less about speed and more about time; staying with the run and covering the ground.

I write to you from midlife, fortunate to have survived a lethal disease that brought my running days to an end. But in my work as a criminal defense lawyer, I still cover long distances. Yes, some cases are sprints, or middle distances. Yet in others, getting to justice is a journey that spans decades. Once I get started, I keep going. It turns out that there is really no choice.

ILLUSION
OF
JUSTICE

OPENING
STATEMENT

On a blustery Wednesday afternoon, Dean Strang and I met at his office in Madison, Wisconsin, for our first discussion about representing Steven Avery, the most famous innocent man in the state's history. It was about 3:00 p.m., March 1, 2006.

At the very moment Dean and I started speaking, a new drama was coming to an end 135 miles away that we knew nothing about, but that would change everything. A sixteen-year-old boy was sitting on a couch in a room of the Manitowoc County Sheriff's Office. His moon face was hidden in his palms, which were pressed into his head. Seated next to him, the boy's mother tried to wrench off the mask formed by his hands, but his fingers would not yield. Leaning forward, elbows on his legs, head in hands, he was bent into the position people are instructed to take during a plane crash. He had spent nearly the whole day with interrogators, offering grunts and "yahs" to one leading question after another. One of his longest utterances was to ask if he could get back for a class at 1:29 p.m., explaining, "I have a project due in sixth hour."

A man spoke to the boy's mother, assured in his tone. "We've been doing this job a long time, Barb, and we can tell when people are telling the truth."

The boy's name was Brendan Dassey, and although his name was unfamiliar to Dean and me then, we would soon be finding out a lot more about him and what had happened that day.

While Brendan was seated, miserably, in Manitowoc, Dean and I spoke about my joining the defense of Steven Avery, who was accused of killing a woman at his family's auto salvage and burning her body. Dean had already been retained. For close to an hour, we had gone over practical matters like the division of labor; what had been learned by the public defenders who had been his lawyers when he was first arrested; the resources available from Avery to hire experts and investigators; and where the case stood. Up to that point, the charges seemed based on strictly circumstantial evidence.

Then the phone rang.

An Avery relative was calling. Dean's end of the conversation, at the beginning, was mostly "uh-huh"s and "yes"s, so I half listened and glanced around the office. On the walls, he had a few pieces of artwork depicting events in legal history, a scholarly interest of Dean's. He also had a standing desk, which not too many people were using at that time. It caught my eye because I'd had back problems a few years earlier. A trophy stood on a shelf, which I would later learn was for hurling. Hurling is an ancient Irish game, a tougher, more physical ancestor of field hockey. Dean didn't play, but a friend had given him the trophy as a present.

He and I were partners in different firms. We had worked together a few times, and I had high regard for his work and acumen. Dean wasn't part of the crowd that hung out in courthouse watering holes, but he was levelheaded and a relentless, hard-driving professional, quick on his feet. Also, he was hard not to like, which was important, because we were going to spend a lot of time together.

Now I could hear his side of the phone call take a turn.

"You've got to be kidding me," he was saying. "Arrested? The nephew? For *what*?"

At age forty-three, Steven Avery had already fallen once into the gulf between what is preached and what is practiced in America's criminal justice system. It took him more than two decades to climb out and less than two years to fall back in.

Steven Avery had spent eighteen years in prison for a sexual assault he had nothing to do with before the real culprit was identified through DNA testing and Steven was unequivocally cleared. Now Avery was facing an even more serious charge: the murder of a young woman,

Teresa Halbach, who had come to his family's auto salvage yard to take advertising photos for a trade magazine. In the story initially laid out by the authorities—before there was a trial, before anyone outside law enforcement had looked at any of the evidence—Avery's guilt was a foregone conclusion. Some of the victim's burned remains were found near a garage used by Avery. His blood was in her car. Her car key had been discovered in his bedroom. But this tidy narrative of detective work grew messier as details emerged about the peculiar circumstances under which the supposedly incriminating evidence against Avery had been gathered. Some of the investigators were not even supposed to have been on the Avery property, or indeed have anything at all to do with the case, because they were connected in various ways to the frame-up that had sent Avery to prison two decades earlier. Once their involvement was revealed, public certainty about Avery's guilt began to erode.

Even before this meeting with Dean, I'd been following the story on television and in the newspaper, like many other people in the Wisconsin area. My connection to it was deeper than most. I had *met* Steven Avery. As it happened, I'd served on the legislative task force that was set up to investigate what went wrong in his wrongful rape conviction, and to recommend reforms.

The Avery family ran its auto scrap yard in a place called Two Rivers, Wisconsin, which is just about halfway between the Atlantic and Pacific Oceans, not exactly the middle of the United States. But it's not far off. About a hundred miles north of Milwaukee and ten miles west of Lake Michigan, the scrap yard is in an area remote enough for a family of modest means to own forty-four acres of land. On it they stored thousands of cars, an inventory of discards that could be sold for scrap or parts. Family members lived in trailers or homes near the yard. It was a business, and it was a life. Not quite a true city, not a suburb, Two Rivers is a world apart, and the Averys lived on its outskirts. And it is in such forgotten places, among people from the wrong end of town or no town at all, that the ideals of our criminal justice system are stress-tested every day.

On that early March afternoon in 2006, no one would have expected that scrap yard, and the people living around it, to set off one of the most far-reaching discussions about the American criminal justice for generations. That millions of people would become absorbed by the Avery case a decade later was, at that moment, beyond conception. Improbably, it became the subject of a ten-hour, ten-episode television documentary, *Making a Murderer*, which riveted viewers in America and around the globe—most of whom had only a superficial understanding of our country's justice system. Like nothing else had before, it drilled deep into a world that was out of public sight, but where Dean and I had worked for decades.

The saga of Steven Avery, which unfolded in a sweeping narrative studded with intricate detail, stunned many as a portrayal of a badly warped American justice system.

Its twists and turns neared Shakespearean proportions, and I will deal with them in depth. But what happened to Steven Avery is not unique. So I write this book to widen the lens beyond that case, to try to show what the world looks like to people who are standing alone and accused and, many times, despised. As a defense lawyer, my place is by their sides. Far too often, to be charged with a crime is to become something less than human. It is my work to demand that my adversaries in court, the many who are honorable and the handful who are not, meet the requirements of the law. But there is much more to it than straightforward lawyering. Defense lawyers must fight not just to protect the legal rights of their clients but also to protect their clients' humanity, a frequent casualty of the leviathan machinery of the courts.

Across most of my career of thirty-five years, law enforcement has been granted a de facto monopoly on wisdom and truth telling, a presumption of virtue that has dragged us far from the bedrock principles on which American justice originated. The founders of the United States of America, who lived in an age of sovereign power that was cruelly and arbitrarily applied, were keen to create a nation that protected its citizens from government abuse and excess. This, John Adams declared in his closing argument for the defense in the 1770 Boston Massacre trial, was the formula for a secure and stable society.

> It's of more importance to community, that innocence should be protected . . . for guilt and crimes are so frequent in the world, that all of them cannot be punished. . . . But when innocence itself, is brought to the bar and condemned, especially to die, the subject will exclaim, "It is immaterial to me, whether I behave well or ill; for virtue itself, is no security." And if such a sentiment as this, should take place in the mind of the subject, there would be an end to all security what so ever.

Along with the ideals of freedom, justice, and human rights, the founding documents embedded the denial of full citizenship to people of color, a moral calamity that endures in our legal system and society long after the offending precepts themselves were struck from the laws. Imperfectly realized from the beginning, it was the more noble vision that made America for many around the world a "shining city on a hill" (the words of early Massachusetts Bay colonist John Winthrop, famously adapted by Ronald Reagan in his 1989 farewell speech).

But with greater regularity than people outside the system might expect, the American criminal justice system leads to results that are unreliable, unjust, and sometimes both. Our courts are less fair and more punishing than they ought to be. Unseen by global audiences of documentary viewers, men and women, some of them barely more than boys or girls, move through the machinery of the system every day on conveyor belts that rarely lead to trial. Instead, the vast majority of American criminal cases are resolved in negotiated pleas: deals made between lawyers for a sentence in exchange for an admission of guilt, rather than take the risk of a harsher punishment after a trial verdict.

Even when cases go to trial, the presumption of virtue accorded to prosecutors can obscure the truth, as I believe it did in the trials of Steven Avery. Most prosecutors are ethical people, dedicated to seeking justice and not simply racking up convictions, but there are many documented examples of individuals who corrupt the system by distorting the truth; by hiding or destroying evidence; and by misleading judges and juries to achieve, and maintain, a guilty verdict at all costs. Often this is done with at least the tacit approval of the officials under whom they serve. And many judges pay lip service to high-minded principles of fairness, yet all the while clearing the path to a preordained end.

That is certainly what happened in the case of Ralph Armstrong, whose story will be among those told in these pages. An innocent man who was convicted of a gruesome rape and murder, he was the victim of misconduct that took many years to surface. Armstrong became my client in 1993, and in March 2006—just as Avery was heading to court—his case was still in my portfolio, and moving toward a spectacular finish. Just before and during the Avery trial, there were extraordinary developments in Armstrong's case. They would resonate for years.

None of this is part of *Making a Murderer*, so Armstrong's story is little known outside Wisconsin. Yet the history of *State of Wisconsin v. Ralph Dale Armstrong* is critical to understanding why we should be wary of the presumption of virtue afforded to prosecutors. Some of them so firmly believe they have the public interest at heart that they cut corners with the truth and the rigors of due process. A defense lawyer must be skeptical when law enforcement or prosecutors, or both, try to control even the most "objective" processes, such as the scientific testing of evidence. Ralph Armstrong's epic odyssey foreshadowed some of the unsettling irregularities that emerged in Steven Avery's case. That it takes years, even decades, for unjustly convicted people to get a court to listen to them ought to be a matter for intense self-reflection by all parties in the system. Even people who are eventually vindicated have lost large, irreplaceable pieces of their lives. We should not mistake this illusion for justice.

Whether convinced of Steven Avery's innocence or guilt, most viewers of *Making a Murderer* agree that the investigation, prosecution, and trial of Teresa Halbach's murder were tainted by law enforcement conflict of interest; biased pretrial publicity generated by an unethical prosecutor; and evidence that led to more questions than answers about what really happened to Teresa. This is a travesty of justice for her, too.

Dean and I did not know all of this about Avery's case at our first meeting. But whether it was real or manufactured, we *did* know that the trouble Avery faced would not vanish on its own. He needed experienced criminal attorneys, and Dean and I were recommended to him by the lawyers representing him in his civil lawsuit for the earlier wrongful imprisonment.

And so it was that I came to be sitting in Dean's office, overhearing his phone call. His bewildered tone revealed more than what he actually said. After a few minutes, he hung up.

"Brendan Dassey has been arrested," Dean announced. "Avery's nephew. They're saying he confessed."

The family member who had called with this information knew nothing else, only that Brendan had supposedly confessed to something that put him in the middle of Teresa Halbach's murder, along with Steven Avery.

We began to think out loud.

Perhaps I should represent Brendan and leave Dean to handle Avery's defense? Dean had been on the case for a week or so and had already been out to the family property.

The prospect of representing Avery's sixteen-year-old nephew was tantalizing to me. Innocent or not, Brendan Dassey clearly needed a good lawyer to represent his interests, separate from those of his uncle. The law enforcement claims of a "confession" would have to be evaluated carefully. I had been practicing law long enough to know that, contrary to popular belief, innocent people do sometimes falsely confess, especially those who are young, or mentally impaired, or otherwise vulnerable. I also knew that Wisconsin state law had recently been changed to require that all juvenile custodial interrogation be recorded, so there would be video evidence of what Dassey had said to law enforcement—and, just as important, what they had said to him. But within a few minutes, we dropped the notion. For the past hour,

Dean and I had spoken as cocounsel, as lawyers entrusted with the affairs of Steven Avery, and so my duty to him had already begun even though the papers weren't formally signed. My involvement couldn't be called off, even after a mere sixty minutes. If Brendan Dassey and Steven Avery were both going to be tried for the murder of Teresa Halbach, each was owed the exclusive loyalty of his own lawyer.

In the months and years that followed, the thought crossed my mind that things might have turned out differently if I had been able to represent Brendan Dassey. That afternoon, though, we were in the dark about what the young man had supposedly said to incriminate himself. His family was just as shocked by this turn of events as we were. How had he come to confess? What did he say had happened? Was there any evidence to show that what he'd said was true?

We did a quick search online and found nothing useful. The special prosecutor handling the case, Calumet County district attorney Ken Kratz, would be making an announcement about the arrest on the evening news. There was not much we could do until we heard his account, so I drove back to my home in the western suburbs of Milwaukee, about an hour's journey. On the way, I heard a radio newscast of Kratz and the Calumet County sheriff, Gerald Pagel, giving a short press conference, and that evening I saw it on television. Both were dressed casually in sweaters, suggesting rapid developments that gave them no time to don jackets and ties; indeed, as I would later learn, they had literally rushed to hold the press conference as soon as the interrogation of Brendan had been completed.

Kratz and Pagel announced that a search warrant had been executed at the Avery property. A "sixteen-year old juvenile"—Brendan Dassey—was being held in a juvenile detention facility.

"The sixteen-year old juvenile admitted his involvement in the death of Teresa Halbach as well as Steven Avery's involvement in this matter," Sheriff Pagel said.

Kratz broke in. "Sheriff Pagel and I will be releasing to the media the specifics of this case. I will be filing, as I indicated, a criminal complaint tomorrow, and by 2:00 p.m., that will be available to all of you."

A reporter wanted to know if some of the same buildings that had been searched four months earlier, before Avery's arrest in November 2005, were being scoured yet again.

"Yes," Kratz replied. "We have done extensive searches on that property, with the degree of specificity that we received this week, knowing exactly what to look for and where to look for it, led to the issuance of today's search warrant."

So, having gotten some information from Brendan Dassey—though what, Kratz wasn't saying—the prosecution was able to go back in front of a judge and get another warrant.

Afterward, Brendan's mother, Barbara Janda, was interviewed on camera. She had a message for her brother, Steven Avery, who she said was surely watching from jail.

"You know, I hate you for what you did to my kid. So you can rot in hell."

In the studio, a news anchor listened to this report.

"What a story!" he said.

Part I

A PIXEL RARELY MAKES THE PICTURE

1

For every hour I spend in the courtroom during a trial, there's another two to five hours—at least—spent in preparation: studying evidence, interviewing witnesses, hiring technical experts, and writing motions arguing that this spadework, or some of it, belongs in front of a jury. It's hard for people not familiar with the practice of law to fathom the amount of time a case that goes to trial consumes outside of the courtroom, and preparation for the Steven Avery case was sure to dwarf the time necessary for most trials.

What this means is that getting involved with a case like Steven Avery's was not a decision I could make by myself. Given its complexity, work on the case would affect my professional and personal lives. Naturally, before I committed to joining Dean in representing Avery, I had to discuss it with my law partner and with my wife. Fortunately, they are the same person.

Kathy Stilling and I met in 1981, on our first day as public defenders in Milwaukee, got married in 1989, and eventually struck out on our own, joined by Dudley Williams. Ours was a boutique firm specializing in criminal defense, with enough serious clients for us to support our family but not so many that we could not give each one a full measure of effort. Our personalities and skills complement each other in the courtroom, so Kathy and I often teamed up over the years on hard cases, although it became harder to do jury trials together once we had young children. A few hours after my meeting with Dean, Kathy and I talked before dinner about what the Avery case would mean for us.

Rare is the scrap yard worker in trouble who can afford private defense lawyers, but Steven Avery was an unusual client by any measure. At the time of his arrest in the Teresa Halbach murder, he had almost no financial resources of his own—what kinds of assets can anyone accumulate during eighteen years in prison?—but he did have a $36 million wrongful conviction lawsuit pending against Manitowoc County, which had prosecuted him in 1985. During the pretrial discovery period for this civil suit, his lawyers had uncovered strong evidence that the authorities in Manitowoc had sat on information about another suspect, the person later revealed by DNA tests as the real culprit. Had Avery been able to go to trial on these civil claims, or at least continue negotiations for a settlement with the county, he would likely have wound up with a substantial pile of money. But with another criminal trial looming, and once again facing the prospect of life in prison, he was at an extreme disadvantage. He needed money, fast, and his civil rights lawyers knew this, too. A deal had been struck to settle the civil suit just a few days before Dean and I met. After fees and expenses for the civil suit, Avery was left with about $240,000. The harsh truth is that every remaining penny would have to go toward his defense.

We would put aside $20,000 for experts, investigators, and related expenses, which we already knew would not be enough. I would receive $100,000; Dean would get $120,000 because his firm, Hurley, Burish & Stanton, was larger than mine and would be the backstop when we ran through the expense budget, as we almost certainly would. It had lawyers in other, more lucrative lines of work besides criminal defense, such as civil litigation and commercial real estate. Given the economics of a law practice, Dean could take on a case that was likely to be a money-loser because his colleagues would be able to pick up the slack. Even with a fee of $100,000, my representation of Avery would put a strain on our firm, which was much smaller. The case would absorb nearly all of my attention for the next year; there were twenty-five thousand pages of documents and hundreds of hours of tapes of phone conversations Avery had while he was incarcerated, and technical evidence that needed to be slowly, carefully scrutinized. If I were to take on the Steven Avery defense, Kathy would have to keep our law practice going, handling all the work already on our calendar as well as any new business that might arrive.

Neither Dean nor I would get rich from this case. At one point, he figured that we had made $9 an hour after expenses. But money was not the point. This was the kind of profound challenge that a good attorney in the prime of his career should not shy away from. Kathy understood. A superb trial lawyer herself, she needed no lessons on why the toughest cases can be the most irresistible. Our biggest concern, though, was neither money nor person-power.

A few years earlier, I learned that I had a form of cancer of the soft tissue, synovial cell sarcoma—both extremely rare and usually lethal—in my right leg. A long siege of treatment and surgery had saved my life, but in the process I had lost a huge amount of tissue in the leg. A large flap of muscle from my abdomen had been disconnected at one end and flopped down to fill in the cavity left behind in my right thigh. It didn't function as muscle anymore. But still: My stomach was literally in my leg.

I was off work for an entire year, while Kathy took care of me and our two young children and largely ran the law firm. The Avery trial would not be my first time back in court. But was I healthy enough for a case that would not only mean the routine, grueling ordeal of a trial but also the added weight of wall-to-wall press coverage? I had been going for CT (computed tomography) scans every three months and they had all been clear, so the doctors had recently dialed them back to once every six months. But I had not yet reached the arbitrary milestone of clear scans for five years, so there was also the ever-present fear that any cancer survivor fights in those first few years—that the cancer could return and disable me again, or worse.

"You can do this," Kathy said. "You're ready."

This was not a "rah-rah" speech from someone just trying to tell me what I wanted to hear. For months and months, Kathy had nursed and fed and watched over me every day; one person fighting for my life, my mind, and my soul like a platoon of marines. No one was better situated than she was to give me a straight answer. If she said that I was ready, I believed her. However, we also had two teenagers in the house: our son, Stephen, then fourteen, and our daughter, Grace, twelve. At these ages, kids probably need more supervision than at any other time.

Neither Kathy nor I had family in town who could watch them. While I was off defending Steven Avery, she would have to run our business and our household. So she added one caveat: With all that she would be shouldering, she would not directly take on any of the work in the matter of Stern Avery.

"You're doing this case on your own," Kathy said. "It's going to be you and Dean."

2

By 2006, Dean and I had known each other for more than fifteen years. We had worked on a number of criminal cases together, representing codefendants, but those had not actually gone to trial. We also had never worked at the same law firm or otherwise had a reason to see each other on a daily basis. This would soon change.

Dean is four years younger than I am, but I'd heard about him early in his career. He had no interest in being a lawyer when he was growing up. He'd wanted to be an editorial cartoonist for a newspaper and pursued that for a while at Dartmouth College. But he changed his plans when he realized a cartoonist can only lampoon others, not solve the problems he points out. Dean went on to law school at the University of Virginia, graduating in 1985. He started in a large civil law firm and spent about a year as a federal prosecutor in Milwaukee before he was lured away by Jim Shellow, one of the nation's leading criminal defense lawyers. Dean spent the next nine years at Shellow, Shellow & Glynn, which, coincidentally, was one of the firms that handled Steven Avery's unsuccessful appeal of his 1985 wrongful conviction. One of the other partners, Steve Glynn, later teamed up with Walt Kelly to represent Avery in his civil rights lawsuit against Manitowoc County.

Dean and I had collaborated several times while he was at the Shellow firm, before he left to become the first federal public defender in the state of Wisconsin—telling the Federal Defender Services of Eastern Wisconsin's board of directors at the outset that he would do the job for no more than five years. Dean did not want to make a career out of the position, but he could see that he was the right person to get the new program off the drawing board. True to his word, Dean left late in 2005 to join the criminal defense division of Steve Hurley's law firm in Madison.

Dean had been there only a few months when he received a call from an Avery family member, asking if he would represent Steven Avery in the Halbach murder case. Dean had to run it by his new employer first, because the demands of Avery's case would take him out of the rotation for other business. Then he asked me to join him in the defense. Avery had been given both of our names on the advice of his civil rights lawyers, and Dean was hoping we could split the responsibilities.

From the outset, I was thrilled at the prospect of working with Dean on such a complex case. I knew we would make a good team and formidable opposition for prosecutors Ken Kratz, Thomas Fallon, and Norman Gahn. We respected each other's intelligence, and neither of us had any doubt that the other would thoroughly complete whatever task he was assigned. This kind of trust is important, because it means you don't ever feel like you have to be doing your partner's work as well as your own. We also shared the same ideals, and still do. Each of us has a deep passion for justice and great compassion for our clients, many of whom are utterly incapable of standing up for themselves within America's criminal justice system. It's frustrating when we see it fail them, but that just makes us dig in our heels and fight harder.

The Avery case would test our faith in this system like few others. It had all the elements of the awesome power of the government juggernaut arrayed against one man, who had been an outcast his whole life. In most small towns in America, there is usually at least one person who is viewed with suspicion by the community, and treated poorly by local officials, from an early age. They become the "usual suspect" in the cops' eyes, and there was a history of this in Steven Avery's life. We both instinctively understood where Avery stood in the world and knew that our place was to give him our best defense. Until we got on the case, though, we had no idea how far law enforcement would be willing to go to ruin Avery and scuttle his embarrassing lawsuit against his home county. We were all that stood between Steven Avery and a steamroller.

I really like Dean and enjoy his company, which is a not insignificant factor if you are going to be doing a six-week trial together. Trials, and the preparation leading up to them, are intense and consuming undertakings, and all the more stressful if you aren't getting along with cocounsel. We did take the precaution of getting separate apartments in Appleton, a small Wisconsin city of about seventy thousand where we would stay while the trial was ongoing, so we could have some time away from each other, but most of that we spent sleeping. Otherwise, we were together in court or together preparing for court.

Professionally, we complement each other's strengths and shortcomings. I've always had a particular interest in forensic evidence issues and scientific testing in criminal cases, so I generally took the lead on those aspects of the Avery defense. Dean is a magnificent lawyer, with an aptitude for legal writing and analysis. He is also extremely well read and calls himself a student of how the legal system treated outsiders and people at the margins of society during America's Progressive Era. Others might say a scholar: He is the author of a book about a little-known trial of anarchists in Milwaukee in which Clarence Darrow played a leading role, and he has been working on a second book about an extraordinary 1918 trial of more than one hundred members of the Industrial Workers of the World labor union.

By nature, I tend to be a little more aggressive than Dean, who is always a consummate gentleman in the courtroom. Almost by default, we slipped into good-cop-bad-cop roles with the prosecutors and witnesses in the Avery case. I had never handled a case against Ken Kratz before this, and I was so outraged by his March 2006 press conferences that I wasn't sure how I would work with him. It soon became no secret that Ken Kratz and I did not get along, although before the trial we were generally civil to each other. Dean was the primary conduit between us, while I preferred to deal with the two other prosecutors on the case, Fallon and Gahn, whom I've always respected.

Dean's eloquence was known to me long before we represented Avery, and *Making a Murderer* captured him speaking naturally and profoundly, in fluid prose. It was no accident that some of the most memorable statements in the documentary came out of his mouth. After Ken Kratz complained that the state would be put at such a disadvantage by a legal ruling that it would be like swimming upstream, Dean famously replied: "All due respect to counsel, the State is supposed to start every criminal case 'swimming upstream.' And the strong current against which the state is supposed to be swimming is the presumption of innocence."

3

An auto salvage yard might look chaotic, but it has its own logic. What some people may think of as oily junk is inventory, an asset to the business—potentially a hard-to-get part for a repair, or a bargain on a serviceable transmission or engine. Scrap aluminum can also be melted down for sale, and the Averys had a smelter on-site for that purpose.

Dean was waiting for me at the Avery scrap yard when I arrived for my first visit, video camera in hand to capture the state of the place. It was a sunny day, unseasonably warm for early March in Wisconsin. I wore a spring raincoat instead of my winter overcoat, and tall, buckled boots because the ground was thawing and muddy. I intended to walk through rows of thousands of junked cars in the "pit," a recessed area of the property and part of the old quarry that used to occupy the land before it was turned into an auto salvage yard. Dean and I wanted to see all of the access points to the property, including dirt roads that led off through neighboring quarries.

Investigators had just been through the scrap yard for a second round of searches. The first had been in November 2005, after Teresa Halbach disappeared, when they shut down the yard and business for eight days. They had just come back now, the following March, after Brendan Dassey's interrogation and confession.

We walked along rows of cars in various states of assembly, then traipsed into the trailer where Steven Avery lived. It had already been searched multiple times and had been left uninhabitable. All the carpeting had been torn up from the floor in the living room and down the hallway into Steven Avery's bedroom, leaving only the padding behind. In the bedroom, sheets and cases had been pulled from the mattress and pillows. Large strips of wood paneling were pulled off the wall behind the bed and to one side of it, near a closet. A few pieces of furniture had clearly been moved around and some drawers left open, but beyond the disorder caused by the searches, both those done in

November and the more recent ones, there was nothing to the naked eye that suggested a violent crime had taken place there. We went outside to look at Steven Avery's garage. Its concrete floor had been recently jackhammered, apparently in the wake of Brendan Dassey's statement.

My camera was a handheld Sony VHS-Hi8, not quite the top of the line but adequate for my purposes. As it happened, I was not the only one at the yard that day with a camera. Two women emerged from the home of Steven Avery's parents, carrying their own video gear. Their names were Laura Ricciardi and Moira Demos, graduate film students from New York, and they planned to make a documentary about the Avery case. A few months earlier, they had read a front-page article in the *New York Times* about this wrongly convicted man who had been exonerated, freed, and then charged in a new murder case. Almost immediately, they'd rented a car and driven out to Wisconsin to follow the story.

By now they had already been at work for more than three months, filming the court proceedings and interviewing the Avery family and other participants in the saga. Dean and I had known about them and their project before this encounter from our discussions with the Avery family, though neither of us realized they would be at the Avery property when we got there. As a rule, lawyers are cautious in dealing with the press. No matter how we hope to shape coverage, journalists cannot be controlled. Material that makes a good story does not necessarily advance the interests of your client. But in this case, Steven Avery had already made his decision: Laura Ricciardi and Moira Demos had written to him in jail, and he'd agreed that members of his family would be available for interviews. That's how they came to be visiting with his parents, Allan and Dolores, when I arrived.

We couldn't stop them, of course, but Dean and I had to decide how much to cooperate with them, Steven Avery's permission and cooperation notwithstanding. So we all chatted in the yard, giving me a chance to take their measure. Both filmmakers impressed me with their intelligence and the seriousness with which they were approaching the project. They had been out in the world before going to film school. Ricciardi had a law degree—at one point she had worked as a law clerk in a federal prosecutor's office and as a lawyer in the Federal Bureau of Prisons—and so was attuned to the legal process. She understood the importance of the privileged nature of communications between lawyers and their clients and respected it. Moira had more experience in the production of television and film. Before going back to school, she'd worked on the crews of television shows and several movies. Though somewhat reserved, she showed a droll side when she did speak.

Eventually, they rented an apartment in the area, close to the Manitowoc County Courthouse and within driving distance of the Avery yard. It was clear that they were in it for the long haul, making an extended documentary that would not air until well after the trials of both Steven Avery and Brendan Dassey. By following our preparation, they could pull back the curtain on pretrial processes that most people are barely aware of, much less familiar with. As far as I knew, only one documentary had gotten into the nuts and bolts of a criminal prosecution from this perspective, a film called *The Staircase*, about a 2003 murder trial in North Carolina. But the defendant in that case, a successful novelist and newspaper columnist, with substantial financial resources for lawyers, experts, and investigators, was from a different world. In their salvage yard, Steven Avery and his family lived apart from even those in small-town Wisconsin. Hardly any attention had been paid to the experiences of people from their economic class or to how their contact with the criminal justice system generally unfolded. The subject was worthy, the risk to our client seemed minimal, and perhaps there might even be benefits.

Although they were cordial and pleasant to be around, from the outset the filmmakers made their own judgments about the case and the story they were going to tell. They were also seeking access to the prosecutor and the offices of the two sheriffs. If Dean and I botched up something important during the case, it would undoubtedly become part of their film—if it ever actually got made.

As I write this book a decade later, it's worth remembering that in early 2006, Facebook was just two years off the ground and still dueling with the dominant social network, MySpace, which it has since vanquished and all but consigned to history. No one had heard of Twitter because the company had not yet been launched. No such thing as an iPhone or iPad existed—except as a concept in Steve Jobs's mind. Above a pizza parlor in San Mateo, California, a company called You-Tube was in the early days of figuring out how to share video online. And television series and movies came into people's homes on cable and broadcast channels, not on the Internet. Or you could carry them into your house by renting a DVD or a BluRay disc in a store. The biggest chain, Blockbuster, had nearly sixty thousand employees at nine thousand locations. A few years before, it had turned down a chance to buy a mail-order DVD rental company called Netflix for $50 million. There were some people in the Internet world saying that, someday, consumers would even be able to stream films and TV series right into their homes over the Internet. But if I had even heard about that prospect then, it was still a long way off.

Bright and committed as the two filmmakers were, they were two students working on a shoestring budget, and they had no expectation of getting any support from a distributor until they had something to show. Their capital was energy and brains, not money. Who knew if they could even *make* a film, let alone if anyone would ever see it (outside of perhaps a few dozen people in an art-house theater in New York City)—or if, in the expediencies of editing, the finished product would be faithful to the events as they unfolded?

Dean and I had a client to defend, and, as far as we were concerned, the most important audience for our work would be the twelve people sitting in the jury box. It was hard to imagine the public at large ever really crawling into the rickety, unsightly machinery of criminal justice. In any event, would people accept that misconduct, sloppiness, and error are as much part of it as any other human endeavor?

4

Dressed this time in suits and ties, Kratz and Sheriff Pagel took the stage for their press conference on March 2, 2006, with great ceremony and a touch of P. T. Barnum's sanctimony. Before getting into the details, Kratz warned, people who knew Teresa Halbach should not listen. And there was more.

"I know that there are some news outlets that are carrying this live, and perhaps there are some children that may be watching this. I'm going to ask that if you're under the age of fifteen that you discontinue watching this press conference."

After a brief, conspicuous pause, presumably so children could be shooed away from the television—or so people would have a chance to raise the volume—Kratz commenced his story. "We have now determined what occurred sometime between 3:45 p.m. and 10:00 or 11:00 p.m. on the thirty-first of October," he said.

Then he and the sheriff regaled the public with what they billed as a chronicle of Teresa Halbach's last hours. At that moment, no one knew for sure what evidence they had drawn on to construct their narrative. In time, though, it would emerge that they had but a single source: Brendan Dassey, sixteen years old, a special education student with a below-normal IQ who had been questioned for hours without a teacher, parent, or lawyer at his side. This is how Kratz began his narrative:

Sixteen-year-old Brendan Dassey, who lives next door to Steven Avery in a trailer, returned home on the bus from school about 3:45 p.m. He retrieved the mail and noticed one of the letters was for his uncle Steve Avery. As Brendan approaches the trailer, as he actually gets several hundred feet away from the trailer, a long, long way from the trailer, Brendan already starts to hear the screams. As Brendan approaches the trailer, he hears louder screams for help, and he recognizes it to be of a female individual. He knocks on

Steven Avery's trailer door. Brendan says he knocks at least three times and has to wait until the person he knows as his uncle, who is partially dressed, who is full of sweat, opens the door and greets his sixteen-year-old nephew.

Kratz continued:

Brendan accompanies his sweaty, forty-three-year-old uncle down the hallway to Steven Avery's bedroom. There, they find Teresa Halbach, completely naked, shackled to the bed. Teresa Halbach is begging Brendan for her life. The evidence that we've uncovered establishes that Steven Avery at this point invites his sixteen-year-old nephew to sexually assault this woman that he has bound to the bed. During the rape, Teresa is begging for help, begging sixteen-year-old Brendan to stop, that you can stop this.

The story was compelling, and ghastly, but what was truly depraved about it—that it was essentially spoon-fed to Brendan by law enforcement—would not become clear until much later.

Kratz's recitation did not resemble how Brendan Dassey told the story, *ever*; it is doubtful that Brendan was even capable of assembling a coherent account, true or false. And when it came to the narrative's awful particulars, we later learned that Brendan had come up with virtually none of them by himself. He had only confirmed them after repeated long sessions with detectives who prodded, pushed, threatened, suggested, and pleaded until this version of events had been assembled, one gruesome moment after the next. Virtually none of this would become known to the public for well over a year. The full scope of those interrogations was a dark secret kept even from Brendan Dassey's own jury. After the trials in the Halbach murder were over, it would become my mission to expose the web of silken lies, promises, and threats that were used to bind Brendan. Untangling it was an arduous task, and it would be years before people paid attention.

But for the moment, I was pinned to the screen, listening and watching.

"After the sexual assault is completed," Kratz said, "Steven Avery tells Brendan what a good job he did. Takes Brendan into the other room and now describes for Brendan his intent to murder Teresa Halbach."

He was painting a picture of agony in her last minutes on earth and leaving no color on the palette untouched. This level of specificity about a crime is normally reserved for a courtroom, where it will be subject to the scrutiny of a judge before being presented to a jury— and then, only in opening and closing statements. There are powerful reasons why ethical prosecutors refrain from putting on precisely this kind of spectacle. It was a one-sided story that would be the lead item of every television news program. Inevitably, such presentations pollute the jury pool with assertions unmediated by a judge and untested by the defense. And, as Kratz should have known at the time of his press conference, from prior searches of Steven Avery's residence, these particular assertions were unprovable.

"Brendan watches Steven Avery take a butcher knife from the kitchen and stab Teresa Halbach in the stomach," Kratz continued. "What Steven Avery does then, while Teresa is still begging for her life, is he hands the knife to the sixteen-year-old boy and instructs him to cut her throat. Sixteen-year-old Brendan, under the instruction of Steven Avery, cuts Teresa Halbach's throat but she still doesn't die."

The story was starting to bother me, and not because it could not have been more awful. In fact, it was *too* awful. Steven Avery stabs her? Brendan Dassey cuts her throat, and she doesn't die? Kratz kept adding new assaults: Avery begins punching this woman in the face, who in Kratz's account had already been raped, stabbed in the stomach, and slit across her throat.

This was not the end, either.

"There's additional information which includes manual strangulation and gunshot wounds," Kratz said.

They strangle a woman whose throat they'd cut? And they shoot her? I am temperamentally inclined to skepticism—or maybe it's a result of decades spent in criminal courts, where every story has a tilt. This one felt so tilted it could collapse. It was, literally, overkill.

At the news conference, a few reporters were able to back away from the flood of horror to ask if this story was shored up by physical proof.

"Is there any DNA evidence backing up the kid's story?" one asked.

Since Kratz was using the press conference to essentially make an opening statement in a trial, the question was perfectly logical. It cut to the core of the entire narrative that Kratz had just recited.

The prosecutor seemed to have anticipated it. "Yeah, we're not going to comment on that," he said, suddenly coy. He drew a breath. "We obviously have a lot of evidence and I guess we can say," he continued, "that there is a substantial amount of physical evidence that now makes sense, fits a lot of pieces together."

In fact, scarcely an iota of Brendan Dassey's story would *ever* be corroborated by physical evidence. But despite two centuries of American jurisprudence on due process, there is almost nothing stopping a prosecutor like Kratz from claiming that a "substantial amount of physical evidence . . . now makes sense" when laboratory test results proved just the opposite in almost every instance.

Scrutiny of the criminal justice system rarely makes it into the public eye. In public, cops and prosecutors are almost invariably seen as wearing white hats. For good reason, Kratz might well have had no worries about being called to account if the story that came out of his mouth at that press conference turned out to be contradicted by virtually every piece of physical evidence. Brendan Dassey never testified against Steven Avery—his account would have been shredded by Dean and me. And where else might Kratz's narrative be challenged? At press conferences, no one can make you answer an inconvenient question. For Kratz, Brendan Dassey was at his most useful as a Gothic specter on dozens of news broadcasts, contaminating the jury pool for hundreds of miles; paradoxically, he would have been most dangerous to the prosecution at the Avery trial, where he would have been both a witness to and an exhibit of investigative excess.

Cops and prosecutors often *are* the good guys. Just not always. And sometimes, they go far afield. It was starting to look like the Avery case was going to be one of those times, and we were soon going to see how twisted their pursuit had become.

The prosecution did not hold a monopoly on the travesties that afflicted Brendan Dassey's case. Some were captured on camera, but a few critical ones were not. The day after Kratz's gruesomely detailed press conference, Brendan was brought into court for his first appearance in front of a judge. Even with all that has happened since *Making a Murderer*, an important part of that day has still largely gone unnoticed and unremarked upon.

When a person accused of a crime goes before a judge for the first time, it is generally a routine proceeding. Under our system, police and prosecutors cannot unilaterally decide if someone can be held in jail after an arrest; within a day, the authorities must appear before the judge and explain, briefly, why they believe this person committed a crime and then address what bail conditions, if any, are suitable. Then the judge decides how to move forward.

The prosecution almost always succeeds in meeting the low standard of proof required at this stage. Often an affidavit or complaint sworn by an investigating police officer will suffice. But that does not mean the defense should write this initial appearance off as a pointless ritual. At this time, the defendant has the right to ask for a preliminary hearing, which forces the prosecutor to call witnesses who can then be cross-examined by the defendant's lawyer. A preliminary hearing is not a trial, and in the overwhelming majority of instances it will not unwind a prosecution before it even gets going. But it is not an exercise in futility, as good lawyers can pick up a few nuggets of insight into the strength of the state's case, or even point out unexpected weaknesses. These can be valuable because most charges are resolved in plea bargaining, and the terms of a negotiated deal often depend on how strongly motivated the prosecution is to avoid a trial. If there are potential weaknesses in the state's case, the defense should try to find them before going into plea negotiations. For any good defense attorney, it's just common sense.

This was particularly true back in 2006, when Wisconsin courts did not yet allow most hearsay evidence at preliminary hearings, so live witnesses could be called and questioned, and the plausibility of their testimony could be probed. On that day, Brendan was represented for the first and only time by Ralph J. Sczygelski, a private lawyer appointed by the court. He immediately adopted Kratz's narrative, with a minor modification, saying of Brendan: "He essentially has been victimized by Mr. Avery as well."

The judge set bail at $250,000 bond, which was well beyond the means of Brendan's mother.

It is customary, during that first appearance, for defense lawyers to request a preliminary hearing even if they do not intend to go ahead with one. These hearings may not be held for up to another ten days, and the defense can drop the request before, or even on the day of, the hearing itself. That was not how Ralph Sczygelski handled it. On the day of that initial appearance, he waived Brendan Dassey's right to a preliminary hearing on the spot. Later, he told reporters: "In my opinion, putting that before the judge and both families would be very horrible and not fruitful in any way."[*]

As it turned out, "both families" he was sparing from the preliminary hearing included one Sczygelski himself was related to. A few hours after waiving this important right to which Brendan Dassey was entitled, Sczygelski withdrew from the case because, it was reported, he had just learned that he was a distant relative of Teresa Halbach. These circumstances bewildered me. Ms. Halbach had been murdered four months earlier, and the case had been one of the leading news stories in the area since. But it wasn't until *after* Sczygelski appeared in court to defend Brendan Dassey against charges of first-degree intentional homicide, sexual assault, and mutilation of a corpse that he learned the victim was a member of his family? Well,

* Associated Press, "Boy 16, Pleads Not Guilty to Brutal Rape and Murder," March 4, 2006, *Beloit Daily News*. http://www.beloitdailynews.com/wisconsin/boy-pleads-not-guilty-to-brutal-rape-and-murder/article_ec782efa-7b0a-52ee-97d2-11582ad540f4.html.

whenever he found out, his representation of Brendan became an un-ambiguous conflict of interest.

A few days later, a lawyer named Len Kachinsky was named as the substitute. Greeted at the courthouse by a swarm of reporters, he was keen to express his horror at what had been done by Steven Avery and his own client.

"We have a sixteen-year-old who, while morally and legally respon-sible, was heavily influenced by someone who was evil incarnate," Kachinsky told them.

At the time he made this statement admitting his client's guilt, he had not yet even met Brendan Dassey, much less spoken a word to him. I didn't know that then, but I did know Kachinsky. Two decades earlier, I had been one of the charter founders of the Wisconsin Asso-ciation of Criminal Defense Lawyers, which had representatives from each of the judicial districts in the state. Kachinsky had signed up as the representative of the Fox Valley area district, which included Apple-ton and Oshkosh. He'd attended some board meetings, then eventually dropped out after a few years. I hadn't spoken to him in ten or fifteen years; now we were about to reconnect, if only fleetingly.

As shocking as Kachinsky's statements had been to the press on his first day, he was still Brendan Dassey's lawyer. The next time he was in court on some routine matter connected with the case, I sidled up to him and spoke about Sczygelski, the lawyer he had replaced.

As I recall, I said, "Len, this guy gave up an important statutory right to a preliminary hearing when he was conflicted out and should never have been on the case. You can file a motion to get the prelimi-nary hearing back. This waiver was void."

Kachinsky just kind of smiled and said, "Oh, okay, I'll think about it."

He was not at all enthusiastic. He was signaling, without explicitly saying, that he wasn't going to file that motion.

If there was any doubt that Kachinsky wasn't going to be aggressive in representing Brendan, this omission made it plain. Asking to with-draw that waiver of a hearing was a simple, obvious thing *any* good lawyer would do, a declaration on behalf of the client. Even if Kachin-sky did not yet realize that Brendan maintained that he was innocent, at the very least the hearing could improve his client's leverage in ne-gotiations: *I'm going to file this motion, we have a right to this, and the lawyer who waived it should never have been on the case to begin with. We're going to challenge this statement from Day 1, including having a preliminary hearing about it.*

Two weeks later, Ken Kratz was in court asking that Steven Avery's bail—which had been set at $500,000 months earlier—be raised to $2 million. Dean Strang countered that Avery should be allowed to put up a mortgage on the family property. Avery had been giving interviews to the press asserting his innocence, and there was no sign that he was going to flee.

The Manitowoc County circuit judge presiding on the case, Patrick Willis, raised it to $750,000. The reason, he said, was new evidence from Brendan's statement showing more violence than previously charged.

"This is no longer a purely circumstantial case," Judge Willis de-clared.

This meant the prosecution of Steven Avery for the death of Teresa Halbach no longer appeared to rest on a chain of circumstances such as the presence of her burnt remains on the Avery property or the drops of Steven Avery's blood supposedly found in her car. Now, through the words of Brendan Dassey, Kratz was claiming direct evidence of Avery's involvement in the crime. It was not obvious to the general public, or even to the judge, that Brendan's account would never actu-ally become part of the official evidence against Steven Avery. Neither was it apparent that Brendan's account was so impossible, so addled, so *contrary* to the physical evidence that the prosecutors would not dare make him a witness.

Nor was there much discussion, if any, in those early days about Len Kachinsky's decision not to bother with a preliminary hearing or the scope of his surrender.

Of course, for people who followed the documentary and could see the entire arc of the case, ten years on, the significance of these events could not be more plain. However, in the rush of claims and jarring moments that make up the start of a trial, it was not easy to grasp their importance. But after having practiced criminal defense work for many years, I know that a single episode or two, especially taken out of context, does not necessarily decide a case; a pixel rarely makes the picture.

My education in seeing the whole picture began in my earliest days in the law, more than twenty-five years before I took on the Avery case.

5

I was the third in a family of seven children, arriving in the world in September 1956. For most of my childhood, we lived in a part of Indianapolis that had not been fully urbanized. Our split-level house on the edge of cornfields had two full bathrooms, plus one half-bath that never worked, and the generally happy and nonstop chaos of a big family.

Our mother, Margaret Mary Bateman, was born in North Carolina. Her family moved to French Lick–West Baden Springs, Indiana, during the Depression, in pursuit of work in the area's famous resort. She met our father after World War II, while she was studying for her master's in organic chemistry at Purdue University and he was there completing his doctoral studies in the same field. His name at the time was Walter Butinsky. Shortly after they married, though, he changed his last name to Buting. We always heard that he did that because he was concerned that even though he had fought in the Battle of the Bulge and won a Purple Heart, a foreign-sounding name could cause problems in the early 1950s, when Senator Joseph McCarthy was conducting witch hunts of so-called subversives. Many years later, a more complicated story emerged, and it seemed that the name change was an act of defiance, or protest, by my father in defense of the woman he loved.

My father was the son of Ukrainian immigrants, Wasil and Eugenia Butinsky, each of whom had been lured from their homeland near Transylvania by flyers that promised a rich American life working in the coal mines of Pennsylvania. They met when they settled in the thriving community of Ukrainian émigrés near Scranton in around 1910. Devout Ukrainian Catholics determined to see their two kids get ahead in the new country, they sent both my father and his sister to college. My father went to Scranton University, which was run by Jesuit priests.

After the war, my father left the Scranton area for his graduate studies and wound up at Purdue. His parents were not pleased that he had fallen for an Irish-American Roman Catholic from Indiana. Weren't there plenty of nice Ukrainian girls in Scranton? My mother and her mother, Grace, decided to straighten out the Butinskys by paying them a visit. They took the train from Indiana to Scranton. When they got to the house, my grandfather answered the door. No one else greeted them. His wife and daughter—my paternal grandmother and my aunt—stayed upstairs.

My mother's mother was royally ticked off, having made the long journey. "You may not approve, but these two young people are in love, and I came here to check you out, to see if you were good enough for my daughter," she said, or so family lore holds.

The Butinskys would not budge. My father was also there, but he could not persuade his mother and sister to come down to greet his fiancée and mother-in-law-to-be.

When they all returned to Indiana, my father wrote letter after letter to his mother, telling her he loved Margaret and asking her to apologize. She did not. Finally, he wrote one last time and told his parents and sister that they were not invited to the wedding.

With his doctorate, my father went to work for Eli Lilly and Company, the pharmaceutical company founded and headquartered in Indianapolis. My mother was fully occupied with running the house and raising the children, the first five of whom arrived in rapid succession. A household of nine like ours was not unusual for that time and place. One neighboring family had fourteen children; another had eleven. We were about midsized.

Our house on Winding Way, on the northeast side of Indianapolis, was within walking distance of the Catholic church, and life revolved around its institutions. All of us went to Catholic schools. We had family members who were members of religious orders. One of my brothers, for a time, thought he might become a priest, and when we were not scuffling, we would "play" Mass. Our mother actually sewed miniature priest vestments for us.

With five boys in the house, all competitive, we also found plenty of nonpious ways to play, quarrel, and battle. I shared a room with two older brothers, Tom and John, who were good athletes. Skinny and gawky, I'd dribble a basketball and it would go flying off my foot. Once, during a wrestling match in our bedroom, I was tossed into a closet door that splintered and broke, like the wall of a saloon in a television Western. Somehow, I was naturally allied with the underdog. All of us had favorite football teams, but mine was the Dallas Cowboys, which sports fans today might not regard as much of a pity case, but back in 1966 the Cowboys were new in the league and unlikely to topple the mighty Green Bay Packers, who they met two years in a row for the NFL championship.

As more children arrived, my father realized that an organic chemist's salary was not going to be enough to support his family. One of his bosses encouraged him to consider patent law, and so for five years he went to law school at night and practiced organic chemistry by day. Having gone through law school myself and knowing its demands, I am struck now that he never seemed absent to me as a child. After being admitted to the bar, one of my father's early assignments was to negotiate a license for Lilly with Genentech, a relatively new biotechnology company that had come up with a way to manufacture synthetic insulin. Years later, when Genentech was head-hunting for a patent lawyer, they wooed my father and my mom to the West Coast, where he worked until retirement.

I followed my two older brothers, Tom and John, into Brebeuf High School, which was run by the Jesuits and, at the time, an all-boys school. I pretty much gave up on team sports and joined the drama club, which was a good way to meet girls from sister schools. Otherwise, they—girls—would not have been part of our daily lives.

Like my brothers, I went to Indiana University in Bloomington. I grew up in the 1960s, when landing a man on the moon and space exploration were dominating much of America's culture, and I was fascinated by *Star Trek* and all forms of science fiction. I had no pretensions of ever becoming an astronaut, but perhaps the study of space would satisfy my interest. My plan was to major in astronomy. After a week it dawned on me that sitting alone on a mountaintop all night looking through a telescope was not socially engaging enough for me. Astronomy was a hobby, not a career. Criminal justice, on the other hand, seemed compelling. Among my favorite television shows were *Perry Mason* and *Judd for the Defense*, legal dramas that depicted the criminal defense attorney as an honorable occupation. So I switched to the Department of Forensic Studies, which included some fine courses on big, important subjects such as criminal and juvenile law and procedure.

My grades were strong, but nobody was mistaking me for a total grind. One major undertaking of my college years was the formation, with a number of friends, of an informal group known as "Ass Kickers Inc." Our idea was to throw a party for students living off-campus, in Bloomington, who were not part of an annual bacchanal held by the fraternities and other campus groups around the Little 500 bike race. (Modeled after the Indianapolis 500, but on bicycles, the race provided the plot for the movie *Breaking Away*.) As treasurer, I managed the funds. By issuing mock stock certificates for "Ass Kickers Inc.," we collected enough the first year to get ten kegs and a band. In my senior year, the event exploded, and it was carried on by friends who stayed behind in Bloomington. Eventually, it became a mini-Woodstock of the Midwest, with over a hundred kegs and seven bands playing long into the night.

Like many in my generation, our childhoods defined by the social unrest of the civil rights movement and the Vietnam War, I idealized my ability to change the world for the better. Even the unspeakable corruption of Watergate did not dampen my enthusiasm. I was about to graduate college with a BA in forensic studies and a minor in history, two subjects that naturally prepared me for law school. I decided that the law would be my career path, and as a criminal defense lawyer I could use my gifts to advocate for the downtrodden in our society, and maybe improve their lot in life. I scored very well on the LSAT, which made me eligible for admission to top-tier law schools.

When I went touring prospective law schools, my travels brought me to North Carolina, where I checked out the state school at the University of North Carolina at Chapel Hill and Duke University in Durham. I got to Duke on a Thursday evening, which would have been a party night back in Bloomington; going out on Thursdays became as much of a habit in my college years as going to Sunday Mass had been as a kid. Yet no one could tell me where to go on Duke's campus to have some fun that Thursday night. They all suggested Chapel Hill. So that's where I went, and I ended up enrolling there.

With a little more forethought, I might have realized that if I wanted clinical training in the law—hands-on experience in court, as opposed to studying precedents and statutes from a book—a big-city school would provide more opportunities. But I got lucky at Chapel Hill. Two of my professors, David Rudolf and Richard Rosen, were starting up a clinical program that sent students into the courthouses of nearby counties under the supervision of actual lawyers. This gave me the chance to speak with people accused of crimes, and to initially appreciate that one of a criminal defense lawyer's most important tasks is to represent his client as a human being and *not* just a criminal defendant. You're trying to help, or cajole, the prosecution, the judge, and the jury into seeing the person standing in front of them as more than a defendant in a criminal case. You're not asking them to overlook wrongdoing but rather to make sure that their gaze does not stop there. Whether in plea bargaining or on trial, you want them to consider what your client is accused of in the context of his or her life. When it's in the best interest of someone to negotiate a plea, you need the judge and prosecution to understand not only if the individual was prepared to take responsibility for what he or she had done, but also how and why things went wrong. This experience also gave me a chance to stand up in a courtroom, and the professors let me know that I was good on my feet.

I am proud to say that I ran for class president during the first week of school at Chapel Hill, and, even though I didn't know a single person for a thousand miles, I won. It was a simple campaign, based on a tried-and-true strategy honed in Bloomington: We're going to throw an ass-kicking party. That was it. After all, we were first-year students with no power, and anything more serious would have been baloney.

It got me into the mix of student life pretty quickly, even though I was not drinking alcohol at the time. Throughout college, I had worked to pay the bills, and in the summer before law school my job was on the second shift at a General Electric factory in Bloomington, making refrigerators. Lunch consisted of vending-machine sandwiches, and after work I'd go to local dives to sample the rotgut whiskey. By the end of the summer, I had an ulcer and had to abstain from alcohol. Not that this made my law school campaign platform of throwing parties entirely altruistic; I just got over the ulcer as soon as I could.

The next summer, between my first and second years of law school, was quite a bit more serious, if not as strenuous as the factory work. Staying in North Carolina would allow me to qualify for the in-state tuition rate of about $600 a year, so I got a job doing research for a professor who was studying how the death penalty was applied. Four years after the U.S. Supreme Court created a de facto moratorium on the death penalty with its 1972 decision in *Furman v. Georgia*, the Court's *Gregg v. Georgia* (1976) ruling brought it back, authorizing a dual trial system in capital cases. First, the jury would decide guilt or innocence, and then it would decide if the penalty should be death or prison. That gave thousands of local decision makers—prosecutors—the authority to seek punishment as they saw fit. This professor's research goal was to chart how they exercised that discretion. In one county, a stupid, drunken bar fight that ended with someone being stabbed to death would be charged as manslaughter; a serious felony, to be sure, but one that did not carry the possibility of the electric chair or a lethal injection. Yet, in another county, the same sort of misadventure would be considered a capital crime.

To collect data for the professor's project, we went to the medical examiner's office in each county, got the records for each violent death, reviewed the police reports, and then tracked what, if anything, had happened in the courts. I vividly recall that one woman had done in her husband by pouring scalding water on him as he slept, a purposely cruel and thoroughly planned killing, but she was not charged with a death penalty–level crime. And yet a Lumbee Native American guy who killed a man with his fists in a drunken bar fight with no clear premeditation faced the death penalty—and got it. I learned a lot about the uneven and unfair use of the death penalty that summer, and how, often, the race of the victim and the accused were decisive factors.

The following summer, I had my only experience working for the prosecution when I served as an intern in the United States Attorney's Office for the District of Columbia. Seeing how good prosecutors approach their work with integrity and honesty continues to help me as a defense lawyer.

With the passage of time, it's intriguing to look back at the landscape of my law school days and early years as a lawyer. I realize now that some of the landmark United States Supreme Court decisions we regard as pillars of our modern legal framework—for instance, *Gideon v. Wainwright* (1963), which found that the Sixth Amendment guarantees the right to counsel regardless of ability to pay, and *Miranda v. Arizona* (1966), which required the police to inform people being arrested of their rights—were then still quite new, less than a couple of decades old. The concrete had not hardened. The justice system was more fragile than I'd thought.

Crack cocaine flared into the national consciousness when I was in law school. Many corrosive ideas originating in the political arena were imposed on the criminal justice system, including mandatory minimum sentences and lowering the age at which teenagers could be tried and punished as adults. Transforming social problems into criminal cases by arresting people became the one-size-fits-all solution to complex issues—but moving those ailments behind bars far too often solved nothing and only deepened the moats that trapped people in difficult circumstances. The United States is the leading jailer of the world, ahead of the reported rates of incarceration in countries regarded as far more authoritarian.* And, as throughout American history, the weight

---

* Roy Walmsley, "World Prison Population List," 11th ed., Institute for Criminal Policy

of judicial dysfunction has fallen heaviest on African American men and other people of color.

New federal laws punished the use of crack cocaine at one hundred times the severity of powder cocaine; that is, the form of cocaine used in black and Latino communities was penalized far more heavily than the one used among whites.[*] Nearly half of all drug arrests in the United States are for marijuana possession, a rate that soared in the first decade of the twenty-first century; although blacks and whites use pot at the same rate, a 2013 study by the American Civil Liberties Union found that a black person was 3.73 times more likely to be arrested for it.[†] In 2014, 6 percent of all black males ages thirty to thirty-nine were in prison, compared to 2 percent of Hispanic and 1 percent of white males in the same age group.[‡] And it's not just drug offenses. Of 455 men executed for rape in the mid-twentieth century, 405 were black.[§] Given these strong patterns, it should come as no surprise that, as of a 2012 Innocence Project reckoning, approximately 70 percent of people exonerated by DNA testing in the United States are minorities. Sixty-three percent are African Americans.[¶] Another analysis done in 2015 revealed that 10 percent of people exonerated by DNA testing had

---

Research, 2015. http://www.prisonstudies.org/sites/default/files/resources/downloads/world_prison_population_list_11th_edition.pdf.

[*] Jim Dwyer, "Rewriting the City's Record on Prisons," *New York Times*, January 2, 2014, A14. http://www.nytimes.com/2014/01/03/nyregion/rewriting-the-citys-record-on-prisons.html?_r=0.

[†] American Civil Liberties Union, "The War on Marijuana in Black and White," June 2013. https://www.aclu.org/files/assets/aclu-thewaronmarijuana-rel2.pdf.

[‡] E. Ann Carson, "Prisoners in 2014," United States Department of Justice, Office of Justice Programs, Bureau of Statistics, September 2015. http://www.bjs.gov/content/pub/pdf/p14.pdf.

[§] Lincoln Caplan, "Racial Discrimination and Capital Punishment: The Indefensible Death Sentence of Duane Buck," *The New Yorker*, April 20, 2016. http://www.newyorker.com/news/news-desk/racial-discrimination-and-capital-punishment-the-indefensible-death-sentence-of-duane-buck.

[¶] Edwin Grimsley, "What Wrongful Convictions Teach Us About Racial Inequality," The Innocence Project, September 26, 2012. http://www.innocenceproject.org/what-wrongful-convictions-teach-us-about-racial-inequality/.

been arrested as minors; all of them were tried in adult court; and of that number—thirty-four—thirty-two are minorities and thirty out of those thirty-two DNA-based exonerees are black.[*]

One of my favorite professors at Indiana, Victor Streib, was an early nationally respected advocate for reforms of the juvenile justice system. He highlighted these issues forty years ago, and today they are an even more pressing part of our national discussion on justice and young people. Brendan Dassey, chronologically a teenager, emotionally and intellectually a child, was treated as if he were an adult.

---

[*] Edwin Grimsley, "Lessons About Black Youth and Wrongful Convictions: Three Things You Should Know," The Innocence Project, May 1, 2015. http://www.innocence project.org/lessons-about-black-youth-and-wrongful-convictions-three-things-you-should-know/.

6

In the 1980s, just like today, a recruitment pipeline was part of the operating machinery at major private civil law firms in the United States. They had regular cycles of hiring new graduates to replace lawyers who retired or otherwise left. At the highest levels, this was a wonder to behold. Recruiters from the big firms fanned out to the campuses of leading law schools and interviewed the top students. Promising candidates were flown, business class, to big cities such as New York and Los Angeles, Chicago and San Francisco and Houston.

Suddenly, students who had been living on ramen and macaroni and cheese for three years were tasting the luxe life. They were put up in four-star hotels, wined and dined, treated to box seats at the ballparks, orchestra tickets for hit Broadway plays, dinner cruises. And if these firms liked you, they tried to hire you. There was no waffling and waiting to see if the firm was going to have a budget for new hires. You got an offer, or you didn't. You were hired, or you were not.

It has always worked differently in public defenders' offices.

In the spring of 1981, as I was finishing law school in Chapel Hill, I did not go on any of these recruiting jaunts. They weren't looking for me, and I wasn't looking for them, because I was only interested in criminal defense. I was shopping for public defense work in cities reputed to have good programs. And I was doing it on my own dime. Like big law firms and prosecutors' offices, public defender services have attrition and turnover. Unlike the big firms, public defenders' offices do not have budgets to inveigle the best and the brightest. Often, they have no idea what their budgets will be from one year to the next.

Seattle had a strong office, so I booked a trip to the Pacific Northwest, flying into Portland where my brother John already worked as a general practice lawyer—a mix of criminal defense, family law, and personal injury law. This meant I could also interview there on my way to Seattle. And, in a stroke of luck, my flight to Portland had a long layover in Denver. Most travelers hate layovers, but the Colorado public defender's office in Denver also had a well-regarded program. That layover gave me enough time to leave the airport, hurry to the office, squeeze in an interview, and still make my flight to the Northwest. This was not a deluxe recruitment junket. If I could have squeezed another city out of that airline ticket, I would have.

That job hunt exemplifies the low value that our country places on public defender services, even though they exist to vindicate the constitutional guarantee that no one, no matter how poor, can be forced to go to court on criminal charges without a lawyer. In Denver, Portland, and Seattle, I had good interviews with all of the defenders' offices, and each one seemed interested in hiring me. But none could be sure they were going to have any positions until their state legislatures passed budgets and their governors signed them. During my interview tour, I also heard that a good statewide public defender program had been started in Wisconsin, and I stashed that in the back of my head. Wisconsin was in the Midwest, with no mountains or ocean beaches—landscapes I had become fond of after three years amid the beauty of North Carolina—and in my mind I'd had my last cold and snowy winter when I left Indianapolis.

By the time I graduated, I still didn't have a solid offer in hand. Complicating things was the requirement that all new lawyers pass a bar examination recognized by the state where they wanted to practice. Many states now use a common test, but at that time Colorado did not. Its test also had an early registration date, which meant I would have to lay out $350—in 1981 dollars—in fees without knowing if I would ever actually work there. This was a comically small amount of money for big law firms, which still hire young associates with the expectation that they'll be spending some of their workweek getting ready for the bar, and even provide tutoring. For me, it was a *colossal* amount of money—more than half of my entire year of law school tuition.

I called the Colorado public defender's office and let them know I couldn't afford to spend $350 if I had no chance of being hired. They told me that they really liked me and wanted to formally offer me the job but couldn't do that until the state budget became law, although they urged me to sign up for the test. I didn't; I just wasn't convinced that a job was really going to come through. They eventually made me an offer, after the test deadline had passed.

When June came, I decided to kick the tires on the Wisconsin program and sent off a letter and my résumé.

A few days later, the deputy public defender, Jim Rebholz, called. "You really should come up here for an interview," he said.

"I can't afford it," I told him. "If I come, what are my chances?"

"We can't pay your expenses, but this particular year, we have made an effort to hire out-of-state law students, to get different perspectives—not just Wisconsin or Marquette grads," Jim said. "So why don't you come up?"

I flew to Indianapolis, borrowed my parents' old Chrysler, and drove to Milwaukee. Most of the bosses were unavailable, and the one who did meet with me, Kevin Dunn, got called to court just as I sat down.

"Come with me," he said.

Later, Kevin brought me to a grand dive bar, Jim Hegarty's, down the block from the courthouse on West Wells Street. There, we were joined by Rod Uphoff, one of the top supervisors in the office, and he and Kevin conducted my job interview over a table in the bar. Before long, a group of the younger lawyers from the office rolled in. Just back from a two-week training program in Houston run by the National Criminal Defense College, they were buzzing with excitement. They had done mock trials from start to finish; questioned potential jurors; given opening statements; conducted direct and cross-examinations of witnesses; and given closing statements. Each day they were interviewed and coached about what they had done, and they saw a demonstration by a master lawyer. Their enthusiasm swept me along. This was a group passionately dedicated to being public defenders, and also to enjoying a beer at Jim Hegarty's. That was a winning combination. I was offered a job with a salary of $19,200. That was half of what big law firms were paying their first-year associates, but not bad by public defender standards—although that is not really saying much. I took it and have never regretted moving to Wisconsin.

But first, I had to finish my summer in Chapel Hill, where I'd already enrolled in a bar exam study course. Wisconsin is the only state that does not require students who attend one of two law schools, Marquette or the University of Wisconsin, to take the bar exam. Because I went to law school in Chapel Hill, I did not receive the diploma benefit, and as an out-of-state recruit I had to take the two-day exam. One day was dedicated to the common multistate exam covering general laws applicable everywhere, and the North Carolina study course would suffice for that prep. I was on my own for the Wisconsin law portion. In my opinion, bar exams are a largely useless measure of one's fitness to practice law. I believe they really function as tariffs to limit the number of lawyers who can come into a state and compete for business. The jurisdictions most sought after by lawyers, for money, power, or warm weather—California, New York, Arizona—typically have higher bar exam failure rates, thereby lowering the chances that too many hungry lawyers will be trying to split the pie. Wisconsin was not a lawyer magnet, and the bar exam pass rate that year was more than 90 percent. That included me.

While waiting in line to register for the exam in Madison, I heard other people talking about working at the public defender's office. Like me, they were out-of-state recruits, from Georgetown, Virginia, Boston College, and other East Coast schools and had all started at the public defender's office that summer, before passing the exam. One of them, Dudley Williams—a Georgetown law grad—would, years later, become my law partner.

On September 1, 1981, I reported for work with three other brand-new lawyers from the University of Wisconsin Law School, including my future wife, Kathy Stilling. I wore my one suit, which I'd bought in law school to have something to wear at interviews, and drove myself to work in my 1971 Buick LeSabre, with over a hundred thousand miles on it; only four of its eight cylinders were working. On cold days, to get it to start, I would jam a pencil in the carburetor flap to add enough oxygen to the fuel so that combustion could take place, and perhaps coax the engine into turning over. When that didn't work, I walked or took the bus.

Our first assignment was to the intake section, where we met people after they had been arrested. We'd find out if they were poor enough to qualify for a lawyer at taxpayer expense and then represent them at their initial court appearances. As new staff attorneys, we spent most of our time making bail arguments. Later, we moved onto misdemeanor cases, working our way up to handling the most serious crimes, felonies. We worked in pairs, one of us in court while the other conducted interviews in the lockup pens behind the courtroom. More than a few of our clients were homeless or living in the craters of their own lives; you breathed their world. Being arrested was another day at the office for them.

But not everyone seemed defeated. One day, a woman arrested on a prostitution charge during a police sting was brought into the lockup. When I met with her, she was spitting mad. An undercover officer had approached her, and the generally accepted rules of engagement in such situations required that as soon as the undercover cop made the deal, the arrest was to be made, before any actual intimate contact took place. If a john advanced into physical intimacy, the prostitute would know that he was not a cop. On the other hand, if he seemed reluctant to actually go ahead with the act he'd just negotiated, she would have time to back out and perhaps avoid arrest. Apparently, the officer in this case had not been so restrained.

"That motherf***ker came in my mouth!" she complained to me. "Only then did he arrest me."

She was so agitated, I believed her. She wasn't too restrained herself. As we stood in court later, she pinched my butt. I kept my composure, and the judge was none the wiser.

After I'd been in Milwaukee for a couple of weeks, I went over on lunch hour to a small local bank down the block. I had no links to the state and only one paycheck stub to show I was working. Ushered over to the bank's vice president, I told him that I needed a loan to buy some suits. How much? Maybe six hundred dollars, I said.

He laughed. "Is that all?" he asked.

I got the money, enough for four cheap suits, just on my signature. It was a moment that would have gladdened the heart of George Bailey from *It's a Wonderful Life*. I was suddenly cutting a much more distinguished figure in court, or at least *I* thought so.

This early stream of cases included some driving-while-intoxicated charges. About a year after I'd started, I had one client charged with drunk driving who was particularly adamant that he had not been intoxicated and that the breath test result had to be an error. The breath test result did seem to indicate a much higher level of intoxication compared to the officers' description of my client's condition. It was based on a reading from one of the most commonly used Breathalyzers in the country, made by Smith & Wesson. I couldn't see anything obviously wrong in the paperwork, but I decided to do a little research on the Breathalyzer instruments themselves.

The first thing I noticed was that the devices looked like something from a bad 1950s science fiction movie, with knobs and switches and a needle that moved up and down, supposedly showing the presence of alcohol in one's breath. We were now living in the 1980s, and although the personal computer had just been invented, most of the electronic devices in use did not look as rudimentary as this machine. With a little research, I learned that these Breathalyzers had serious defects because their components were not shielded from radio interference. They had been designed so many years earlier, when law enforcement departments had relatively few radio communication devices—particularly handheld walkie-talkies—that no one thought radio interference to be a problem. But now every officer had radios, and would often use them in the same room where another officer was administering the test. Some studies had shown this made the needle on the Breathalyzer dial waver and that the test results could be skewed. Remarkably, these Breathalyzers had not been recalled, and police departments all over the country were still employing them daily. Perhaps this was the explanation for my client's apparently abnormally high reading.

What I needed in order to challenge the reliability of these readings was an expert on the shielding of electromagnetic fields—someone like Heinz Schlicke, who I'd learned in the library was probably the leading authority in the United States on the subject at the time, and the author of the book *Essentials of Dielectromagnetic Engineering*. German-born Schlicke's path to the United States was an interesting one. He had a doctorate in engineering sciences and had been a lieutenant commander in the *Kriegsmarine*, the navy of Nazi Germany, specializing in radar and methods of shielding submarines from detection. Near the end of World War II, he was sent to Japan on *U-234*, a U-boat submarine carrying uranium oxide and advanced weapons. Before it got there, Hitler had killed himself in a bunker and Germany's unconditional surrender was announced. The submarine was captured off Newfoundland by the U.S. Navy, and its crew—other than two Japanese officers on board, who committed suicide—were repatriated to Germany the following year. Schlicke was invited back to the United States as part of Operation Paperclip, an effort by American intelligence officials to make sure that German scientists, technicians, and engineers, such as the rocket expert Werner von Braun, did not go to work with the Soviet Union. Schlicke's assignment in the United States, at the Office of Naval Research, was in stealth technology. Later, he traveled around the country visiting nuclear power plants and worked for the Jet Propulsion Laboratory, with its huge magnetic fields.

Heinz Schlicke was clearly the right person for the job, but how could I get him to testify in a misdemeanor drunk-driving case in Milwaukee? Well, it so happened that after this world-famous ex-Nazi electromagnetics expert finished working for the U.S. government, he accepted a job with the Allen-Bradley Company, based in Milwaukee, which specialized in industrial automation. He lived on the city's north shore. I sent him the information about the defective Breathalyzers, then spoke to him on the phone. He was appalled by the lack of shielding on the devices. So, would he testify in my drunk-driving case?

"This is too stupid for me," he said in his thick German accent.

"Yes," I said, "but who better than you?"

When Schlicke realized people were actually being prosecuted and going to jail based on readings from shoddy equipment, he agreed to help.

Another lawyer in our office, Kathy Stilling, had a similar case and so we made a joint motion to preclude the evidence from these Breathalyzers. Several days of hearings were stretched out over several months, and while our motion was pending, nearly all of the other drunk-driving cases in the state were put on hold. Siding with us, the judge found that the machinery and its results were unreliable. That meant nine hundred cases were either dismissed or plea-bargained. It was the first case I'd handled that made lawyers take note of my skills.

This was also my first in-depth case working with a scientist. More important, I got to know Kathy better. Our friendship deepened, and before long we undertook another strange venture together.

Among the peculiarities of a criminal lawyer's work are the frequent close encounters with death. Every year, Wayne State University in Detroit holds a conference on the medicolegal investigation of death. It is a prestigious conference, for many years hosted by Dr. Werner Spitz, a Wayne State professor made famous through his work on the assassinations of President John F. Kennedy and Martin Luther King Jr. for the House Select Committee. In many areas of criminal law, forensic pathology is crucial—for example, the time of death can be estimated by things such as the degree of rigor mortis or the life-cycle stage of maggots found in the body. Pathology may help figure out whether the deceased was trying to attack someone at the moment of death, a highly important detail when a survivor claims to have acted in self-defense. As strange as this field is, it has its own experts and lines of study, and at its annual meetings the latest research and demonstrations are shared. Homicide detectives and prosecutors attend to learn about them; why shouldn't defense lawyers? Kathy and I decided to go, paying our own way, and so we drove to Detroit.

The conference was a bizarre *Rocky Horror* show of pathologists, many of whom seemed socially inept—nothing like the wisecracking pathologists you see now on TV series such as *Bones*. We'd get into an elevator and try, and fail, to make small talk. There were very few other lawyers present. The most memorable part of it was a field trip to a medical examiner's office in order to observe an autopsy in progress. This turned out to be a moving experience that has stayed with me.

With his long hair, the deceased looked like a Western rendition of Jesus. He was a thirty-three-year-old man who had died of a single gunshot wound in the center of his chest; the bullet went right into his heart. His face and skull were intact, and you could see that he was a nice-looking man. His torso had been opened, and I was shocked at the slightness of the protective layer between the outer skin and inner organs. All the life-sustaining processes of these organs were shielded by just a thin exoskeleton. We watched for maybe a half hour, and then someone asked how this man had come to be killed. Less than twelve hours earlier, he had been shot by his mother in an argument. As I started hearing about this man, who was not much older than I was at the time, who had been fully alive just a short while ago, I started getting sick. This was more than a dissection of flesh. This was a human story, flayed open. I had to excuse myself. In the hallway, I leaned against the wall to regain my composure.

Though I have spent many hours since studying gruesome photographs of victims, this would be the only autopsy I ever attended. One was plenty.

7

While I was still cutting my teeth in the public defender's office in Madison, a miscarriage of justice was unfolding 140 miles away on the western shore of Lake Michigan. I knew nothing about it at the time. It was impossible to know that just under two decades later, it would intersect with my life and career.

This story began on a late July day in 1985, when Penny Beerntsen, a member of a prominent family in the small lakeside town of Manitowoc, Wisconsin, went for a jog along the shores of Lake Michigan. At around 3:50 p.m., a man jumped her, then beat and sexually assaulted her. The attack had taken about fifteen minutes. Two Good Samaritans passing by found her naked and bleeding in the woods.

In Wisconsin, the county sheriff has jurisdiction throughout the county, whereas municipal police departments have authority to investigate only those crimes committed within the confines of the city or town where they are located. Manitowoc County includes the City of Manitowoc, which has its own police force. But the Lake Michigan beach where this assault occurred was outside of town and thus within the jurisdiction of the Manitowoc County Sheriff's Office. Deputy sheriff Judy Dvorak was assigned to Beerntsen's case and quickly focused in on Steven Avery, then twenty-three, a member of the family that ran an auto scrap yard on the outskirts of town. He'd had a number of prior run-ins with the law, including convictions for burglary (he had broken into a bar and stolen two packs of beer, two cheese sandwiches, and $14 in quarters), and the abuse of a cat. In January 1985, he was also accused of ramming the car of his cousin Sandra Morris, who happened to be married to Manitowoc deputy sheriff Bill Morris (and a friend of the investigating deputy sheriff, Judy Dvorak), and then threatening her at gunpoint after she purportedly spread rumors that he'd had sex with his wife on his lawn and had exposed himself.

Steven Avery was, to say the least, not well liked in the Manitowoc County Sheriff's Office.

Avery did superficially resemble Beerntsen's description of her attacker, although he was not necessarily a close fit; she initially described a man who was taller than Avery and who had different color eyes. Manitowoc sheriff Tom Kocourek directed the department's sketch artist, Gene Kusche, to meet with Beerntsen in an effort to make a composite drawing from her description. Kusche later admitted it was his first composite drawing and the only one in his career ever used in court. After Avery's 2003 exoneration, allegations were raised about whether Kusche actually created the drawing from a booking photo of Avery in the sheriff's office rather than creating it from Beerntsen's description of her assailant. The sheriff then included a photograph of Steven Avery in an array that was shown to Beerntsen next to her hospital bed, and she identified him. She later picked Avery out of a live lineup as well. He was the only person included in both the photo array and the live lineup.

Steven Avery said he had been shopping forty miles away, in Green Bay, shortly after the crime was committed on the afternoon of July 29. With him were his family, including twin infants just a few days old and three other children. He even produced a cash-register receipt from the store, time-stamped 5:16 p.m., roughly an hour after the attack. In all, he had sixteen alibi witnesses. Why weren't they believed by the authorities? Perhaps because they were people like Steven Avery; they remembered where he was, and when, because they'd seen him after *Divorce Court* had ended on television, or because they were supermarket cashiers, or relatives of his infamous clan. The victim—and sole eyewitness to the crime—was a member of a respectable and wealthy family.

To overcome the timing conflict, investigators staged a drive from the crime scene, in a state park about a mile from the nearest parking area, to the Green Bay supermarket. They proved that in theory, it might have been possible for Avery to have been in both places without necessarily violating the laws of physics. But he would have had to speed ten miles over the limit with five children and their mother in the car, all of them presumably waiting while he hopped out to commit the assault.

Penny Beerntsen did not waver on the witness stand as she recounted the terrible attack, and she maintained that she was confident that Steven Avery was the culprit. And if there were any lingering doubts, a state crime lab technician buttressed her identification, reporting that a hair found on one of Avery's shirts was consistent with Penny Beerntsen's. This hair match was treated as a certainty, not a possibility, even though hair identification for generations had been one of the greatest sources of error in crime labs.

The first crime laboratories in America were opened around 1930, as part of an effort to reform police work and bring an end to practices such as the "third degree"—the brutal interrogation process in which a suspect might be beaten or physically tormented. In 1932, J. Edgar Hoover, then head of the Bureau of Investigation (later to be known as the Federal Bureau of Investigation, or FBI), set up the Technical Crime Laboratory.

Scientists from the agency, Hoover wrote in 1938, were "performing feats which would startle the imagination of a Sherlock Holmes. With microscope, ultraviolet lamp, test tubes, spectrograph, refractometer and parallel light rays, science tracks down American's most vicious criminals. . . . Bloodstains, human hairs, scrapings from under finger-nails, burnt letters and threads of cloth tell tales of the dead to scientists trained in crime detection."

One practitioner, Dr. Wilmer Souder of the National Bureau of Standards, assured readers of the June 20, 1936, *Scientific News Letter* that he had identified the author of a kidnapping ransom note with such mathematical certainty that it could be expressed as a number almost beyond human conception. Only one person in thirty billion-billion could have handwritten that note, or, as he put it, "I found the fraction to have one as a numerator, over 3 followed by 19 ciphers as the denominator." The calculations, he claimed, were done "on a very conservative rating." Then Dr. Souder declared: "This, from a mathematical standpoint, confirms the identification 'beyond all reasonable doubt.'" For the ordinary mortals called to sit on juries, the only task left for them was to decide the merits of the scientists and their arithmetic, their test tubes and parallel light rays and ultraviolet light rays. Not just when it came to handwriting analysis, but also when comparing two hairs, or threads of cloth, or bite marks. The science looked powerful, and for decades the authority of these various specialists went unchallenged. Yet, so much of it was smoke and mirrors—high-end bunk.

In coming up with astounding fractions such as one in thirty billion-billion, handwriting analysts pointed to things such as how the writer crossed the t or looped the bottom leg of a y. They might say that a certain kind of loop only appeared in, for instance, one person in ten. With each additional trait—say, the horizontal crossbar on the t goes across the very top, instead of through the middle of the vertical stroke—a new frequency would be available. An analyst could maintain that one person in three crosses their t's in that way. So now there are two traits and two frequencies, the loop in the y—$\frac{1}{10}$—and the crossbar height on the t—$\frac{1}{3}$. Basic statistics has you multiply these two fractions to come up with the odds of a single person having *both* these traits. The more traits analysts included, the more fractions are multiplied, and therefore the lower the probability that a given person will have them all. That's how Dr. Souder could come up with the cosmic fraction for the ransom-note writer. This is all sound reasoning, except for a couple of flaws: no one actually *knows* how often people cross their t's at the top, or loop their y's. These frequencies are essentially made up. And the "product rule" of statistics, which allows one to multiply frequencies together, cannot be validated, either, because you cannot assume that these traits are completely independent of each other. It may be that most people who tend to cross their t's at the top also happen to loop their y's.

Bite-mark analysis is another discipline of forensic science that DNA testing proved to be deeply flawed. A plaster casting of a bite mark on skin doesn't account for the variation in elasticity or underlying tissue structure of the skin itself; it is hard to get two dentists to agree that the cast is of the same mouth or even, for that matter, of the same species. Nevertheless, testimony by "forensic odontologists" became a foundation of wrongful-conviction death row cases, especially in the South. However, as DNA testing arranged by the Innocence Project and other organizations began to pry open the reliability—or lack thereof—of this and other forensic techniques, their weaknesses could no longer be ignored.

Hairs are often shed during crimes, making them a tantalizing source of clues to the identity of the criminal. But how are these clues decoded? Before DNA testing, technicians compared features of hair collected at a crime scene to samples taken from the suspect and victim side by side under a microscope. Examiners looked for about twenty features to distinguish one hair from the other, and if enough features of the two hairs were the same, or similar enough, the examiner would declare that they were "consistent" or a "match." The certainty of hair comparison was held in awe for generations of criminal cases. But no one could say definitively how many features had to line up for the hairs to be identified as from the same person, nor how often a particular feature of hair occurs in the population. Even hairs from the same head can sometimes be impossible to match. And the results also depended on who you asked. Given the lack of actual standards, one examiner might say that a hair "matches" or is "consistent with" a second hair, but the next could have another answer entirely. Imagine if laboratory tests in medicine were so unreliable that you got a different answer if the same test was conducted by a different lab. The ability to consistently replicate results is a foundation of scientific procedure. As far back as 1978, a research branch of the Justice Department conducted proficiency testing of ninety state and local crime laboratories to see how often they could correctly identify a piece of evidence. Among the worst results were found in hair examinations, with error rates running as high as 68 percent. That is, they were right only one-third of the time. They could have saved time and flipped a coin; at least the odds would improve to fifty-fifty. These embarrassing results did nothing to limit the use of such evidence. Hair examination, as practiced for most of the twentieth century, could go into the dictionary as the definition of junk science.

But yet there it was, helping to cinch a case of rape brought against Steven Avery. After all, if Avery really had been forty miles away in a grocery store, how could the victim's hair have even gotten onto his shirt?

The jury found him guilty. Protesting his innocence all the way to prison, Avery continued to fight.

Every nucleated cell in a human body contains a complete set of DNA, a chemical compound that directs growth, development, and function. The human genome consists of about 3.2 *billion* bases of DNA, divided into an estimated thirty thousand segments—known as genes—each with enough information to produce molecules, usually proteins. Genes are passed on from our mothers and fathers, and they express traits, or characteristics that are the result of slight variations from one person to the next. Some of them are quite obvious, such as hair or skin color, and some of them less so; for instance, one variation of a gene can make a person susceptible to a debilitating form of sickle cell disease, a group of blood illnesses, while a slightly different version of the same gene can help the person resist malaria.

Because a complete human genome is in every cell, a genetic profile can be developed from semen, skin, blood, or other biological evidence found at a crime scene and that may have been left by the criminal. This profile can be compared to that developed from the DNA of a suspect; if they match, and the test was properly conducted, the person can be definitively placed at the scene.

At the time of Steven Avery's conviction in December 1985, DNA testing was an exotic process used in biotechnology companies, not for criminal trials or investigations. The earliest forensic DNA tests, arriving in the late 1980s, required large, intact biological material. Those early tests also could not identify the source of a hair because most of a hair shaft has no living cells. The roots are likely to have intact cells, but the hairs collected at crime scenes usually are no longer attached to them.

Even so, DNA tests on other evidence, such as blood and semen, were showing the inherent weakness of hair comparisons. When convictions were overturned based on tests of those tissues, which did have cells that could supply nuclear DNA, it would often emerge that the wrongful conviction in question had relied in no small part on erroneous hair comparisons. Two men, Ron Williamson and Dennis Fritz, were convicted in 1988 of rape and murder in a small Oklahoma town in large part on testimony from a state crime lab official who said seventeen hairs "matched" one or the other of the men. In truth, none of the hairs came from either man, a fact established in the laboratory in 1999. Williamson came within five days of being executed. Both were exonerated, and the case became the subject of a bestselling book, *The Innocent Man* by John Grisham.

Steven Avery would have to sit in prison and wait for science to catch up.

8

The right team in a trial is greater than the sum of its parts; collaboration becomes a force multiplier. Daily life in the public defender's office taught the skill of collaboration—how not to micromanage another person—and its value, or at least its potential, particularly in serious felony trials, which we worked in pairs. This was one of the many practical professional lessons I learned during my time there. And while every day in that job was an education in being a lawyer, it also taught me that the canvas of humanity includes people whose upbringing was far different from my own. Like all my colleagues, I tried bunches of felonies, homicides, armed robberies, and sexual assaults. For many of my clients, whom I was meeting in the intake section of the court system and getting to know in rooms at the jail or in visits to holding cells behind the courtroom, childhood was not defined by the fortune of having two parents whose joint nurturing was also greater than the sum of their contributions.

One day, about seven years into my job, I stood in a courtroom before a jury, questioning a police detective who had thirty years of experience. He was in tears. Jurors were sobbing. At the defense table, my cocounsel, Kathy Stilling, was sobbing. Next to her, our client wept.

He had killed his ten-year-old son.

The boy had been born in Chicago and was immediately abandoned by his mother. His father raised him alone, but under the strains of single parenthood he lost his jobs and, eventually, their home. They moved to Milwaukee for its shelter system, but the shelters were intended to be places to sleep, not homes, and everyone had to be out by 7:00 a.m. This meant back on the street by seven every morning, even into the jaws of the Wisconsin winter. Once a month, a community advocacy group would issue a voucher permitting them to stay in a cheap hotel, which allowed them to stay indoors awhile longer.

On one winter day, the boy was sick with a bad cough, but they had already used their hotel voucher for that month. So the father pretended he was someone else so he could get a voucher for a second day and keep his son out of the cold. He got caught.

The advocates reamed him out in front of his son: *He should be in school anyway. What are you doing? You obviously can't take care of this boy. We're going to have to take him away from you.*

The boy started crying. *Don't let them, don't let them!*

That night, this father and his son found a squat in an abandoned building. The boy began crying and pleading with his father. *Daddy, don't let them take me away from you, please, please, please. No*, the father said, *they won't take you away from me. I won't let them. We will be together.* Then he snapped, slit his son's throat, and cut his own wrists. Before he bled out, the police found him. He'd cut his wrists, he told the detectives, so he could keep his promise and be with the boy in heaven.

The case came to trial, and Kathy and I argued that he should be found not guilty by reason of insanity. In Wisconsin, and in most states, if a mental condition or disorder makes you unable to conform your conduct to the requirements of the law, or if you are unable to know right from wrong, you cannot be found criminally guilty, and instead of a prison you go to a mental institution for treatment. But our client with no home also had no regular doctor and no health records to speak of—no evidence of a preexisting mental condition.

Even before the trial started, people in the jury pool were crying. One told us that she had been homeless for a time. Another man signaled that he had something to discuss in chambers, out of the earshot of the others being questioned. He was going through a divorce, he told the lawyers and judge, and he did not believe in divorce. As an alternative, he believed in murder-suicide. The judge took in this information coolly, then referred the man to a mental health counselor elsewhere in the building. Needless to say, he was not returned to the pool of potential jurors.

Homicide trials deal with the minute details of a moment of great torment; as the event is teased apart into clinical fractions, its horror can be blunted. Not so in this trial. Never have I felt such raw despair and anguish in a courtroom as I did while trying this case. Witness after witness who had encountered the boy and his father in the homeless shelter community attested to his great love for his son. No wonder the detective who first interviewed the man had choked up on the witness stand.

Ultimately, the jury found him guilty and not insane. Between the conviction and his sentencing, he devolved mentally in jail. He was committed for treatment and never regained his competency. He ended up in the same sort of treatment facility he would have been in if we had won the trial. I've always felt God had a hand in that outcome.

Throughout this saga, it felt like we could have been wandering, bereft, through the pages of Genesis where God tells Abraham to offer up his son Isaac to him. At the last minute, when Isaac has already been bound and laid on the altar, an angel of God stays the hand of Abraham. There was no such ending for this man, no guidance for us in that story. All we knew was that our place was by the side of this wounded man, this Abraham in a stairwell.

After that trial, we needed a break. I took Kathy to a beautiful resort in Wisconsin, and proposed to her.

She said yes.

Toward the end of my tenure as a public defender, I was assigned as lead counsel on a class action lawsuit over nightmarish conditions in the Milwaukee jail, which was built during the Depression and seemed not to have been taken care of ever since. Most jails hold people who have been charged with a crime and can't make bail, or generally are serving sentences of less than a year. (Those with longer sentences typically go to state prison.) Bail is supposed to be used only as a means to ensure that a person returns to court for a case, and not as an early round of punishment. Nevertheless, in many jurisdictions, it has become a way for the system to jail people without trial, and it disproportionately affects the poor; if they can't post bail, defendants have to sit in custody. Those who can are allowed to go home while their case is pending.

Unable to make bail, people of modest or no means are thus automatically pressured into getting their cases over as quickly as possible with a guilty plea, even if they are innocent. Waiting for a trial to show the court they are not guilty becomes a luxury they cannot afford. As a public defender, I had many clients forced to sit in jail for weeks or months because they couldn't even post $50 or $100 cash bail. At some point, the time served pretrial may approach, or even exceed, the maximum punishment they could get if convicted. There is a strong incentive for such defendants to just plead guilty, even if they are innocent, so they can get out of jail. The conditions in county jails are usually worse than in state prisons; there are few exercise opportunities, few educational or vocational programs, no jobs for inmates to cut down on the boredom. Sometimes, people stuck in jails will plead guilty because going to prison will improve their daily living conditions.

In 1988, the Milwaukee County jail was used exclusively for pretrial detainees, and it had an intractable vermin problem. Roaches contaminated the food. The place did not seem to invite a breath of air, and when an expert on jails climbed into the chases, wearing overalls, he found all the vents clogged with years of gunk and dirt. The old-fashioned layout, of cells in a long line, did not permit guards to see all of the detainees, as modern jail pod arrangements do. The result was an abnormally high suicide rate. I worked on the suit with the American Civil Liberties Union and the Legal Aid Society of Milwaukee, which provides legal assistance to poor people in civil cases, and in the end we prevailed. The county decided there was no salvaging the old place and built a modern jail.

This jail litigation gave me an opportunity to do some good and get out, for a while, from under the endless line of cases that arrived every day. We were expected to take on fifteen new felonies a month, whether or not we had closed any of those already part of our load. And back then, cases were not weighted for difficulty. A monthlong homicide trial counted as only one felony, the same as a garage burglary and theft of a bicycle, which would likely mean only a plea and a sentence of probation. I was stumbling under the weight.

One day in 1989, I came back to the office in a foul mood.

"How was your day?" someone asked.

"First of all, I ran twenty to twenty-five felony cases through intake," I said, with a sheaf of case forms in hand. "It sucked. Then there's this guy with a ridiculous story."

At intake, I'd normally sniff around for some cases that I could tell would result in a reasonably quick plea bargain. Technically, the only real issue at the intake sessions was bail, but I'd quickly scan the complaint and ask the client if it was true. That way, I'd know if it was likely to plead out, meaning it could count toward my quota but I would not have to lug it around for months.

The guy with the ridiculous story had been arrested for a burglary in an apartment house. Witnesses identified him as having been in the building at the time of the break-in. He was not a stranger in the neighborhood; he managed a building across the street. Yet, there he was, caught red-handed behind the locked doors of a place where he was not supposed to be. That was the account given in the sworn complaint by the police officer. My client, on the other hand, gave me some cock-and-bull story about having to see someone in the building, which, according to the criminal complaint, was not backed up by the officer's own investigation.

"So he says he is innocent," I told my colleagues. "He's not going to take a plea, there's going to be a fight, it'll have to be a trial, and he's obviously as guilty as sin."

Kathy spoke up, quietly. "I'll take the case," she said.

"Fine," I said. "Knock yourself out."

The upshot was that an investigator sent out by Kathy found out that the man's story was 100 percent true. He had a legitimate reason for being in the building, and he was unequivocally innocent. The case wasn't plea-bargained, it was dismissed outright. It was a good result for this man, and a sobering one for me. What kind of lawyer was I becoming if I judged people in the first five minutes of meeting them?

The hard truth is that this happens every day, all over the country. Public defenders, under immense pressures that are a direct result of the lack of resources, are prejudging guilt and innocence when they shouldn't. This episode made me realize I could no longer be the lawyer I wanted to be under the constant weight of too many cases and too few resources. It was time for me to leave the public defender's office.

There were other changes in store, too.

"Which judge do you think should marry us?" Kathy had asked me after I proposed.

My answer surprised her, and probably surprised me, too. "I don't know if I'd really feel married if I wasn't married in a church," I said.

"What church?" she said. "You don't go to church!"

This was true. I had left the church in my twenties; I no longer went to Mass and basically had stopped practicing. Catholic elementary and high school were in my rearview mirror. Kathy was baptized in an Episcopalian church but grew up largely unchurched. In the eight years we had known each other, neither one of us had given any sign of active practice in any faith tradition.

"Sometimes I go," I said, thinking of a family occasion here and there.

In truth, I had begun feeling uneasy about my drift from the church. For almost two years I had been reading various theological articles and books—works by Catholic biblical scholars such as Raymond E. Brown, John P. Meier, and the French Jesuit priest Pierre Teilhard de Chardin, as well as several of C. S. Lewis's books, including *Mere Christianity* and *The Screwtape Letters*, and parts of classical writings from Augustine and Thomas Aquinas. I was realizing that over the centuries many brilliant minds have explored the great questions of life and faith, and, despite my Catholic education, my understanding was stunted. Something inside me was calling me to understand other faiths and reexplore my own religious traditions. But I operated in a secular profession and didn't yet see how my own religion and faith could help those entrapped in the justice system. I wasn't comfortable discussing these feelings with my friends, not even Kathy, who wasn't Catholic at that time and had no other faith tradition.

At least, not until this moment.

"Well, we'll get married in a church, because I want you to feel married," she said.

We were married in August 1989. Our first child, a boy, was born three years later. We named him Stephen after Saint Stephen, the great voice of advocacy in the New Testament and the first martyr. Brought before the high court in Jerusalem and accused of blasphemy, Stephen argued that, contrary to the views of the high priests, the laws of Moses were being fulfilled by Jesus. His speech is among the longest in the Acts of the Apostle. (He was still found guilty and stoned to death.) Two years later, our daughter was born, and we named her Grace Elizabeth, for Kathy's grandmother and mine.

Within a year of getting married, both Kathy and I had left the public defender's office and gone to work in different private firms. This was an interim step before we set up our own firm, joining forces with Dudley Williams, another member of our class at the public defender's office. Dudley and I struck out on our own first while Kathy stayed at her other private law firm, where she could draw a salary. As young parents with new obligations of child rearing, we weren't ready to put all of our financial eggs in one basket. After two years it became clear our law firm could succeed, so Kathy left hers and joined ours.

Ever since, our goal has been to maintain a practice that allows us to give each client a full measure of representation and not take the shortcuts that are inevitable in the high-volume work of public defenders' offices. We deliberately do not carry on a high-volume practice. Instead, we take fewer cases and charge more. This structure lets us really dig into the intricacies of a case, although it also means some nervous months when the phone doesn't ring with new business that will pay enough for us to comfortably practice our model. But I've found that success and more clients follow when you take the time to provide the full representation each client deserves.

Going into private practice did not curtail our interest in public affairs around the law, however. Kathy and I had joined the National Association of Criminal Defense Lawyers years earlier—three decades later, we're still active in the organization—and now I had time to serve as a director of the NACDL and also to be president of the Wisconsin Association of Criminal Defense Lawyers. It was a trip to an NACDL conference in 1992 that would end up launching me on an epic case that I carried with me for decades: *State of Wisconsin v. Ralph Dale Armstrong*.

Part II

PRESUMED GUILTY

9

If, for some reason, you ever have the urge to become invisible in a crowd, try bringing a baby to a conference of lawyers. Our son, Stephen, was just three months old when Kathy and I went to the August 1992 annual meeting of the National Association of Criminal Defense Lawyers in Colorado. Three months is probably the only age that a child could be prudently taken to such a gathering; Stephen was portable but not mobile, and his infant-scale fusses were manageable. If we hadn't brought him, one of us would have had to stay home, and neither of us wanted to miss the conference. We relished connecting with others in the defense bar to think and talk about the issues that we had in common with very few other people. Moreover, I was a member of the association's board. Of course, all such gatherings have their hierarchies, their divos and divas, and lawyers with small practices in Wisconsin are not necessarily sought out in the mingling sessions—especially when they're dandling an infant across their knees.

I went to the conference that year with an agenda: to get the association to speak up for the indigent defense bar—the lawyers in private firms who are appointed to represent poor people when public defenders' offices cannot handle the case for one reason or another, including conflicts of interests with other clients. Salaried staff public defenders (like my wife and I were when we began our careers) handle only about 60 percent of cases when defendants cannot afford to hire their own lawyer, and the remainder are apportioned to private attorneys on a list. Public defenders and the indigent bar together handle about 80–90 percent of all criminal cases in the nation. Public funding for indigent defense was in a truly pitiful state in 1992 and has actually worsened since then. The economic downturn of 2008 caused more defendants to qualify for indigent representation, but less money was available for governments to fund programs. In 2009, Attorney General Eric Holder noted at a meeting of the American Bar Association that resources for public defender programs lagged far behind other justice system programs. In 2016, Wisconsin had the lowest hourly rate for assigned counsel appointments in the country: $40 per hour. Out of that sum, attorneys must pay overhead such as rent, utilities, staff (if they have any), and insurance. A national law office study done years ago established that the average overhead for small firms was $64 per hour.* And that's before the lawyers can pay themselves a penny. Even more shocking is that when I moved to Wisconsin to begin my law career in 1981, appointed private lawyers were paid $45 per hour for time spent in court and $35 for out-of-court work. Factoring for inflation, Wisconsin lawyers nowadays are making about $7 per hour in 1981 dollars. Is it any wonder the number and quality of lawyers willing to take such cases has plummeted?

Honestly, the subject did not excite much enthusiasm among many NACDL members. The NACDL is now a leading champion for indigent defense, but back in 1992, it was dominated by lawyers from the private defense bar; hardly any legal aid or public defender organizations had the money to send people to such meetings, and neither did the private attorneys on indigent defendant appointment lists. But Kathy and I had met doing that kind of work, and knew firsthand how the crushing caseloads and poor reimbursement made the system less just. So we were there, in part, to push the organization to speak up for the women and men in the trenches of the courts, and also to lobby for an increase in the measly hourly rate for private lawyers who took on assigned cases.

At one session shortly after I joined the NACDL board, a charismatic, mop-haired man came over to chat with Kathy and me. It was Barry C. Scheck, who, with his partner Peter J. Neufeld, was among the pioneers in the use of DNA testing to reopen old convictions. At the time, few lawyers grasped how it could work, much less its signifi-

* Kelli Thompson, "The Wisconsin State Public Defender Organization," IFLA Conference, November 1, 2009. http://www.laf.org.tw/ifla2009/panel_discussion/The_Wisconsin_State_public_defender_organization_en.pdf.

cance. In the late 1980s, Scheck and Neufeld realized that technology was making it possible to get DNA profiles out of old evidence. The principles of harvesting ancient DNA would become part of mass culture, thanks to a 1990 novel by Michael Crichton (which was made into a film) about creating a dinosaur from ancient dinosaur blood that, conveniently enough, had been the last meal eaten by a mosquito before the bug was preserved in amber. That book was *Jurassic Park*. Working with far more prosaic material—old crime scene evidence, typically rape kits—the two lawyers from New York had been racking up exonerations for people who had been imprisoned before DNA testing technology was available. If the central issue of the trial had been the identity of an assailant, and biological evidence like semen or blood had been left during the course of the attack, a DNA test could definitively say if the right person had been identified.

As word spread about their work, Barry and Peter began getting letters from prisoners around the country asking them to look into their cases. They created something they called the Innocence Project, based at the Benjamin N. Cardozo Law School at New York's Yeshiva University, where they both taught. Students in a clinical law course researched transcripts and files to determine if a conviction rested largely on an identification. If it did, then the lawyers would apply to get the old evidence released for these newly available tests.

By 1992, Scheck already had great stature within the legal community, but at the NACDL he saw us as members of his tribe. He had started out as a Legal Aid lawyer in the Bronx, so he understood the challenges indigent defenders faced. And at the Colorado meeting, instead of striding past with a quick hello, he stopped to chat with Kathy and me as we pushed a baby carrier with a small infant. He stood out from the crowd as someone who was just as interested in Stephen as he was in public defense.

A year later, toward the end of 1993, I heard from Scheck again. The Innocence Project at Cardozo was getting flooded with requests from prisoners for help, and he and Neufeld were making alliances with local lawyers around the country to work on the cases together.

"There's an interesting murder case from Madison, Wisconsin, involving a man named Ralph Armstrong," Scheck said. "The students have gone through the transcripts and the records, and we think there might be something here. The state's evidence seemed pretty thin. Can I tell you about it?"

"Sure," I said.

The annual June lull was settling on Madison. From the city's center of gravity, University of Wisconsin–Madison, the class of 1980 had just been sent into the world. The singer Jackson Browne was making a video on State Street, outside a smoke shop called The Pipefitter. Plenty of young people who had found summer jobs in town or campus were still around, drawn to the adult freedoms of college life without the pressure of actual classes. On the twenty-third of June, a Monday, the temperature was close to ninety, and a heat wave was forecast for the week.

Charise Kamps, nineteen, who had just finished her first year at the university, was back from visiting her boyfriend, Brian Dillman, in Iowa. Kamps and one of her best friends, Jane May, decided they would go waterskiing on Tuesday afternoon. They worked together at The Pipefitter; May lived upstairs from the store, and Kamps was in a house less than a five-minute walk away. On that Monday evening, May had a small get-together at her place. Kamps was there, of course, and so were a few friends from The Pipefitter, as well as May's boyfriend, Ralph Armstrong, who was a doctoral fellow in educational psychology. There was also one special guest, in from Texas: Armstrong's younger brother, Stephen. The brothers had not seen each other in several years. They could have been cut from the same substantial block of granite. Ralph Armstrong was six foot two and powerfully built—a friend would say that he had once seen him tear an entire deck of cards in half—with long wavy hair; at six foot five and 250 pounds, Stephen Armstrong was taller still, but with a very similar hairstyle. Earlier that day Charise Kamps declined a friend's dinner invitation, saying she "had a date" with Stephen Armstrong.

Other than this brotherly reunion, the get-together in May's apartment would have been common among young men and women in those years and, indeed, many years. They had pot, beer, and cocaine. Thus fortified, they made their way to Namio's Supper Club on South Park Street, where they ate and drank for nearly three hours, until close to 9:00 p.m. The night was not over, however. Ralph Armstrong and Charise Kamps decided to get more cocaine, but first they dropped Jane at her apartment and Stephen Armstrong back at Ralph's apartment. By 11:00 p.m., Kamps was home alone, reading a book and speaking on the phone with May about the next day's waterskiing trip. They planned to meet at The Pipefitter at around 1:00 p.m., where Ralph and Stephen Armstrong would pick them up. Jane May felt Kamps seemed uncharacteristically in a hurry to get off the phone.

Around noon the following day, May got a call from Charise Kamps's boyfriend, Brian Dillman, who said he was home in Iowa and had been unable to reach her by phone. He had called the night before at 2:00 a.m., and then at 2:30 a.m., and her line had been busy both times. When he tried again a few times that morning, it was still busy. Would Jane mind checking up on Charise? She had just gotten herself ready for the waterskiing trip but, slathered in suntan lotion, wearing a bathing suit top and shorts, May made her way to Kamps's third-floor apartment on Gorham Street. She found her friend naked, facedown on the bed, and covered in blood. On the floor was her crumpled bathrobe, also bloodied. The belt of the robe, detached from the garment, was draped across her back.

May ran downstairs and along the four blocks to The Pipefitter, where another worker called the police. Then she returned to the apartment on Gorham Street to wait for them. Not long afterward, Ralph and Stephen Armstrong rolled up at The Pipefitter as promised, to collect the girls for the waterskiing trip. Just at that moment, May rang the store and spoke to Ralph Armstrong.

"She said, 'Get over here right away. Charise has been raped and murdered,'" he testified. "I said, 'I'm on my way.'"

He and his brother got in the car for the short drive. On the way to join May at the crime scene, Stephen Armstrong later told a reporter for *the Capital Times* newspaper, "Ralph said, 'That girl we had dinner with last night was raped and killed.'"*

When the police brought Jane May in to be questioned, the two Armstrong brothers picked up what Stephen called "decent clothes" from her apartment above The Pipefitter so she could put them on over her waterskiing outfit. At the police station, they were both also questioned about the events of the night before along with the others who had been with them. Not surprisingly, given the drugs and alcohol consumed, the details and accounts were frayed. Some said Ralph Armstrong and Charise Kamps were flirting with each other during the early-evening gathering at Jane May's, with Armstrong going as far as to sit in her lap; he had tried kissing her, but he was rebuffed. Another person said no, *Charise* had lightheartedly sat in *Ralph's* lap. Ralph Armstrong himself claimed that he was not interested in Charise Kamps sexually but that he did think she was attractive. Her boyfriend, Brian Dillman, had called her during the party. Armstrong had borrowed $400 from Dillman for the purchase of a car, and Dillman would later testify that he overheard Armstrong giving Kamps money toward the repayment of the loan.

After the meal at the supper club, Armstrong told investigators, he went up to Kamps's apartment for a few minutes and had a beer. They went out to buy cocaine, a meeting confirmed by the dealer. Then, he said, he and Kamps had gone back to Jane May's apartment, where everyone watched a little bit of the ten o'clock news. Before long, May was ready to sleep, so Kamps left around ten thirty. Armstrong wasn't tired, so he'd left a few minutes after Kamps for his own place where, he said, he visited with his brother for a while. He claimed he had gone back to May's apartment at around 1:00 a.m., using a fire escape at the back because he did not have a key to the front door. The last time he

---

* Rob Fixmer, "The Gorham Street Slaying: Some Pieces of the Puzzle," *Capital Times*, July 9, 1980.

saw Kamps, he told the police, was when she was leaving May's apartment at around ten thirty.

After an hour, officers read the brothers their rights. The police had discovered a minor warrant from Texas for Stephen Armstrong and wanted to hold him overnight. Matters were far more serious for Ralph Armstrong. Besides being one of the last people to have seen Kamps alive, he was on parole. A decade earlier, when he was eighteen and living in Albuquerque, New Mexico, he and several other young men had committed a series of sexual assaults on four women over a period of several months. Armstrong served about eight years in prison in New Mexico, where he had rehabilitated himself and was considered a model prisoner. He was eventually paroled, with a full scholarship to the graduate program in educational psychology at the University of Wisconsin.

Now, in the midst of a murder investigation, Armstrong had admitted drinking and using cocaine the night before, which were violations of his parole terms. He was immediately detained on the parole violation, and the investigation continued. The police searched every inch of Ralph Armstrong and his life, but they found no evidence of the crime in any of his belongings, his home, or his car, although a two-day search of the vehicle yielded a packet of marijuana and traces of cocaine. A laboratory technician rubbed the cuticles of Armstrong's fingernails and toenails with Hemastix, three-inch strips treated with a reagent that changes colors in the presence of chemicals contained in blood, but this is not a definitive test. There were several positive results, though not enough blood—if that's what the Hemastix *had* detected—for any typing.

Stephen Armstrong acknowledged that things looked bad for his brother, but he told the *Capital Times* that he was sure that Ralph Armstrong was innocent. "Whoever did that to Charise has to be a lunatic," he maintained. "Ralph's not a lunatic. He's a brilliant guy who likes to party, get high, and have fun, just like a lot of people do. And sure—sometimes he gets a little rowdy," Stephen added, pointing to a hole Ralph had once punched in a closet door. "He's got a bad, bad temper.

So do I. But the thing is, he's not a murderer. With a prior conviction and being on parole, though, he's guilty until proved innocent. Meanwhile, whoever did it is still running around loose. That's what (bothers me)."*

It would be many years before people would realize that Stephen Armstrong was speaking the truth. Just as with Steven Avery, one could easily see how Ralph Armstrong might be viewed as a likely suspect. But for anyone who doubts the plausibility of the more aggressive elements of our defense of Steven Avery—our suggestions that there had been illicit tampering with evidence, a stubborn refusal to look at other suspects, the junk masquerading as science that pervades the judicial system—Ralph Armstrong's case provides a template of mistakes, misconduct, and breathtaking twists. His struggle for vindication had to wait for several generations of biotechnical advances. But his story is not simply one of redemption and revelation found in a test tube. It includes an idealistic prosecutor who became so blindly committed to an outcome that he conjured entirely different narratives when evidence emerged to prove the opposite of what he had originally claimed; a hypnotized (and unreliable) eyewitness; two women fleeing from a house with their small children after a chance meeting with the real killer, fifteen years after the fact; a secret plan by the defense to set up a lunch meeting where an essential DNA sample could be surreptitiously collected from a reluctant person involved in the case; and a mysterious e-mail that came to me out of the blue, twenty-six years after the murder, while I was working on the Avery trial. In its final hours, there were two revelations that even now, a decade later, I have a hard time believing.

---

* Ibid.

10

A young woman just beginning to explore the promises of the world had been strangled in her bed. Her attacker had been sadistic in his assault, using a blunt instrument to violate her. Few crimes in Madison's history were as shocking as this one. The mystery of who had done it was not long-lived, at least for the investigators; the question they faced was proving it.

As word of the murder raced through Madison, the Dane County District Attorney's Office dispatched John Norsetter, an idealistic young prosecutor, to the scene. He took control as crime-scene specialists meticulously documented the condition and contents of Kamps's apartment on Gorham Street. The investigation began at the front door. No signs of forced entry. Brian Dillman said Kamps always kept the door bolted shut. A backgammon set had been knocked over, but everything else seemed to be in place; later, Dillman would notice that a tapered glass flower vase was missing from her nightstand. On the kitchen table, investigators found a small mirror, a razor blade, and a silver straw, the essentials for snorting cocaine. Fingerprint technicians dusted the room, and on a bong they located two fingerprints. One matched Ralph Armstrong's. Two officers searched for the $400 that he had given Kamps the night before. They looked "in just about any conceivable place we figured there could be money hidden," one of them said. "Drawers, dressers, cabinets, anything." The only money found was $136, in a pocket of a pair of jeans in a pile of clothes. No blood was found in the bathroom or anywhere in the apartment other than the bed, leading the authorities to conclude that the killer had not cleaned up there after the crime.

Most important was the collection of trace evidence from Charise Kamps's body before it was moved; the history of her murder would be discovered in, on, and around her corpse. She was photographed on the bed. The killer had smeared lines of her own blood from her buttocks to her legs, and also on her face. Later examination determined that she had been battered around the head, and her anus, vagina, and throat showed injuries from the insertion of a blunt object. The pathologist would estimate that she had died between midnight and 3:00 a.m., and the likely cause of death was strangulation. In all probability, the murder weapon was her bathrobe belt.

Two head hairs were recovered from the belt. Semen and blood were found on her bathrobe. Hairs were also gathered from blood and fecal matter next to the body; from the sink drain in the bathroom; and from the fan in the apartment, which had been spinning in the desultory heat. The area around the bed was vacuumed, a process that pulled in what were later toted up as seven head hairs, six head hair fragments, twenty pubic hairs, two pubic hair fragments, seven animal hairs, and three body hairs. During the postmortem examination, the pubic area of the victim was combed in search of foreign hair.

While this investigation of the crime scene was going on, various witnesses helped fill out the narratives of people who had been with Charise Kamps.

A drive-through bank teller said that, the morning after the murder, Ralph Armstrong deposited $315 in his bank account but had not been his usual chatty self; to the investigators, that was the same money Armstrong had given Kamps the night before, which now could not be found in her apartment. Armstrong explained to investigators that his brother was the source of the cash, a repayment of money that he had fronted for Stephen's visit. If he had not engaged with the teller during the transaction, Armstrong said, that was because he had been speaking with his brother at the time.

In a building next to Charise Kamps's, detectives found a witness who they believed could definitively place Ralph Armstrong going into her apartment after midnight, during the timespan when she was murdered. Riccie Orebia, a troubled prostitute who identified as female at the time of the trial and was not the sturdiest plank in their case. She said he had been sitting on her porch from around 11:00 p.m. until nearly 4:00 a.m., and that at about 12:45 she saw a white car with a black top pull up and disappear from view, apparently turning into a parking lot across the street. The driver had dark, shoulder-length hair. A few minutes later, Orebia saw a man cross the street from the parking lot and go in and out of Kamps's building several times, the last time without a shirt on.

Orebia's observations plainly would become central to any narrative of the murder of Charise Kamps. She assured the detective that she had a good memory of what had happened. The man had been about five foot five, maybe five foot seven. He'd had long dark hair. His physique was powerful; a flat stomach and strong arms. *Any facial hair?* She wasn't sure. Of course, Orebia would have to officially identify the suspect in person. Before that, though, the detectives had work to do with their witness.

Ralph Armstrong was indeed a powerfully built man, with a luxuriant head of long, wavy hair. Beyond those two features, though, Orebia's description was highly problematic. She had emphasized the physique of the man she saw going into the Gorham Avenue building— the glistening skin of his bare torso, his muscular arms, no tattoos. Yet, on Ralph Armstrong's right arm, the symbol of a phoenix was plainly tattooed; on his left upper arm, an obvious inscription read WE ARE EVERYWHERE TITAN. Another tattoo on his right calf depicted women climbing a flower. By the standards of 1980, Ralph Armstrong was a heavily inked man, a fact that would not have escaped the notice of a person like Orebia who was, based on the closely observed description she provided, captivated by the male form.

Potentially even more significant was Orebia's reckoning of the height of the man she'd seen. Orebia herself was five foot five. She said the person was five foot five or maybe a bit taller than himself, around five foot seven, while Ralph Armstrong, at six foot two, was seven to nine inches taller. Even putting aside the differences in the precise foot and inch measurements, there was still a stark discrepancy in the relative heights of Armstrong and the man Orebia described. Orebia said she had seen someone like herself, much shorter than the average man; by contrast, Ralph Armstrong was well above average height. This was not a quibble over an inch or two.

Surely, Orebia could not be summoning up an accurate recollection. The detectives turned to a psychologist in Madison, Dr. Roger McKinley, who had been an evangelist for the use of hypnosis as a way of enhancing memory in criminal investigations. On June 29, five days after the murder but before Orebia had been asked to look at any suspects, Detective Robert Lombardo arranged for Dr. McKinley to question Orebia under hypnosis. Before the session, Lombardo gave the psychologist a description of the suspect, Ralph Armstrong, and a rundown on what he saw as the pertinent facts. Then the detective followed McKinley into the session with Orebia. The hypnosis session was recorded on videotape.

Psychologist: How tall are you?

Orebia: Five five.

Q. And would you say this person was taller than you?

A. Yes.

Q. How tall is your father?

A. My father?

Q. Or somebody you know. Do you know somebody who is six feet tall?

A. Yes.

Q. Was this person the same height as a person who is six feet tall?

A. No.

Q. Was he taller?

A. Taller than six feet?

Q. Yes.

A. No.

Q. Shorter than six feet?

A. Yes.

Q. So, he's some height between five five and six feet.

A. I wouldn't go that far.

Q. How far would you go?

A. I would go between five five and five eight.

The detective passed McKinley a note that read, *The suspect is taller than that.*

McKinley prodded Orebia on her description. "Look at him carefully because the question of height is important," McKinley said.

Orebia stuck with her estimate, but McKinley was not prepared to yield to Orebia's memory and told her, "You don't have to be positive," and continued to put questions to her about the man's height.

Q. Why don't you just imaginarily put your six-foot friend next to him in your mind.

A. I think five eight is too big. He wasn't that tall.

McKinley continued to imply that Orebia's answer was wrong, repeatedly mentioning a height of six feet. The detective also made his opinion clear. At one point, commenting on one of Orebia's answers,

Detective Lombardo can be heard to say, "I doubt that." And as if their badgering of Orebia and vocal skepticism about her responses were not enough, McKinley and Lombardo also had four photographs in the room during the session. Three were of Armstrong's car and one was of Armstrong himself. The doctor and the detective passed the pictures back and forth in sight of Orebia.

The very power attributed to hypnosis—putting people into a state of consciousness in which they are open to suggestion—is antithetical to eliciting reliable, authoritative memories. Add to that the open skepticism expressed by the doctor and the detective, and the display of photographs, and the entire exercise amounted to little more than a highly effective process for contaminating Orebia's memory. It was tantamount to sneezing into a test tube.

Four days after the hypnosis session, an extraordinary in-person identification session was staged. Detectives told Orebia that they had a suspect and asked her to sit on her porch as she had been on the night of the murder. The plan was to have Armstrong and "fillers" (who were really police officers) walk from the parking lot up to Kamps's building. But Armstrong's lawyer warned him that the lineup would be staged to make him stand out and advised him not to cooperate with the procedure by passively resisting. This way, it could be explained in court that his conspicuous uncooperativeness was why the witness had selected him in the lineup. So Armstrong went limp, refusing to take his place in the parade. Two officers got under his arms and dragged him across the street. Along the way, his shoes fell off. To give the process some semblance of objectivity, the four police officers rounding out the lineup pretended to go limp when they walked as well, but one of them simply walked with an officer on each arm. Armstrong was the only participant obviously being carried and dragged by the officers, so he did indeed stand out from the other "fillers." The detectives reported that Orebia gasped when she saw Armstrong. In court, Orebia denied gasping and said she had simply belched.

After the parade, the five people were arrayed in front of a van so that Orebia could see them all at once. Two of the "filler" officers appeared to be much older than the person Orebia had described. Two others had short hair; they shared wigs, which were immediately spotted by Orebia, who knew her way around wigs. All four officers had fake tattoos. In a photograph taken of the lineup, the wigs worn by the "fillers" are obviously askew, and Armstrong is the only one being held up by police officers.

The procedure, Orebia later said, was "rigged." Months later, she swore affidavits recanting her identification of Armstrong, saying she had made it only under pressure from the police. By the time the trial came, however, she had recanted this recantation and was back to stating that Ralph Armstrong was the man she had seen going in and out of Charise Kamps's building around the time of the murder.

Ralph Armstrong's trial marched quickly to the wrong destination. It featured pictures of a gory crime scene; abundant physical evidence; even a witness, albeit a shaky one, who identified the only suspect going into the victim's house at the time she was killed.

Time and again, the prosecutor, John Norsetter, described the physical evidence in damning terms. The semen was part of his evidentiary panorama, beginning with a stain on Charise Kamps's bathrobe that originated from a man with Type A blood. That covered a large percentage of the population, including Brian Dillman, her boyfriend, but also Ralph Armstrong.

"It came from a person with Type A blood who secreted his blood type in his body fluid, in his semen, in his saliva, in his tears," Norsetter told the jury. "Ralph Armstrong's a Type A secreter."

His hands and feet also incriminated him, Norsetter said, recalling the testimony of a technician named Jill Wegner.

"The defendant's fingers were tested down at the police station. Jill Wegner ran the Hemostix around the cuticles and under the thumb and under the nails and around the cuticles of every finger and lo and behold, there was blood under every fingernail, every single one.

"That was Charise Kamps's blood."

Certainly, that was a drastic overstatement of the testimony: Wegner had said that her test only indicated a presumptive presence of blood, not the type. Other nonblood substances could have triggered the same result. If it was blood, it might well have been Armstrong's own. He had cut himself on the day of Charise Kamps's murder when he fell in a footrace with his brother. Moreover, a few hours before Kamps's body was discovered, both Armstrong and Jane May testified that they'd had sex. May was having her period and was being treated for a condition that caused an unusually heavy flow. So Armstrong might well have had blood under his nails for reasons having nothing to do with the murder of Charise Kamps.

The harvest of the scene had yielded hair in the sink, the fan, and in small bits of fecal matter found near Kamps's body, none of which could be said with any certainty to have come from one person, but some of which were linked to Ralph Armstrong by a laboratory technician, who said the hairs were "consistent" with or "similar" to Armstrong's—the same pseudoscientific discipline that would condemn Steven Avery five years later.

"There is no explanation of why that hair was found in every place that the defendant was," Norsetter said.

Well, actually, there is: May testified that she and Ralph Armstrong shared a hairbrush and that she had brought it with her on occasions when she stayed with Charise Kamps.

Norsetter showed the jury a photograph of Kamps's naked body, facedown, blood smeared along her back, buttocks, and thighs. Her robe belt was draped across her back.

"Two of the defendant's hairs were on this robe [belt]," Norsetter said.

It was untrue, devastating.

One by one, none of the claims was proof positive, a smoking gun that could prove Ralph Armstrong had killed Charise Kamps. But they were not considered individually. Faint and blurry as single elements, they somehow achieved greater clarity when viewed as parts of a mosaic, their suggestiveness solidifying into certainty: witnesses who thought Armstrong and Kamps were flirting that evening;

a bank teller who received a $315 deposit when $400 was missing from Kamps's apartment; a witness who might have seen Armstrong coming and going from the building after midnight; a bong with his fingerprint on it; an apartment where hair "consistent or similar" to his was found; semen on Kamps's bathrobe that was consistent with his.

In his closing argument, Norsetter overreached even his own expert's opinion. "The physical evidence [of] Ralph Armstrong at the scene ties him irrevocably to the murder of Charise Kamps," he insisted.

Those ties were not irrevocable. But they would take decades to undo. Convicted of murder and rape, Armstrong was sent off to prison for life plus sixteen years.

While in prison, Ralph Armstrong, who is a voracious reader, learned that DNA tests were being used to revisit old biological evidence and that the results contradicted the original evidence used to convict other prisoners. Acting as his own lawyer, in 1990 Armstrong asked that the physical evidence used to convict him be tested with this new technology. A friend helped him cover the costs. At the time, the tests were still in their earliest stages and required large volumes of intact DNA, and so would work only on biological evidence that had not heavily deteriorated. Armstrong was in the first generation of convicts to seek them out. It took him the better part of a year to get the testing done and bring the results to court, which he did in February 1991. They seemed to be far more illuminating than the original laboratory evidence in the case.

For instance, the lab had determined that the semen on Charise Kamps's bathrobe was produced by someone with Type A blood. Most people's blood types can be detected not only in their blood but also in their saliva, mucus, or semen. Since Armstrong had Type A blood, the prosecution argued that the semen on the bathrobe could have been his. It was not very strong evidence, as the semen also could have been left by anyone with the same blood type, including Kamps's boyfriend, Brian Dillman. The DNA test, however, was much more specific. It showed definitively that Ralph could not have been the source of that semen.

Another year went by before the same judge who had presided over the original trial decided that this new DNA evidence was not important enough to grant Armstrong's motion for a new trial. The case went to the Wisconsin State Court of Appeals and languished for another year before the court declared that the semen stain, which could not have come from Armstrong, was "an insignificant piece of circumstantial evidence linking Armstrong to Kamps and to her apartment." Far more important, the court found, was the eyewitness—Orebia, the hypnotized prostitute who changed her (at the time of the trial) mind repeatedly about whether Armstrong was the man she had seen going in and out of Kamps's apartment building—and "other physical evidence, such as blood and hair samples found on his body and at the crime scene, [that] also inculpated Armstrong." So the court of appeals also decided Ralph Armstrong was not entitled to a new trial based on the new DNA evidence.

When Barry Scheck called me in 1993, Armstrong's appeal was pending before the state supreme court.

"The original case had some voodoo testimony about hairs found at the scene matching Armstrong's," Barry said to me. "The main witness, the neighbor, was a transvestite prostitute, who was hypnotized before she identified him. It seems pretty thin."

It sounded that way to me, too. Barry was looking for a local lawyer to work with the Innocence Project in filing briefs and wondered if I would be interested in joining forces with him.

"I'd be happy to work with you on this," I said.

For the next fifteen years, I would be working on that case, off and on, with Scheck and the Innocence Project. Whenever it looked as if Ralph Armstrong had enough proof to warrant a new trial, the courts in Wisconsin found some reason not to grant one. From the perspective of the appellate courts, evidence that is discovered *after* a trial and guilty verdict is like finishing a meal and then being served a new course of food after coffee and dessert—the system is not well equipped to digest it. Therefore, appeals courts do not, generally speaking, reevaluate evidence but rather decide if the original trial process was constitutional and administered fairly by the judge. The primary interest of most appellate courts is "finality" of judgments, not real justice, and in the vast majority of cases, appeals courts ratify whatever took place at that original trial, no matter how unreliable.

Indeed, some courts hold that "actual innocence" is not enough to warrant a new trial. The DNA shows us the mistakes made by police, prosecutors, defense lawyers, witnesses, and juries. It has also revealed how ineffective the appellate courts are at vindicating the rights of people who come before it. In a study of the first two hundred DNA exonerations, Brandon Garrett, a law professor at the University of Virginia, mapped out the journey of the wrongly convicted people before they were finally cleared. In 86 percent of the cases, no appellate court found fault with the original trials, or if they did, they declared it to be "harmless error."[*] Those courts—widely, but mistakenly, regarded as the backstop of our judicial system—won't substitute their judgment for that of the lower court or the jury, even if new evidence makes that conviction or court judgment highly suspect. Over the years, appellate courts have created legal obstacles limiting their review of "discretionary" decisions and have imposed convoluted "tests" that must be overcome for a defendant to gain a reversal of his conviction.

At the time Scheck called me, one of the few universally recognized experts in forensic DNA testing was Dr. Edward Blake, a scientist in California. Blake had just worked on a New York rape case in which a man in prison was excluded as the source of a semen stain, but the district attorney would not concede that this proved his innocence because the semen could have come from the victim's husband and not the rapist. The logical next step would have been to get a reference sample from the husband, but as this was a new area of law, the defendant had no power to compel the husband to provide a sample, and

---

[*] "Judging Innocence," *Columbia Law Review* 18, no. 1 (January 2008): 55–142.

even now, a quarter century later, this remains an unsettled issue in many states. That case had dragged on for a couple of years until the husband voluntarily provided a sample, which showed that neither he nor the convicted man was the source of the semen. Since the woman had no sexual partners other than her husband, the only explanation was that it had been left by the rapist. The conviction was overturned.

In Ralph Armstrong's case, that first round of DNA testing also did not include a reference sample from Brian Dillman. Even though the results had excluded Armstrong as the contributor of the semen, this in itself did not necessarily prove he had *not* assaulted Charise Kamps. Dr. Blake took the reasonable position that it was essential for us to get a DNA sample from Brian Dillman so that we would know if he was the source of any other evidence that might be tested, such as the hairs found on her body and also on the bathrobe belt that was apparently used to strangle her. Interestingly, during the original police investigation, blood was drawn from Brian Dillman and it could serve as a reference sample for his DNA, but, for some unexplained reason, it had disappeared.

How could we get a new blood sample?

The prosecutor on Ralph's case, John Norsetter, told us that he had no objection and that he would ask Dillman on our behalf. He reported back that Dillman was thinking about it, and this dragged on and on. Finally, we came up with another plan.

If someone could collect a glass Dillman had drunk from, or the butt of a cigarette he had smoked, then we might be able to secure a testable sample of his DNA. Among Ralph Armstrong's friends from his days in Madison, a few people continued to believe in his innocence, and although it had been many years since any of these friends had seen each other, one of them called Dillman and asked to meet him for lunch. The plan was for the friend to surreptitiously pick something that might have a trace of Dillman's DNA. He agreed to the lunch. At the last minute, though, he canceled.

Finally, we went to court seeking an order to force Brian Dillman to provide a sample, although we were not sure we even had the right to do so. The judge scheduled a hearing that Dillman did not show up for. He did, however, send a lawyer who said Dillman was willing to provide a sample. We agreed to share the test results with his counsel.

In the end, Ralph Armstrong was definitively eliminated as the source of the hairs found on the belt of the bathrobe. So was Brian Dillman. John Norsetter, who had been most agreeable to all of these tests, seemed very surprised when the results came back excluding Armstrong. But he would not consent to a new trial. So we went back to court.

Part III

JUST A LAWYER

11

As the calendar entered a new century and a new millennium, our law practice was continuing to grow. I was beginning to think about adding other young lawyers to the firm. We opened a satellite office on the north shore of Milwaukee, closer to our partner Dudley's home. Meanwhile, favorable forensic tests continued to come in on Ralph Armstrong's case. Barry Scheck and I were getting ready to file a motion for a new trial in Dane County Circuit Court. September 1, 2001, marked the twentieth anniversary of my admission as a lawyer in Wisconsin. But my life was about to turn upside down in ways I'd never contemplated. I was about to experience what my clients must feel, what it's like to put your entire faith in the expertise of someone else when your life is on the line.

On the Friday before Labor Day weekend in 2001, a radiologist stepped into the room where I had just finished having a CT scan. I'd had X-rays and scans before, and the usual routine is that a technician will come out, tell you it's all done, and that Dr. So-and-So will be sending a report to your personal physician, which means a delay of several days or more. You almost never see the radiologist in person on the day of the exam. You rarely find out on the spot what mysteries have been divined.

If you do, it usually means the answers aren't good. "You've got something in there," he said. "It may be benign, but it's quite large; it may be malignant."

Kathy had been right. Two weeks earlier, at the beach on the Outer Banks of North Carolina, she'd noticed a bump on my thigh.

"That's getting bigger," she'd said.

I had barely registered it a few months before, then pretty much forgot about it. I was preparing to try a high-publicity homicide trial in the middle of September. Our beach vacation was to be my last respite before that began.

The bump did not hurt at all and appeared to be less than an inch in size.

"It's probably a cyst or something," I said, and promised to get it checked out. My primary doctor looked at it, but he did not seem alarmed. Nevertheless, he referred me to an orthopedic specialist for his opinion. That doctor ordered this CT scan later the same week, which I'd insisted on going to by myself.

"You really need to see a cancer specialist," the radiologist said. "An orthopedic oncology expert." It had not occurred to me that there were such specialties within specialties.

He gave me a big manila envelope with the images. I went home in a daze. Since it was Friday afternoon of a holiday weekend, there was no one immediately available to consult. I was surprised when the doctor who'd ordered the scan called me from his cell phone on Friday evening, while on his way to Northern Wisconsin for the long weekend.

"You need to go see Don Hackbarth. He's *the* guy. I'll try to reach him this weekend and ask him to get you in as soon as possible."

He called me back on Saturday night to say he'd already spoken to Dr. Hackbarth and I should call his office on Tuesday. All this extraordinary haste on a holiday weekend really made Kathy and me even more nervous.

I called Dr. Hackbarth first thing on Tuesday, but the next available appointment was on Tuesday of the following week. At home, I pulled out the films and tried to read them: cross sections of tissue in each leg, dozens of thumbnail images, impossible to make sense of. I was pretty sure that I could see some form in the right leg that was not visible in the left. Kathy and I scoured websites for information. Sometimes these growths were benign, and surely that would be the case with me; I felt fine. As a matter of fact, I was feeling more fit and trim after the beach vacation than I had in a long time. We were in a modestly hopeful state as the appointment with Dr. Hackbarth approached. Even so, this time Kathy was coming along; as I'd learned working alongside her in court, having her there would do me good.

We arrived at the orthopedic clinic at Froedtert Hospital in Milwaukee early. Dr. Hackbarth took a quick look at the lump on my leg, then stuck the images into a light box, scanning them for a moment.

"We'll need to get a biopsy, probably tomorrow," he said. "I can tell you right now, this is almost certainly malignant. It's a soft-tissue sarcoma. I'm guessing it's one of two types, and they're both quite rare and lethal. We used to just take people's legs with amputation, but we've gotten better at this. We will try to save your life, and your leg—but you will definitely have a long year ahead of you with various kinds of treatments."

As I stood over his shoulder, he went through the individual images that showed the abnormality and pulled up a full-length picture of both legs that I hadn't noticed before. The difference was stark. I couldn't tell what was me and what was tumor. The growth ran so high up my leg that an amputation might involve not just the leg but my hip, too. In any event, Dr. Hackbarth said, he was going to do everything he could to avoid that.

Just then, he got paged and gently excused himself.

"I'll let you guys talk about it," he said. "I'll come back in a few minutes."

A sinkhole had opened beneath our lives. Our son, Stephen, was nine; Grace, our daughter, was seven.

"Don't panic," I told Kathy. "It's not definite until the biopsy."

Clear-eyed, Kathy would have none of my whistling in the dark. "He knows already," she said. "That's why he's telling us the other stuff."

Then Dr. Hackbarth opened the door, with an expression on his face that hadn't been there a few minutes earlier. It was now about 10:30 a.m., Milwaukee time.

"That page was from my wife," he said slowly. "A plane has hit the World Trade Center, and it's collapsed."

At first, Kathy and I gave each other a look that said, *This guy is nuts; let's get out of here!* But as we talked further, it became clear Dr. Hackbarth was telling the truth.

In the car on the way home, the radio broadcasts were full of one alarming piece of news after another. A second plane had hit the other twin tower. The Pentagon had also been hit. Nobody knew where the president's plane was. People were in bunkers. A plane had gone down in Pennsylvania. The government had ordered all airliners to land and not to fly again until further notice.

This was a horrible national tragedy. I felt awful for everybody. Kathy and I had been in New York less than a year earlier for another NACDL conference. We went to the World Trade Center and ate at Windows on the World. And yet I couldn't help but think I was going to be dead in a few months. I was forty-five years old, and until now I had not given mortality much thought. I was absorbed by Kathy, by the two little kids in our lives, and by work. What had I done to leave my mark on the world? My life had been a meaningless blip.

Back home in the bedroom, I turned on the *Today* show to follow the unfolding personal and global calamities. Kathy came in and out; it was too horrible to watch. My biopsy was scheduled for the next day. Often, biopsies are just simple procedures to extract pieces of tissue. Not this time. The tumor was braided around my femoral vein. The biopsy would be a fully anesthetized surgery.

Almost exactly a year earlier, when my father had been in the final months of bladder cancer, a priest had come to anoint him and pray. During my childhood, this sacrament had been called extreme unction, or a "final anointing," emphasizing that it was meant for the dying; now, it is known as the Anointing of the Sick. The ritual for my dad had been moving and settling, comforting and reassuring. I wanted an experience like that before going in for the biopsy, and I wanted our kids to be there.

After the morning's news of the attacks, their school had brought students to the church for prayers. Stephen was in fourth grade and Grace, second. We picked them up and went into a chapel, where the associate pastor gave me the sacrament. Kathy and I were worried about alarming them, especially because they had just lost their grandfather to cancer a year before. We didn't mention the word "cancer" itself, but we did let them know I was going to have surgery and that it was serious.

The sacrament, and the quiet time with our children in church, brought me and Kathy some peace.

During my father's illness I spent a lot of time in the medical library at the hospital reading journals that weren't easily available online. I had also developed some proficiency over the years mining medical articles in preparation for the testimony of expert witnesses. Now I was back in that same library, on behalf of myself, but I couldn't stick with the task.

I quickly learned that if you're going to get cancer, you don't want it to be a rare type. There's not enough money or impetus spurring research. For my cancer, there was no clear-cut treatment. Depending on the specialist, the approach would be different, but they all relied on old-line chemotherapy that destroyed both cancerous and good tissue almost indiscriminately. The drugs might as well have been battery acid. We had to consider the choices and decide quickly which one to go with and where to do it.

The first time I read the statistics on surviving five years with this cancer, I got physically ill and went into an emotional tailspin.

"You've got to stop doing this," Kathy said.

But somebody had to do the research. Because I could not face the grim numbers, Kathy and my oldest brother, Tom, took it on.

In the meantime, we wanted a second opinion. Our first choice was a doctor in New York City, but because of the terrorist attacks, flights had been canceled indefinitely. Instead, we arranged to meet with specialists at the Mayo Clinic in Rochester, Minnesota. It was reachable by car, about a five-hour drive. By the time we saw the oncologist and the surgeon at the Mayo Clinic, the biopsy had confirmed the suspicion of Dr. Hackbarth: The tumor was malignant, a soft-tissue sarcoma subtype known as synovial cell sarcoma. The people at Mayo recommended several months of chemotherapy, plus radiation, and then surgery. I'd have to move to Rochester and live there alone during that time, because Kathy had to take care of the children. This was a depressing prospect for someone already struggling with nothing but bleak news.

Near the end of my afternoon with the Mayo specialists, I realized my leg was really hurting although the biopsy surgery site on my leg was healing fine. Was I thinking about the tumor and conjuring the pain? It seemed too acute to be self-induced. When Kathy took a look, she was shocked; my entire right leg was inflamed and hot. Even I could see that something was wrong. But no one at the Mayo Clinic was prepared to deal with a patient in crisis, or at least my crisis, particularly as it was by then past 5:00 p.m. and they were closing. They suggested we go back to the hotel and come back in the morning when the clinic would reopen.

"Not a chance we're doing that," Kathy interrupted. "What alternative option is there to figure out right now what's going on with his leg?"

Well, we could go to an emergency room, but there wasn't one on the Mayo Clinic campus. We'd have to go to Saint Mary's Hospital, a few miles away. How should we get there? Call a cab, we were advised. Then, as it does now, that seemed a startling response to a patient in clear distress, but we had no choice.

At Saint Mary's Hospital, the emergency room staff did not waste a second when they saw my leg. They quickly discovered a giant blood clot stretching almost the entire length of my thigh, a life-and-death emergency. A part of the clot could break off, travel to my lungs, and kill me. If Kathy had accepted Mayo's first suggestion to come back the following day, I could have died in our hotel room overnight. But the people at Saint Mary's could not have been better. They started me on blood thinners to dissolve the clot and admitted me to the hospital for five days to be sure the medicine did the trick. A few days later, the doctors from the Mayo Clinic cancer center stopped by my hospital room and suggested that hey, since I was already in town, why not just go ahead, start the chemo treatment with them, then have the tumor removed in Rochester under Mayo's care?

"Not a chance," I said.

That blood clot experience had two important effects on me. For one, it helped shake me out of the funk of self-pity caused by the shock of learning that I had a rare and lethal form of cancer and, even if I managed to survive, I could lose my leg. I decided there was a lot of living left to do, even with only one leg. When I got home, I was confined to a wheelchair for a while. I learned to wheel myself around the house, researched how to retrofit my car with handles to activate the foot pedals, and plotted where I could install an elevator in the house we'd built just two years earlier. If Raymond Burr from the *Ironside* television series could navigate the criminal justice system in a wheelchair, I could too.

The clot also helped me to see that I needed to be home in Wisconsin for my treatment, where I would have my children and wife around me. It wasn't just that we were dismayed by Mayo's response to my blood clot emergency. My doctor back in Wisconsin, Don Hackbarth, had impressed me with his refreshing, humble approach to his mission. He doesn't have the bravado typical of surgeons. I like that about him.

"I believe God works through my hands," he told me once. "I can only do what God wants me to do."

I returned to Froedtert and met with a team that included a chemotherapy oncologist, radiation oncologist, and Dr. Hackbarth, who served as captain of the ship. I knew from our research that my best chance of survival was an aggressive approach. With renewed hope and an optimistic outlook, I told the oncologist to blast me with his highest-octane chemotherapy.

"Bring me to the brink of the precipice before you yank me back," I said.

"Don't worry," he replied with a wry smile. "You will not feel undertreated."

The oncologist was right about that. Before the tumor itself could be removed, I had chemotherapy so strong that it required hospital inpatient administration for five days, followed by two weeks of retching illness before I had recovered enough for another blast. After two months of this, I certainly did *not* feel undertreated.

That was followed immediately by twenty-five daily doses of high radiation. Because radiation has a cumulative effect on the body, there are ceilings on how much people can take in their lives. Even exposures that take place years apart—dental X-rays at twenty and orthopedic X-rays at fifty—are added together. I got the lifetime maximum in less than one month. My hair fell out and my skin peeled off.

Kathy later told me that one day in the car, Grace had asked: "Momma, what are the chances that Daddy is going to die?"

"No, no," Kathy said, "Daddy's not going to die. He just has to have this treatment." Grace wasn't satisfied.

"But Momma," she asked, "what are the chances that he may die?"

After Kathy ducked the question again, Grace repeated it a third time. Kathy finally answered directly, with perhaps more assurance than she felt.

"The chances are good that Daddy's not going to die," she said.

That last answer seemed to satisfy Grace. But, not really, as we found out a few days later. Her seven-year-old brain had been absorbing all the changes in our lives, and in me, and she had a new question.

"Momma, if Daddy dies, and you die, what is going to happen to me?"

Again, Kathy tried to avoid the question, eventually responding when Grace asked a third time. She had aunts and uncles around, Kathy said, and plenty of cousins, a response that Grace took in stride. At seven years of age, this child of two criminal defense lawyers had intuitively mastered the old lawyer's trick for witnesses who avoid answering a question: Just keep repeating it. By the third time, they usually will answer it.

In February, one month after my radiation treatment had ended, it was time for the surgery. The tumor had been growing for a long time, the doctors said, possibly ten years. It was older than my kids. Centered near the groin, it was so big that they had to remove the femoral vein and hope that neighboring veins would take over the flow of blood from the leg back to the heart.

On the day of the surgery, Dr. Hackbarth came in early to read the latest pathology reports on the exact borders of the tumor and to visualize how the surgery would go.

His preparation sounded similar to what we do before a homicide [trial], when we work our way mentally through all the possible permutations of evidence, Kathy wrote to friends and family.

Before I was put under, Dr. Hackbarth explained, as he had previously, that he would try to save my leg, but once he opened me up and could see the tumor, he might conclude that this wasn't feasible if he were to save my life. So he wanted me to sign away my leg in advance if he had to amputate. I hesitated and turned to Kathy.

"Why don't you wait on that decision and come out and ask Kathy before you amputate?" I suggested.

"Oh no you don't," Kathy said. "You aren't putting this on me. I'm telling you right now if he comes out and says it's his leg or his life, and you leave it up to me, you won't be waking up with two legs."

All right, then. I managed to smile as I signed the consent form, then dropped into a drugged sleep.

Vascular and plastic surgeons worked all day and into the evening. Just teasing apart the blood vessels that were tangled with the tumor took six hours. Much of what had been my thigh was gouged out, and to fill in the missing tissue, the doctors disconnected from my rib cage a sheath of muscle that connects the sternum to the pubis, the rectus abdominis. Then they flopped it down to the cavity where my thigh had been. Its purpose was not to serve as a muscle that would move my leg; it was needed as fresh tissue for the parts of my thigh that had been nearly destroyed by the blasts of radiation and would have a hard time healing after surgery.

Kathy stood vigil in the waiting room with either my brother Mike, our law partner, Dudley, or an old friend from the public defender's office, Kathy Zebell, keeping her company. After the tumor was finally removed, Dr. Hackbarth went down to the pathology lab, clucking like a mother hen over it in his keenness to confirm that it had been cleanly removed, with no edges left behind.

By the time the surgeons came for Kathy, the waiting room had closed. They had been working on me for thirteen and a half hours.

"He's in the recovery room and very combative," one of them reported. "Don't worry, it happens a lot when they're under that long."

Kathy later told me that she'd found me struggling with a male nurse, so much so that they feared I would dislodge a line. She started talking and calmed me down, but I was in cuckoo-land for the next few days. In my hospital room, the Winter Olympics were on television.

"That should be me," I said. "I'm a bobsledder. I should be there at the Olympics."

Kathy looked at me.

"I'm a downhill skier," I said, changing sports. "I broke my leg. It's too bad I can't be there. Maybe next time."

"Jerry," Kathy said, "what are you talking about?"

"I'm a skier, aren't I?"

"No," she said. "You're in the hospital because you have cancer. You are a lawyer."

A lawyer. Hmm.

"That doesn't sound very interesting," I said.

Much of what happened was a blur to me. I don't recall waking up from surgery, or when I first realized that I still had both legs. Kathy kept our friends and family abreast of developments by e-mail. In the big picture, the news was good. The removal of the tumor had been a success, and follow-up pathology reports showed that its edges were clean, meaning a smaller chance that there were fugitive cancer cells that escaped the chemo, radiation, and surgery. But there was a mysterious complication.

12

He is not making the rapid and smooth progress that we hoped, Kathy's e-mail read. He has been running a temp the last few days.

The doctors checked for a clot, tested my blood, studied the incision and the drains. My pain was pretty well controlled by some heavy-duty narcotics. We even nicknamed one of the physicians "Dr. Feelgood" because he was easygoing about prescribing medications.

Kathy wrote: They have weaned him down a bit so his active hallucinations have slowed but we have had some wacky conversations the past few days. And, she acknowledged, it wasn't just me who was disappointed that I wasn't a skier. So am I, she'd noted.

The fever and its mysterious origin persisted. My doctors feared the abdominal muscle flap wasn't healing properly in the leg, so a new incision was made in search of a cause. Nothing. I kept getting ice packs and antibiotics as a precaution. Finally, two weeks later, they operated again and made a ridiculous discovery. A sponge had been left at the bottom of the original incision.

The doctors who came to tell me the unhappy news could not have been more embarrassed and miserable, and with good cause, Kathy wrote in another e-mail update. First, if you are going to leave a sponge in someone you don't want it to be a lawyer. But they also really like Jerry and he had a big complicated surgery in which they gave a lot of heart and energy. Due to their error, I'd had two unnecessary surgeries and a lot of extra misery.

Looking back, the error is an interesting one. Sponges left behind in surgical patients have been a hazard for decades; on average, it happens twice a year per hospital. The costs of tracking them down and reopening the patient add, on average, $63,631 to a hospital bill, a federal study found. So it has long been standard procedure in operating rooms to keep a careful inventory of everything that goes into a patient so that it can be accounted for.[*] But sponges are devilishly hard to find if the patient has been closed up because on an X-ray they look just like other tissue. Then someone came up with the idea of putting a tiny metal marker in the sponges, so if one does get left behind, it can be located with an X-ray.

In my case, the operating room staff did a count at the end of my surgery and realized that they were missing a sponge. They brought in an X-ray machine before I was fully closed up but did not catch it. Meanwhile, a sponge was discovered in the operating room trash. Ah-ha! There was the missing sponge, or so they thought. I was wheeled off to the recovery room. Yet there I was, days later, with a miserable fever, unable to leave the hospital or make recovery progress. In fact, that sponge in the trash had nothing to do with my surgery and probably shouldn't have been there. The missing sponge was still inside me and it had missed detection. This was a cautionary tale about how it's possible to infer the wrong conclusion from circumstantial evidence.

The X-ray did not reach all the way to the end of the incision because it is two and a half feet long, Kathy wrote. Upon closer inspection, the sponge had actually appeared on the X-ray, but its distinctive little metal marker was in the corner of the image, covered with the name plate identifying the film as being of me. In general, the medical profession is far more proactive than the criminal justice system about identifying systemic errors, facing them squarely, and setting up measures to curtail or elim-inate them. Hospitals have weekly sessions to review unexpected deaths or prolonged stays. That's why there was a metal clip on that sponge. More recently, some hospitals have begun using RFID (radio frequency identification) tags on sponges to keep track of them. Even though the metal clip did not work for me, studies show a significant decline in lost sponges and other forgotten surgical paraphernalia as new tracking technologies are adopted. In my line of work, wrongful convictions are

---

[*] Lenny Berstein, "When Your Surgeon Accidentally Leaves Something Inside You," *Washington Post*, September 4, 2014. https://www.washingtonpost.com/news/to-your-health/wp/2014/09/04/when-your-surgeon-accidentally-leaves-something-inside-you/.

almost always systemic failures, with many contributing causes, but the kinds of reviews needed to understand them—and come up with solutions—rarely happen.

I wasn't happy about the sponge error, but luckily it caused no permanent damage. I was alive and still had two legs. The surgeons did a remarkable job of removing the tumor without spreading cancer cells elsewhere in my body. And they stitched up my rearranged anatomy without causing me to lose all function in that leg. To this day I am very grateful for their skill and dedication. I always will be.

The next months brought rounds of infections, chemotherapy, white blood cell counts in free fall, shuttling between doctors and home. I was off work for nearly a year. Kathy had set up a hospital bed in the guest room, and it became a secondary living room. She spread a towel on the floor so the family could eat meals there. Except for me. I ate in bed or, more accurately, I slurped in bed: I was on a diet of high-calorie shakes. Rather than use packaged versions, Kathy concocted her own from protein powder stirred into ice cream and chocolate.

She also learned wound care, how to clean the central intravenous line that had been installed in my chest, and all the other tedious tasks of looking after a gravely ill person. Hers was a triple burden; in addition to nursing me back to health and taking care of two young children, Kathy also—along with our partner, Dudley—handled existing and new clients at the law firm. Much of our usual referral business from other lawyers dried up because people felt they didn't want to overburden Kathy, but we also needed the business to pay for health insurance and all of our other obligations. In the end, we had very little income after expenses that year, but nobody was laid off and all the bills were paid.

One side effect often experienced by cancer patients—"chemo brain," a fog in the mind—hit me hard. Reading or watching television became impossible. It was too hard to follow. When the kids came home from school, they would climb into the bed with me and read books. Their presence was consoling, but often all I could do was lie there with my eyes closed, unable even to really speak. After they had turned in for the night, Kathy would lie next to me. Eventually, I was able to watch some television, and so every evening Kathy and I tuned into reruns of *Everybody Loves Raymond* before I dropped off. Comedy at the end of each day seemed to help me sleep better.

Our neighbors and parish community rallied. People at church signed up to bring in meals three times a week. (Kathy finally had to make a request: no more lasagna or desserts. Everyone likes baking desserts.) My siblings Tom, John, and Mike, along with their spouses, Terry, Bjorn, and Rina, came to visit at different times to pitch in. At one point, Kathy had a trial in a courthouse an hour from home, which meant she would have to stay overnight. My brother Mike arrived to stay with the kids and me. As soon as Kathy got to her hotel, she realized that she'd left behind all the suits she was going to wear. Mike drove them up to her.

I had to learn to walk again without the regular package of muscles that control the hip. This required rigorous, regular physical therapy, with sessions several days a week. Friends from our parish volunteered to drive me. One woman in particular took me to many of my appointments, even when they fell on days when her kids were not in school. She just brought them along, and they all waited while I went through the sessions. Once, I suggested that she really shouldn't make her children sit through such a boring afternoon.

She said, "No, I want them here to see this is part of life's little sacrifices when we need to help others."

These gifts of time, mostly from stay-at-home moms, made it possible for Kathy to keep running the office.

About five weeks after the surgery, Kathy sent an e-mail update:

Slow and steady wins the race to be fully functional. Jerry gets stronger every day. His ability to move his leg, even to pull his legs together in the absence of several of the muscle groups that would ordinarily power the leg, is nothing short of miraculous. Sometimes I think he does it by sheer will. He is even walking a few steps without the benefit of a walker.

The first time he pulled that stunt, I developed a few more gray hairs but he looked so proud of himself I didn't have the heart to give way to my hysteria.

When I was able to mess around on my laptop again, I discovered an article about my type of cancer. The numbers on survival were even more dismal than I had believed. On arriving home that day, Kathy immediately saw that there was something the matter.

"What's wrong with you?" she asked.

"I'm doomed," I said.

"What do you mean you're doomed?"

"You've been hiding this from me all along. I found these articles," I said, spouting statistics.

"I haven't been withholding from you, although, yeah, I've seen a lot of bad stuff," she said, examining the article. "You're reading that wrong. You're completely misunderstanding what this says."

In fact, I had inverted the statistics in my head, making them even worse.

"Stop doing that," Kathy said. "You're not going to do any more research."

As the months piled up, and I got through more brutal rounds of chemo treatment, I started to feel better and began to once again see a horizon that did not end at the hospital bed in the guest room. One day, through the window overlooking the wetlands behind our house, I could see the prairie grass swaying in the breeze. That wind was energy that had traveled around the earth with incalculable force; the grass was its vector, a physical sign. I thought, *There's a God who created this complex and beautiful movement and energy.* Throughout the ordeal, my faith became even more important. I told myself I would never again take life for granted. I would appreciate every day, and not go back to sweating the small stuff that everybody normally does. From what I've heard, this shifting of priorities is common among cancer survivors and combat veterans. Life provides a new lens for seeing the world.

Still, getting better means that old routines come out of hibernation;

familiar, easy, comfortable, but not necessarily what is important. You have to distinguish between what is necessary and what is mere force of habit. Fortunately, our vague plans to bring in associates and expand the firm had never gone beyond the talking stage. Taking on all that overhead would have made it very hard to keep the practice going, and given what we had just been through we decided we weren't going to go that route. Instead of plunging back in, I would work part-time to be more available for the kids and school activities, family life and vacations.

When I first went back to the office, I had piles of unread e-mails from criminal lawyer groups, state bar association committees, and other organizations in which I held leadership positions. Going through them after so many months, I realized that nothing had changed. *These guys were still fighting over the same stuff.* Maybe I needed to change my career. Could this all have been a sign from God that I was wasting my life on the wrong things? After all, why had I survived this cancer when a lot of people had not? There had to be a bigger plan here somewhere, if I could only discern it. Then I remembered a neighbor, a Lutheran minister, who used to come down and talk to me regularly when I was home sick, as did my Catholic pastor.

One time, the minister said to me, "You know, maybe *this* is the plan. Continue doing what you're doing. You're doing a lot of good. Helping people at difficult times in their life. Maybe there is no plan for you to do something different. This is what you need to keep doing."

I have always looked at the career of a criminal defense lawyer as more of a vocation than a job. But cancer was a wake-up call. It helped me understand how people must feel when they find themselves wrongly accused as a defendant in court, totally dependent on an expert—their defense lawyer—to guide them through the labyrinthine criminal justice system. It also drove home one of its fundamental problems. I was fortunate to have access to the best experts. I've often thought that people without my education and means, without my support system of a strong family and loving wife, without a community that embraces them, might not fare so well in a similar situation. This is also true of defendants. For those without education and means to hire an expert legal team, without the support system of a strong family and loving spouse, without the support of their community, the deck is stacked against them from the start.

Reflecting on the minister's words, I realized that is what I would have to do: Focus more on making a difference in people's lives, using the tools of mind, personality, and spirit given to me, for however long I could. By the skill of my doctors and nurses, the goodness of heart of friends and family, the power of my wife's love, and the grace of God, I was on my feet again.

As Kathy put it in one of her updates:

Gone are the glorious fantasies of being an Olympic skier or bobsledder. He now fully realizes that he is just a lawyer ("That doesn't sound very interesting"), but he is a happy lawyer, back in the bosom of his family.

13

I had not been back in the office more than a week when a piece of mail arrived from the clerk of the Wisconsin Supreme Court, informing me of the schedule for oral arguments in two cases that had been pending in court for quite a while. Both were appeals of convictions, and the briefs had been submitted months and months earlier. I had asked the court to postpone arguments while I was recovering, and they'd readily agreed. Now they were getting ready to start their fall 2002 term. Word had gotten out that I was back, so the court put both cases on the calendar.

The mail from the supreme court announced that the date for one of the arguments was just about a month off.

Well, I thought, *I'm right back in it.*

One case was particularly compelling. My client had been convicted by a jury of a sexual assault, though he continued to insist on his innocence. He was placed on probation, given one year of jail time, along with a condition that he be released from jail to attend sex-offender treatment classes. I was then retained to represent him on appeal. At the first treatment session, he was told that part of completing the program was taking responsibility for the offense. He refused, on my advice, asserting his Fifth Amendment right not to be compelled to incriminate himself. His appeal was still pending and such an admission would undermine his claim of innocence if he were granted a new trial.

The sex offender program wasn't interested in his constitutional rights, however, and so he was kicked out. Then his probation was revoked for not cooperating with the program. This sent him to prison. I argued repeatedly at the probation revocation hearing, in the trial court, and in the court of appeals that my client's right not to incriminate himself extended beyond the actual trial and through his appeals.

At each level of appeal, I thought this was a no-brainer, that I was certain to win. The United States Supreme Court had long ago held that a state could not revoke a person's probation for the legitimate exercise of the Fifth Amendment privilege. And yet, as I had seen with Ralph Armstrong, and as Steven Avery experienced on his long journey to vindicate his 1985 conviction, the appellate system is stacked against criminal defendants. By 2002, my client had already spent nearly four years in prison waiting for the case to climb onto the docket of the state supreme court. The seven justices unanimously agreed that he did not belong in prison. They overturned the revocation of his probation and rushed out a decision to make sure he was released as quickly as possible.

Yes, I was back in the rat race. But it's not bad when you can win the first sprint.

Another big case of mine had been moving through the appellate pipeline while I was recovering. It arose from a sensational series of events that took place ten years before Steven Avery's prosecution for Teresa Halbach's murder, yet these two cases share much in common, especially the intensity of pretrial publicity.

On April 28, 1994, James Oswald and his eighteen-year-old son, Theodore "Ted" Oswald, robbed a bank in Wisconsin's Waukesha County, which is a suburban area just west of Milwaukee. They fled but were pursued by two police officers who stopped their vehicle. The Oswalds, armed with semiautomatic rifles, got out of their car and shot at the officers, killing one of them, a police captain. A chase ensued, during which the two suspects broke into a home, abducted a woman as a hostage, and continued to flee in her van. A local television station was following the pursuit on a police radio scanner and heard that the police were about to set up a roadblock nearby. A reporter and photojournalist with a camera arrived at the site of the roadblock just in time to broadcast the takedown live on television. As the suspects approached in the stolen van, they accelerated and rammed into a police car blocking the road. Police opened fire at the stopped van, and the Oswalds' hostage jumped out into a hail of bullets. Miraculously, the woman was not seriously hurt. Accelerating again rapidly, the suspects drove the van a few hundred feet farther until they smashed into a tree. They were captured alive.

That local television station had scored an exclusive tantamount to filming the final shootout between the cops and Bonnie and Clyde. Dramatic footage of the gun battle and the crash was replayed hundreds of times in the months leading up to the Oswalds' trial. Even if that had not been caught on tape, the case would still have generated an enormous amount of pretrial publicity. A bank robbery, father-and-son suspects, the tragic shooting of a police captain very close to retirement, the chase and its spectacular conclusion: All of these elements made it easily the most notorious case in the county's history. Serious consideration was given to moving the trial from the courthouse to the county's exposition center in order to accommodate the large crowds of observers and media that were expected from all over the nation.

James Oswald's bizarre philosophy and parenting practices galvanized even more interest in the case. As the ancient Spartans did with their children, he'd commenced "warrior training" on Ted's seventh birthday, sledge-hammering an entire litter of puppies to death right in front of the screaming child to "toughen" him up. Eleven years of unrelenting physical, mental, and emotional abuse would culminate in this bank robbery and homicide.

Ted Oswald was tried separately from his father because his defense was that his father had coerced him into committing the crimes. He was represented by the public defender's office, and his case went to trial first. His lawyers chose not to ask for a change of venue because, as some of the pretrial publicity had portrayed him as a victim of his father's abuse, they theorized that a local jury might be more receptive to the coercion defense.

Lawyers have two ways to winnow the pool of potential jurors before a trial during a process called voir dire (a name that originates from an old jury oath with the Latin *verum dicere*, "to tell the truth"; in old French, *voir* means the same as *vrai*, or "true," does in modern French). If a person clearly cannot be expected to hear the evidence with an open mind because of an obvious or self-professed bias, the lawyer can ask the judge to excuse that person "for cause." Both the prosecution and the defense also have a limited number of wild cards to play, each of which allows them to excuse a juror without the approval of the judge. These are known as peremptory challenges, and if the judge will not excuse someone "for cause," one of these peremptories can be invoked. Naturally, because the number of peremptory challenges allowed are limited, both sides try to hoard them and, whenever possible, convince the judge to dismiss potential jurors "for cause" instead.

Before Ted Oswald's trial, questionnaires went out to more than 156 prospective jurors. Eighty percent said that, based on the media coverage, they believed Ted was guilty. Six jurors stated that the trial would be a waste of taxpayer money. Nine expressed the view that the defendant should have died in the gun battle or that he should get the death penalty, which was not an option in Wisconsin. In an eerie fore-shadowing of the response to the Steven Avery case, the widow of the police captain submitted a petition with thousands of signatures to the legislature, asking them to reinstate the death penalty that Wisconsin had abolished in 1853. One of the prospective jurors had even signed the petition.

Just as would be done for the Avery trial, prospective jurors were questioned one by one. The very first man to be questioned told the judge and lawyers that he had seen the replay of the gun battle and cap-ture of the suspects so many times that his mind was firmly set and he had a very strong opinion of guilt. When asked if that opinion could be changed at trial, he said: "I guess it would have to be a very strong point to change my mind at this point." Remarkably, the prosecution fought hard against the defense's motion to exclude this juror for bias, and the judge refused to dismiss him. The defense was forced to use one of its few peremptory challenges to remove the juror. Similar exchanges occurred with other prospective jurors. All who made it through, even those who'd survived a motion to strike them "for cause," returned to the jury assembly room where they mingled with the still-to-be-questioned jurors under instructions *not* to discuss the matter among themselves unless and until they were selected and had sat through the entire trial.

Near the end of four days of jury selection, a prospective juror who had not seen the TV footage was finally found. He claimed not to have read much about the case, either. As a matter of fact, he said, he had learned more about the case while sitting in the jury assembly room and listening to prospective jurors talk about the defendants than he'd known before he was summoned to court. "According to what I hear, the young man is guilty of what he is being accused of and things like that and everything and I just think it's just a waste of time."* This sent up a red flag. Widespread discussions about the case were already going on, even before a shred of evidence had been presented. Moreover, what he disclosed was very detrimental to the defendant's right to a fair trial. At this point, the defense attorney demanded that the court requestion all of the previously qualified jurors to see if they were biased or if they had been exposed to the biases of others. Once again, the lead prosecutor objected and the judge refused to investigate.

After a three-week trial, Ted Oswald was convicted of all charges and given two life terms *plus* 565 more years. The local community and media were largely pleased. My firm was hired for the appeal, and so I embarked on a ten-year odyssey in the appellate courts.

In Wisconsin, an appellate lawyer must go back to the trial court after conviction if he or she finds new evidence or wishes to introduce legal issues the judge has not previously ruled on. We'd discovered a prospective juror who was not selected to serve, and she supplied more details about the comments made in that jury assembly room. She had heard two or three men talking about how the defendant was obviously guilty and that the trial was a waste of time and taxpayer money. One of these men wound up serving on the jury.

In the motion for a new trial, I presented statements from her and other witnesses. The trial court turned us down. The court of appeals at first tried to duck the issue, instead asking that the Wisconsin Supreme Court take the case. The supreme court refused and returned the case to the court of appeals, which eventually denied my appeal

---

* *Oswald v. Bertrand*, 374 F.3d 475, 479 (7th Cir. 2004).

and affirmed Ted Oswald's conviction. The Waukesha community was, once more, satisfied.

The Wisconsin Supreme Court again refused to hear the appeal. I then moved out of the Wisconsin system and into federal court, where I asked a judge to issue a writ of habeas corpus—a broad power the judiciary has to demand that the state produce a prisoner before the court so it can determine if he or she is being lawfully detained. This avenue for appeal had been severely narrowed during the 1990s, so it was now much more difficult for a federal court to reverse a state court conviction unless the state court's decision was deemed "unreasonable." My first brief was filed in early 2001, before I was diagnosed with cancer. Oswald's case was randomly assigned to Judge Lynn Adelman, then sitting as a district court judge in the federal courthouse in Milwaukee. The state of Wisconsin's response was filed in November of that year, when I was in the middle of chemo treatments. I'd received an extension until the end of January to file my final reply brief; working from home while recuperating from radiation treatment, I filed the papers just four days before surgery.

The decision came in early 2003, a few months after my return to the office, and it was a resounding win for the defense. Judge Adelman ruled that the defendant's constitutional right to due process and a fair and impartial jury had been denied. The state was ordered to retry Ted Oswald within six months or release him from custody (an unlikely prospect). Waukesha erupted in criticism of the judge. Commentators said he was a liberal activist judge appointed by President Bill Clinton, and they predicted that Adelman's decision would be overturned when the state appealed to the Seventh Circuit Court of Appeals in Chicago, which was known to be far more conservative.

In June 2004, the Seventh Circuit decision came down. Again, a complete victory for the defense. Everyone was shocked. The opinion was written by Judge Richard Posner, who had been appointed by President Ronald Reagan and had a national reputation as a conservative legal scholar and judge. He agreed entirely with Judge Adelman, the so-called liberal activist, that not only had Ted Oswald not received a fair trial, but also that the Wisconsin state courts were asleep at the wheel, both during the trial and on appeal. More than ten years before Oswald's trial, he noted, the United States Supreme Court clearly stated in *Smith v. Phillips* (1982) that a criminal defendant's right to "due process means a jury capable and willing to decide the case solely on the evidence before it, and a trial judge ever watchful to prevent prejudicial occurrences and to determine the effect of such occurrences when they happen." When that juror spoke up near the end of jury selection, the trial judge had failed to investigate reports of the jurors' "marathon bull sessions on Oswald's guilt," Judge Posner wrote, ruling that it was highly probable that some, maybe even all, of the jurors who tried Oswald were biased:

> The response to the jury questionnaires against the background of enormous publicity concerning the most sensational criminal episode in the county's history, the fact that Oswald seemed so obviously guilty as to make the necessity for a trial questionable to a layperson, the tumult induced by [one juror's] vocal complaints, the flagrant disobedience of the judge's instructions that the prospective jurors not discuss the case in advance of the trial, the likelihood that [one identified juror] and perhaps other reluctant jurors would vote to convict regardless of their actual views if that would make the trial end quicker, the fact that, at least according to [the disclosing juror at the end of jury selection], the improper discussions had already produced a consensus that Oswald was guilty as charged—these things, taken not separately but together, created a sufficiently high probability of jury bias to require on the part of the trial judge a diligent inquiry.

The Waukesha county prosecutor, "who made every possible effort to prevent the judge's determining whether jurors were biased," was also criticized for his overzealous advocacy.

It wasn't that Judge Posner believed Ted Oswald was innocent. He didn't think much of the claim that Ted was bullied by his father into committing the crime, which he disparaged as a "Patty Hearst or Manchurian Candidate defense," when someone killed an innocent person to save his or her own life. Such defenses had a storied history of failure, Posner noted, citing the case of shipwrecked passengers who were convicted of murder when they "ate the cabin boy rather than starve." Nevertheless, he wrote, "even a clearly guilty criminal is entitled to be tried before an impartial tribunal, something the jurors in this case may well have failed to understand."*

The Wisconsin State Court of Appeals was criticized in particular for sanctioning the inadequate "perfunctory" investigation by the trial judge into the allegations of misconduct going on in the jury assembly room: "Oswald was entitled to be tried by a jury that undertook to decide his guilt on the basis of the evidence rather than of what they had learned from the pretrial publicity about the case and analyzed over a four-day period while waiting for the trial to begin. It was natural that having seen the videotape of Oswald's crimes, laypersons would assume his guilt was open and shut. But a jury that decides guilt before the trial begins is little better than a lynch mob."

I battled the state of Wisconsin for a few more months as they made a futile attempt to get the United States Supreme Court to review the Oswald case. Ted Oswald was indeed reconvicted at a second trial, with a different lawyer, during which victims and witnesses were forced to relive traumatic events, all because state and local authorities cared so little about ensuring the fairness of the first trial. The reputations of the county prosecutor and state court judges were sullied by permitting a defendant's constitutional rights to be so trampled.

The lesson of Ted Oswald, alas, was quickly forgotten. Only one year later, Manitowoc County authorities would make a similar mockery of justice with the prosecution and trials of Steven Avery and Brendan Dassey. And in Brendan Dassey's case, it would again take a writ of habeas corpus issued by a federal court to right the wrong done to him.

---

* *Oswald v. Bertrand*, 374 F.3d 475, 481 (7th Cir. 2004).

14

Ted Oswald's case proved I could stand up in court and win an argument. It was satisfying but vastly different from the full body-and-brain immersion of being in a courtroom, day after day, on an actual trial. Nearly a year went by before I had the chance to see if that was something I could manage.

The client was a twenty-three-year-old man, charged in a sensational homicide. An escort had disappeared, and it turned out that the last person on her call list was this young man. When the police got to his house in a suburb of Milwaukee, he'd said that no, she wasn't there, and invited them inside. The place was immaculate. Not a drop of blood anywhere. So the police started looking around outside. One alert officer noticed a bag with a little blood on it in the dumpster. Inside the bag were female body parts. But that wasn't all. There was also junk mail addressed to the defendant in the same bag. As they searched further, they discovered other bags, more body parts from the same unfortunate person. They also found a list of things to do: *Call up escort. Kill escort. Cut up body. Dispose.*

The man was clearly insane. His case was attracting enormous attention. The issue in a trial would not be whether he was innocent of the crime but whether he could be found legally culpable given that these were the acts of a very disturbed person. The idea of an insanity defense is rooted in the belief that a person's conviction and punishment depend on a defendant's willful misconduct. If a person is so mentally deranged or otherwise incapable of controlling his or her conduct, then it is unfair and not morally proper to punish the individual. Treatment is offered instead of punishment. Contrary to public opinion, the insanity defense is rarely invoked. Only about 1 percent of defendants raise the defense, and it is estimated that it succeeds only 20 percent of the time it is invoked.

At trial, our challenge would be to persuade a court that the man had severe mental illness, even though it had never been diagnosed before the crime. Procedures vary from state to state, but in Wisconsin the defense has the burden of proving that a defendant has a mental disease or defect sufficient to exclude criminal responsibility for the conduct. It would not be simple; even Jeffrey Dahmer, a cannibalistic Wisconsin serial killer who had murdered seventeen men and boys, was found legally sane and culpable for his acts.

At this point, I was still having scans every three months to see if any trace of the cancer had escaped the surgery or chemotherapy. I could get sick again at any moment. Could I commit to take on such a big case? Kathy and I talked it over and agreed to do it together. If I did get sick, she could carry on.

First, though, we had to figure out what was going on with our client. This was not the first violent drama he'd been involved in. At age two, his life had been saved by a police officer. A woman had run into the street, frantically screaming that her husband was trying to kill her, and the police arrived to find the man on the couch smothering their two-year-old son with a pillow. They stopped him, the boy survived, and the man went off to prison. The child was put into foster care, and his foster parents fell in love with him and adopted him. None of them knew about this Gothic family history until he turned eighteen and was able to inquire into the background of his biological parents. Five years later, the police found those body parts under his junk mail.

With help from the dean of American forensic psychiatry, Dr. Robert Sadoff, and months of meetings, we broke through a very complex delusion disorder. For some time, our client believed the forces of the Antichrist were present in the world. To most people, these forces looked just like anyone else, but *he* could see the difference. He could tell them apart from regular people, and they—the Antichrists—knew that he knew. Anytime he would try to tell someone else about them, they'd thwart him. For example, the defendant went to Mass regularly and afterward would try to approach the priest to speak with him. But the Antichrist forces, in the shape of two old women, would swoop in and start talking to the priest in order to block him. Of course, they were just a couple of elderly ladies saying, "Hello, Father, how are you?" but in his derangement, he saw Antichrist figures intruding everywhere.

This delusion explained the murder. The Antichrist forces were trying to get him imprisoned for life so he could no longer fight against them, and so they'd compelled him to kill the woman. For two weeks, he had been able to resist them by making up to-do lists like the one found in the police search. He would get partway through a list, but as long he stopped himself before completing it, he could avoid doing what they wanted him to do. The police had found many sheets of paper with such lists. Reading them, you could see that it was getting harder and harder for the defendant to stop, that he was getting farther down his list, until finally he went through with the plan.

The court appointed a psychiatrist who reported that the client's problems were not so serious as to make him legally incapable of committing the crime—that is, he understood that what he was doing was wrong and was capable of stopping himself from going ahead with the killing. For instance, the court psychiatrist pointed out, the man had to pull himself together to clean up the crime scene. The state hired its own expert who, after examining the defendant, agreed with the defense. So our expert and the prosecution's expert were in agreement on the complex mental illness that the man was suffering from. We went to trial. We won. He was committed to a locked facility for treatment. But it was a hospital, not a prison. He was treated like a patient, not an inmate, and he's progressing very well.

It looked like I could still try a case.

Part IV

ONE STEP FORWARD, TWO STEPS BACK

15

The anniversary of a cancer diagnosis is probably impossible to forget no matter the day on which it falls, but there was no way I could miss mine. Every year, we recall and mourn the terrorist attacks of September 11, 2001. Seeing the harrowing footage always brings me back to the turmoil of those first hours, when I was simultaneously watching the broadcast reports of the attacks and trying to absorb the news that part of my own body had been invaded and taken over by disease.

Two years later, on September 11, 2003, a man walked out of prison after spending eighteen years behind bars for a crime he had nothing to do with. His name was Steven Avery. Helped by the Wisconsin Innocence Project, Avery had cleared his name with DNA testing, which at the time my Innocence Project client, Ralph Armstrong, was still trying to do. In the early narratives of what went wrong in the 1985 prosecution of Avery, an erroneous identification by the victim was prominently cited. But as layers of detail were peeled back, the story became more complex and ever more fascinating.

By 1995, a decade after Steven Avery's conviction, new scrutiny of old biological evidence with DNA testing was forcing the reversal of convictions that had occurred years or decades earlier across America. This was due largely to the efforts of Barry Scheck, Peter Neufeld, and the Innocence Project—and inmates such as Ralph Armstrong—who pioneered its use in the late 1980s and early 1990s. In 1995, Avery's lawyers from the Wisconsin Innocence Project had arranged DNA tests of scrapings collected from underneath Penny Beerntsen's fingernails, on the theory that they might include skin cells or other biological traces of her attacker. Avery's blood was drawn for comparison. The DNA tests showed that he was *not* the source of any of the collected material from the fingernail scrapings, but the trial judge, upheld by an appeals court, ruled that even if this information had been available to the jury in 1985, it would not have made a difference in the verdict.

To be successful, an attempt to overturn a conviction based on new evidence must demonstrate three things: that this new evidence truly was not available before or during the trial, that it is germane to the basic issues being tried, and that there is a "reasonable probability" a jury would have come to a different verdict if it had known about it. To deny Steven Avery a new trial, in 1996 the court of appeals came up with a new version of what a "reasonable probability" meant and said he had not met this redefined burden of proof. (Nearly a decade after that, the Wisconsin Supreme Court would overturn this more difficult standard.

By 2003, there was another, even more revealing result from DNA testing of pubic hair collected from Beerntsen after the crime. It had not figured in the trial, as it had never been attributed to anyone. When it was subjected to mitochondrial DNA testing, that pubic hair excluded Stern Avery and turned out to match the genetic profile of a man with a long history of criminal sexual predation. His name was Gregory Allen, and unknown to Avery or his defense lawyers, the City of Manitowoc Police Department had strongly suspected he carried out that attack on the beach. In the summer of 1985, the Manitowoc city police were monitoring Allen twice a day because they thought he was the likely culprit in a series of disturbing episodes of prowling and lewd behavior—"a dangerous individual with a potential for violence," according to a Manitowoc police report. On the day of the assault at Lake Michigan, the police had checked on his whereabouts once but, because of other calls, did not make the second check. However, the City of Manitowoc Police Department was not in charge of investigating the attack at the beach. That fell under the jurisdiction of the Manitowoc County Sheriff's Office and the Manitowoc County district attorney.

Through several channels, both the sheriff's office and the district attorney's office were told that Allen ought to be considered as a suspect. The deputy chief of the City of Manitowoc Police Department said that he had personally visited Sheriff Tom Kocourek to suggest that Allen should be investigated but that Sheriff Kocourek told him that Allen had been ruled out. It appears that the sheriff's office never considered Allen in any substantive way, even though it, too, had a file on the misdeeds he was suspected of. The Manitowoc district attorney, Denis Vogel, was warned by his aides that Allen was a much closer fit to the physical description given by Penny Beerntsen. And Beerntsen herself received a phone call from someone in the City of Manitowoc Police Department who suggested that a suspect other than Avery ought to be considered. That person also asked if Beerntsen had received any unusual phone calls. In fact, she had. After her assault, her home phone had rung several times, usually just a few minutes after she'd stepped in the front door, with calls of a sexual nature. The City of Manitowoc Police Department officer told her that this was consistent with the stalking behaviors of which Allen was strongly suspected. By then, Steven Avery was already in custody and so could not have made the calls. Learning this, Penny Beerntsen contacted the sheriff's department and would later recall that someone there told her not to worry, that they would follow up with the police.[*]

After Avery's exoneration in 2003, the *Milwaukee Journal Sentinel* and other news outlets began to uncover the backstory of the 1985 wrongful conviction. In response to those reports, the Wisconsin Attorney General's Office announced an investigation. Then one day, I got a call from a Republican assemblyman, Mark Gundrum, who was the chairman of the judiciary committee for the Wisconsin Assembly. He had decided to convene hearings and was setting up a task force including prosecutors, police officers, victims' advocates, law professors, and criminal defense attorneys. Gundrum explained to me that the goal of the Avery Task Force was to study what had gone wrong in the Avery case and determine if criminal justice reforms could help prevent future wrongful convictions. Would I be willing to take part?

---

[*] Peg Lautenschlager, Memorandum, Wisconsin Department of Justice, December 17, 2003. http://www.stevenaverycase.org/wp-content/uploads/2016/03/WI-DOJ-Report-on-Avery-1985-Case.pdf.

I was game.

Another member of the task force was a prosecutor, Norm Gahn, who would later be a member of the team prosecuting Steven Avery for the murder of Teresa Halbach. Norm was a natural choice for the task force, as he was well known among prosecutors as an expert on the use of DNA. In fact, Gahn was one of the first prosecutors to come up with the idea of using a DNA profile of an assailant in criminal complaints if the suspect's legal identity was not yet known. This meant that once charges were lodged, the clock stopped running on the statute of limitations. Even if it took years to arrest the person who matched the genetic profile, prosecutors could plausibly state that they had diligently pursued a trial. This innovation was much admired and imitated around the country by district attorneys.

Steven Avery's redemption came on the heels of other DNA exonerations across America, and many of these wrongful convictions—including his—were built on, in substantial part, mistaken eyewitnesses. People were realizing how fallible that evidence was. The Avery Task Force brought in experts from around the country to come up with other, fairer procedures for having witnesses look at suspects that would avoid cues, conscious or not, suggesting that there was a "right" answer.

For instance, in double-blind lineups and photo arrays, the detectives involved in the case should not conduct the lineup or show images to the witnesses. Instead, a detective who had no knowledge of the case would administer it. This is easy to do with photo array lineups. Individual pictures could be placed in separate, sealed envelopes and randomly numbered. This way, no one would know which envelope contains the suspect's photo as the eyewitness goes through them. Another possible reform was to present photographs or people to witnesses one at a time, sequentially, rather than the classic simultaneous lineup in which all the participants file onstage at the same time while the witness watches through a one-way window. A number of studies have shown that witnesses are more likely to make a false identification when they are asked to look at groups of individuals or pictures; social scientists believe the simultaneous lineups encourage witnesses to weigh one possibility against another and make a relative judgment about who *most* looked like the remembered culprit.[*] Ultimately, the task force came up with guidelines that the Wisconsin Department of Justice strongly recommended be used by all police agencies. I had wanted them to be mandatory, but the compromise was that the state would publish them as a "best practices" protocol.

During one task force meeting, we heard from both Steven Avery and Penny Beerntsen. Penny had forthrightly agreed to have her identity and picture made public. This was the first time she had encountered Avery since the trial two decades earlier, and she apologized for her error. Steven Avery hugged her and said, in effect, "This mistake wasn't yours; it was the police who were responsible, not you."

Another important reform enacted by the task force would, in time, provide critical understanding into the next case involving Steven Avery. But it almost never came to pass.

---

[*] National Academy of Science, "Identifying the Culprit: Assessing Eyewitness Identification," National Academies Press, 2014, pp. 16–29. http://www.innocenceproject .org/wp-content/uploads/2016/02/NAS-Report-ID.pdf.

16

For more than fifteen years, I had been fighting for the mandatory recording of the complete interrogations of suspects in police custody. My interest was propelled by a case I handled in 1990, right as I was leaving the public defender's office and going into private practice. Though it attracted little notice at the time, its echoes would be heard nearly a quarter century later in the cases of both Steven Avery and Brendan Dassey.

My client was a Cuban refugee, one of tens of thousands of Cubans who had left the island in the Mariel boatlift of 1980. Fidel Castro is widely believed to have stocked some of the boats by opening Cuba's prisons and mental institutions, and my Marielito client was clearly suffering from mental illness. He barely communicated with me, even through an interpreter. I argued to the court that he was not competent since he was unable to assist his counsel, and he was committed to a locked hospital for observation. The doctors also got little out of him—so little, in fact, that they could not conclude that he was incompetent—and the judge agreed, meaning the man would stand trial. He was charged with the homicide of a jewelry dealer during the robbery of a jewelry store. There were two other defendants, and although my client was not the shooter, as a party to the crime he was deemed equally responsible. When questioned by officers in the Milwaukee Police Department, my client had supposedly made incriminating remarks, but had he *really* said what they claimed he'd said? The officer had taken notes in Spanish and then destroyed them. An officer said he'd translated the *Miranda* warning into Spanish, but he hadn't kept a copy of that translation, either. If the entire process had been recorded, we would know for sure if the police were telling the truth. But it wasn't.

Of all the police departments in Wisconsin, the Milwaukee Police Department was the most resistant to recording interrogations. At this client's trial, police witnesses testified that it was explicit policy *not* to record any custodial interrogations, even though they had access to plenty of dictation machines and tape recorders. I argued that this policy showed that the Milwaukee Police Department was deliberately hiding the truth from the jury, not just in this case but also in others. Even without the alleged confession, the state's evidence against the defendant was strong and the jury convicted him. But these twelve ordinary citizens took the unusual step of issuing, along with their verdict, a joint statement highly critical of the Milwaukee Police Department's policy. It set off a debate on TV and in the newspapers for several days about whether it was time to change that policy. It didn't happen then, but cracks were beginning to appear. In time, about one in four wrongful convictions reversed through DNA testing would turn out to include statements by innocent people implicating themselves.[*] We needed to see what really went on in police interrogation rooms to understand why innocent people came to falsely confess.

That police interrogations are not recorded may come as a surprise to many people outside the criminal justice system. For years, even if a confession was recorded and used as evidence in court or to extract a guilty plea, there was no general requirement that the entire police questioning that preceded the admissions also be taped. Usually, the recording would begin only *after* the detectives had questioned a suspect, and *after* they had extracted admissions of guilt. This meant we never saw or heard what happened *before* the camera or tape recorder was turned on. These so-called sew-up confessions were presented in isolation, and there was no way to know if they were the product of coercion that had not been recorded. Any psychological browbeating that might have been part of the process would never be seen by the jury, or by the public watching the dramatic snippets of tape on television news.

---

[*] The Innocence Project, "False Admissions or Confessions." http://www.innocence project.org/causes/false-confessions-admissions/.

Around the time the Avery Task Force was meeting, a juvenile case challenging the practice of pulling kids out of class for questioning without a parent present was working its way up to the Wisconsin Supreme Court. The supreme court came very close to ruling that statements obtained under such circumstances would no longer be admitted in court, but it ultimately declared that trial courts should consider the failure of police to contact the parent to be a coercive element. This was a toothless compromise because trial judges had been given the same instruction from the Wisconsin Supreme Court more than thirty years earlier. Over the decades that followed, it became obvious that trial courts were only paying lip service to the warning, and they were likely to do so in the future. Wisconsin judges, the vast majority of whom are former prosecutors, are often elected on law-and-order promises. For many of them, try as they might, it is very difficult to ignore the negative political consequences of throwing out a confession on the grounds that it was coerced. The pressure not to do so becomes even more acute in high-profile cases. Yet that is how Wisconsin's highest court left the matter while the task force was studying interrogation: Police could continue to question juveniles without a parent or lawyer present, and the trial court was later supposed to decide if, under the total circumstances, that practice was coercive.

However, the state supreme court did take one big step. It decreed that all future interrogations of juveniles must be electronically recorded, a ruling that would prove vital to the fight for Brendan Dassey's innocence because it ensured that his interrogation would be recorded in its entirety. Without those recordings, the state's presentation of Brendan's statements at his own trial would have been even more misleading—detectives could have described Brendan's admissions much as Kratz did in those press conferences, as if they were a coherent narrative flowing from the lips of a young man just waiting to unburden himself. In reality, as the millions of viewers of *Making a Murderer* now know, Brendan's statement was the product of detectives who coached him, fed him "facts," and pushed and pushed until he said what they wanted to hear.

The defense attorneys on the Avery Task Force, including me, and an academic member of the committee, University of Wisconsin Law School clinical professor Keith A. Findley, wanted a broader electronic recording requirement that included adult suspects. We brought in people from different states and police departments who were already recording interrogations. Most of these authorities thought it was great. An enormous amount of energy can be spent before trials arguing whether or not a defendant's statement is voluntary. Without any reliable record of how the questioning that produced the statement took place, these pretrial hearings can amount to swearing contests, which the police invariably win. Recordings would provide the judge or jury the best evidence of not only what was actually said by the police and suspect but also *how* they said it. The visiting law enforcement officials, some of whom had initially been skeptical about recording interrogations of adult suspects, told us that in addition to curtailing pretrial hearings on the admissibility of statements, it had helped debunk false accusations of coercion and misconduct against police. Judges could just look at the video.

Despite all of these strong witnesses, the task force was reluctant to act. Some of its members embodied an institutional resistance to change. And after all, a false confession was not an issue in Avery's 1985 wrongful conviction, so why should we urge these changes? This problem wasn't on our agenda. It was clear to me that the cause was nearly lost, but I was so angry that I marshaled one more pitch. This was an opportunity the task force could not afford to miss. We had spent a lot of time considering the issue, and the merits of the reform were, it seemed to me, beyond dispute. If we didn't act now, what had been the point of all that effort? No one had a serious reason to oppose it, but the collective sentiment was that we ought to kick it down the road and leave it for some future panel to deal with. Having gone through a crash course on the precious value of time, I felt that this was the worst posture of all for the task force to take.

This chance to enact reform might not come up again for a decade or more. *Why wait?*

There was kind of a pause. For a moment, I considered that I had been scolding the rest of the commission for being shortsighted.

Then Norm Gahn spoke up. I'll give him credit for this to my dying day.

He said: "I agree with Jerry. I think this is an opportunity we need to take."

Between the two of us, I believe we saved the day for recorded interrogations.

The task forced decided that it was going to call for recording to be mandatory in all felony cases, and ask the legislatures to make sure that the state paid for it, so that the cost did not fall onto counties as an unfunded mandate. This provision would be written into the statute, allowing a small number of exceptions, for things like mechanical malfunctions, that the court could consider; otherwise, if the police had failed to record the interrogation, the judge would tell the jury that recording was a requirement of law and that, as it had not been done, they could draw whatever inference they wanted.

Prosecutors were really against this. They thought it was the kiss of death. But for me, that was the point. We needed deterrence. And it made an impression. One prosecutor went around the state training police officers on the requirements of this law, warning them that they should not expect to be able to wiggle out of the obligation to record. He would not try a case only to have a judge tell the jury that the state had not done things properly.

The various reforms proposed by the Avery Task Force were bundled into a bill. Wisconsin's governor, Jim Doyle, praised our work and said he would sign the bill as soon as it passed both houses of the legislature. There were also efforts at reparations for Steven Avery. At the time, Wisconsin law provided $5,000 per year in compensation to wrongly convicted people, up to a maximum of $25,000 (or five years). For Avery, this would have amounted to about 16 cents an hour for the eighteen years he had wrongly spent behind bars. A special bill was drafted to award him $428,000. Meanwhile, he was brought around the legislature as an honored guest and given a souvenir book signed by elected officials. State Senator David Zien even welcomed Avery into his office, where he gave him soda pop, beef jerky, and pork rinds and apologized to him on behalf of the state. The package of reforms passed the state senate on October 31, 2005. It was known as the Avery Bill. A few weeks later, the governor signed it into law.

By then, though, its name had changed to the Criminal Justice Reform Act. And the special compensation bill had disappeared.

17

While these hearings on Steven Avery's wrongful conviction were getting under way in early 2005, I was also preparing to argue Ralph Armstrong's case before the Wisconsin Supreme Court. The Innocence Project had been helping me prepare the briefs, but I had been handling the court hearings and endless motions for Armstrong's appeal on my own, without compensation, since that 1993 phone call from Barry Scheck. It had taken us more than ten years to get to this point.

Through a painstaking series of DNA tests, we had by 2001 discredited every single piece of physical evidence used to convict Armstrong. The tests showed that neither the hair nor the semen collected from around Charise Kamp's body were Ralph Armstrong's, as the state had claimed at the trial. The hair was not from her boyfriend, Brian Dillman, either, though once we obtained a new reference sample from Dillman, DNA tests of the semen on the bathrobe crumpled on the floor proved that he was the source. What the state had said was Charise Kamps's blood from under Armstrong's nails, detected by "presumptive" tests, also turned out not to be her blood or, for that matter, blood at all.

We were still struggling four years after these tests were completed because the original prosecutor, John Norsetter, refused to concede that all of this new evidence warranted, at a minimum, a new trial for Armstrong. We had gone back to court in 2001 with the DNA test results to plead for a new trial, but then the prosecution changed its story. Contrary to what Norsetter had told the jury in 1981, he and his colleagues now said that neither the semen nor the hair was connected to the murder and that there were innocuous reasons for their presence. The hairs could have drifted in from anywhere. Since the semen was Dillman's, it must have been deposited on her robe at some time before the murder during consensual intercourse. The trial court bought the argument and turned us down.

In 2004, incredibly, the state court of appeals embraced the state's turnabout, ruling that the erratic eyewitness testimony of Riccie Orebia, not the physical evidence repeatedly cited at the trial and now discredited, was the foundation of Armstrong's conviction. Throughout history, mistaken eyewitnesses are the most common reason that the wrong people are convicted; such errors had been a factor in 70 percent of the first 344 people whose convictions were overturned by DNA evidence.* Just one year earlier, Steven Avery, sent to prison on the testimony of a mistaken eyewitness, had been exonerated—hence the Avery Task Force focus on this issue. Nevertheless, the appeals court turned to a manifestly unsure witness to uphold Ralph Armstrong's conviction. "The misleading hair and semen evidence did not 'so cloud' or distract the jury from deliberating this issue," the court held. Likewise, the DNA evidence excluding Armstrong and Dillman as the source of the hair "is not important enough testimony bearing on the controversy to warrant a new trial." The system's default switch for "finality" had trumped the changed understanding of the physical evidence. Science in 2001 had demolished the version of reality that had been presented in court in 1981, but the judiciary clung by the flimsiest of witnesses to the original fiction.

That brought us to the spring of 2005. For the argument before the supreme court, Barry Scheck flew from New York to share the argument with me. The court listened carefully to the state's most important claim—that the physical evidence was not all that important in obtaining the conviction—and in a sweeping, detailed decision called it "disingenuous," and found that "at trial, the State did more than simply use the physical evidence to establish an inference of guilt; it used the physical evidence assertively and repetitively as affirmative proof of Armstrong's guilt." And, after analyzing the full record, the court completely rejected the state's claim:

---

* The Innocence Project, "Eyewitness Misidentification." http://www.innocence project.org/causes/eyewitness-misidentification/.

To bolster Orebia's identification, the State flaunted powerful conclusions before the jury that the physical evidence conclusively and
irrevocably established Armstrong as the murderer. However, the
jury was presented conclusions based on evidence that are now
found to be inconsistent with the facts. The key hairs on the bathrobe belt that was draped over Kamps' body are not Armstrong's
and the semen found on Kamps' robe is not Armstrong's. In addition, there is no indication that any blood that may have been on
the hemosticks was that of Kamps.

In July 2005, the supreme court reversed Ralph Armstrong's conviction. However, as his case returned to the circuit court for a new
trial—or possible dismissal, if the state decided not to retry him—
John Norsetter would still be the lead prosecutor. He told me that
the state wanted to test more of the crime scene evidence before
deciding whether to prosecute Ralph Armstrong again. Within two
weeks of this decision, I wrote to him to discuss the handling of
the remaining evidence; I was extremely concerned about this for a
couple of reasons. If the state moved forward with additional testing,
it was essential that an effort be made to preserve as much evidence
as possible. DNA technology was improving at a sprint, and many
prosecutors in Wisconsin and elsewhere were not fully caught up on
its expanding powers. Every year, the tests became more sensitive,
which meant that they could be done on smaller and smaller samples, and also more discriminating, which meant that more markers
of the DNA could be identified and, therefore, it was increasingly
less likely that the wrong person would match. Moreover, I did not
have confidence in John Norsetter's ability to be objective and I was
concerned that there not be any tampering by the police or prosecution. Whenever physical evidence from the original crime scene
was sent for testing, we insisted on being party to the entire process.
Norsetter agreed that, any time the state wanted to examine or test
evidence, we would be notified in enough time to witness the opening of sealed packets and their repackaging. In fact, we signed a

stipulation to that effect with the prosecution, and it was filed as an official order of the court.

In every way possible, I put the state on notice that it was not to mess with this evidence. But it did so anyway.

In the midst of the preparations for new testing of evidence in Armstrong's case, I heard about the incredible turn that Steven Avery's life had taken in November 2005, from wrongly convicted man to newly accused murderer. It would be four months before I would join Dean on the defense team, so in December 2005, when I set out for the clerk's office in Madison to review the evidence that the prosecution wanted to retest in Ralph Armstrong's case, I was still just an interested spectator to the developments in Avery's case.

On arriving in Madison, I was surprised to find that all of the exhibits had been removed from the clerk's vault and placed in a room, unsupervised, with the chief police investigator on the case. I had looked at the exhibits once before, more than five years earlier, but the clerk had been careful to bring the exhibits to me and remain in the room the entire time. The clerk's office apparently had no concerns about leaving them alone with a police detective.

In January 2006, I learned that, on two occasions, state investigators had handled the evidence without telling us—and even had an analyst from the state crime lab examine the exhibits shortly after the supreme court's reversal the summer before. This was contrary to the standing court order from five years earlier, which also required the lab to turn over the report of any examinations they conducted. I was furious. I wrote to Norsetter and complained about this exhibition of bias on the part of the crime lab, and demanded that an outside—and truly independent—crime lab be employed. The prosecutor's office refused, stating that the Wisconsin lab would continue to handle examinations of the evidence, acknowledging that the state would be "proceeding at its peril." Then, in March 2006, I was retained in the Steven Avery case and would be juggling both that and the Armstrong case as developments unfolded in parallel.

A Wisconsin crime lab analyst issued a report, in April 2006, confirming what we already knew: Ralph Armstrong was "eliminated as the source" for everything she had tested. But there was one more possibility, which had been overlooked all those years—an unnoticed semen stain on the bathrobe belt that apparently had been used to strangle Charise Kamps. The result of testing this second semen sample (found on the belt, not the robe) was not as declarative, the crime lab analyst said, but the male profile developed from it was also not consistent with either Armstrong or the victim's boyfriend, Brian Dillman. At the time of her murder, Charise Kamps had no other consensual sex partners, so this newly discovered physical evidence was a bombshell. The robe belt was draped over the victim's back by the killer, and since the newly discovered semen stain on it matched neither Armstrong nor Dillman, that DNA likely pointed to the actual culprit. I expected the case against Armstrong to be completely dismissed at the very next court hearing.

Two months later, in June, the state surprised me by formally announcing that it was going to retry Ralph Armstrong. I told the court about the new semen stain and the DNA tests that excluded both Dillman and my client as its source, implicating an unknown third party. I announced that the defense would have the stain tested by our own experts, who would try to develop a full profile. The court agreed and scheduled another status hearing some months down the road.

A few days after that June hearing, Dane County prosecutors, a Madison Police Department detective, and the Wisconsin State Crime Laboratory analyst who authored the April 2006 report held a private conference. During this meeting, John Norsetter told the detective to go to the clerk's office, remove the belt from the evidence vault, and bring it to the state crime for further testing that, he hoped, might find some trace of Ralph. He asked for testing that looked just at DNA from the Y chromosome, which only men have because it is passed from father to son. Such tests are not very discriminating because all paternal male relatives, including brothers with the same father, will have the same profile.

This Y-DNA testing did not even go so far as to definitively identify male Armstrongs. It produced only a partial profile, which did not exclude Ralph Armstrong. It could hardly be said to prove his guilt, given that it was incomplete. But the result meant that John Norsetter finally got what he'd wanted: a piece of evidence that did *not* prove Ralph's innocence. Far worse for us, though, was that in the process of conducting these tests, the technician had consumed the remainder of the stain. That meant there was nothing left for us to test. Of course, at the time, I knew nothing about this testing. If I had, I would never have agreed to it. It was a flagrant violation of the court order and our agreement with the prosecution.

Why and how Norsetter had chosen that destructive test and, moreover, why he had behaved so sneakily were mysteries to me then. More than a year would pass before I'd learn the shocking circumstances behind his actions. But even then I was furious. When I spoke to him on the phone, he seemed indifferent, even though what he'd done seemed, to me, to be clear prosecutorial misconduct.

In the fall of 2006 I filed motions to have all charges against Ralph Armstrong dismissed, and also to suppress the original eyewitness identification from the hypnotized witness.

By then, I was already months deep in the Steven Avery case, with no hint that, amid that cyclone of work, yet another critical surprise twist awaited in the odyssey of Ralph Armstrong.

Part V

SWIMMING UPSTREAM

18

The matter of the *State of Wisconsin v. Steven A. Avery* unfolds over tens of thousands of pages of court transcripts, legal briefs, and many cartons of exhibits. By early 2016, entries on just the docket, a kind of running index, stretched well past sixty pages. The *Making a Murderer* series began streaming on Netflix late in 2015, and during bad spells of weather, people binge-watched all ten episodes. Online communities posted the entire court file online—every word, every decision—and engaged in lengthy debates about what mattered and what didn't. Even notorious cases of modern times, such as the trial of O. J. Simpson, have not been subjected to such crowd-based atom-by-atom analysis.

The Avery case got all this attention not because it is more important than many other cases, but because its details were propagated and amplified through popular culture with tools that did not exist until well into the second decade of the twenty-first century. As I write in the summer of 2016, it is neither blasphemy nor hyperbole to say that no criminal case since the trial of Jesus of Nazareth has been as closely studied by so many people. Certainly, few people who pick up this book will be unaware that Steven Avery was convicted. Those readers know that Avery maintains that he had no role in, or knowledge of, the violence done to Teresa Halbach and that any evidence to the contrary could only have been planted.

My purpose here is not to retry the case day by day, much less summarize its sprawling record. Instead, I will highlight what I saw as the central issues in the prosecution and defense of Steven Avery. Many of the critical episodes began before the trial and are best understood when followed in their entirety. Inevitably, my perspective was shaped not only by the facts peculiar to the investigation but also by my experiences on the front lines of criminal defense work.

No one could ignore the glaring irregularities in the construction of the prosecution case. Dean Strang and I firmly believed it was not possible to explain them away. On close inspection, virtually every piece of what looked like damning prosecution evidence was riddled with flaws. Taken together, they form a panorama of rampant bias, conflicts of interest, misconduct, sloppy practices, and grotesque over-reach.

In our offices, and later in the furnished apartments we took for the duration of the trial, Dean and I scrambled to keep up with the avalanche of material that the prosecution was providing to us as state and federal law require.

Under the Constitution, people accused of crimes have the right to confront their accuser and the evidence against them, and by statute law enforcement is required to share the fruits of its investigations with the accused and his or her lawyer. These materials, known as discovery, are supposed to lower the possibility for a trial by ambush, in which the prosecution presents surprise witnesses or evidence surfaces without giving the defense a chance to do its own investigation. As with many things in the criminal justice system, the mandatory sharing of discovery materials is seen by some prosecutors as another opportunity for gamesmanship—for instance, either by swamping the defense with essentially irrelevant materials or severely limiting the number of reports committed to writing. By the time I signed up for the case, the prosecution had already turned over several thousand pages of discovery. The volume grew every week or so, eventually reaching more than twenty-five thousand pages, more than one thousand printed photographs, and still more CDs of digital pictures.

In Appleton, the ground-floor apartment I rented for the duration of the trial became our central repository for the files. I set up two cafeteria tables for work space. The materials were in large cardboard bankers' boxes and more than thirty large three-ring binders, which filled the shelves of a shallow closet. I set up boxes of the photographs, indexed carefully, on the worktables for easy access.

Yet, for all of this Mount Olympus of material, there was but a single, half-page report from Sergeant Andrew Colborn of the Manitowoc County Sheriff's Office. Sergeant Colborn had played a central role in the supposed discovery of evidence incriminating Steven Avery, but his few paltry lines were not filed until months afterward. As we would come to learn, this was typical of the Manitowoc authorities. Every significant piece of evidence in the case—the ignition key to Teresa Halbach's RAV4, for instance, and the bone fragments found in Avery's burn pit—was first reported by Manitowoc County Sheriff's Office investigators, none of whom were even supposed to be on the scene. Despite this pivotal involvement, Manitowoc investigators filed a mere twenty pages of reports. The thousands of other pages of investigative reports all came from Calumet County or the Wisconsin Department of Justice Division of Criminal Investigations (DCI).

That Sergeant Colborn had played a prominent role in Manitowoc's history with Steven Avery, beginning with that 1985 wrongful conviction, had come to light only in the weeks before Teresa Halbach's death. After his exoneration, Steven Avery filed a civil rights lawsuit against Manitowoc County seeking $36 million in damages. By the fall of 2005, depositions for this suit revealed long-buried evidence of misconduct and neglect by local law enforcement officials, who effectively framed him for the attack on Penny Beerntsen, and that his time in prison might well have been prolonged by the cavalier attitude of Manitowoc County officials, who continually ignored strong indicators that they had convicted the wrong man. Just three weeks before Teresa Halbach disappeared, Avery's civil lawyers questioned Sergeant Andrew Colborn and Lieutenant James Lenk under oath about a phone call Colborn had received at the county jail in 1994 or 1995 from another law enforcement department. The caller had said that Manitowoc County prosecuted the wrong man for a rape. Colborn made no effort to investigate the information. On the day of Steven Avery's release in 2003, eight years after the phone call, Sergeant Colborn consulted with his superior, Lieutenant Lenk, and together they went to speak to the Manitowoc sheriff. Only then, eight years after the fact, did Colborn and Lenk write a short report about this phone call. The sheriff then sealed it in his vault. Avery's civil rights lawyers were alleging that the last eight years of his wrongful incarceration were due to the failure of Colborn and his superiors to follow up on the lead presented to them.

Given how deeply implicated the Manitowoc County Sheriff's Office was in Steven Avery's 1985 false conviction, the current district attorney and sheriff conspicuously disavowed any involvement by their offices in the new case even though Teresa Halbach's vehicle was discovered in the Avery auto salvage yard, which was in their jurisdiction. The investigation would be handled entirely by the sheriff's office in Calumet County, a neighboring jurisdiction, and the Calumet County sheriff, Gerald Pagel, told reporters on November 10 that Manitowoc had done almost nothing of substance in the investigation of Teresa Halbach's disappearance.

"I want to emphasize that Manitowoc County's role was to provide resources to us as they were needed," Pagel said. "Items on property [sic] to conduct searches they provided equipment, and that's their role and their only role in this investigation."

This turned out to be strikingly untrue, especially for Sergeant Colborn and Lieutenant Lenk. Both of them volunteered to search Steven Avery's personal home, as opposed to one of the many other buildings and residences on the salvage yard property. Colborn was present when Lenk supposedly "discovered" Teresa Halbach's car key in Avery's bedroom—after his trailer had already been thoroughly searched six times. And Colborn was recorded calling a dispatcher on his personal cell phone to confirm the license plate number of Teresa Halbach's missing vehicle—forty-eight hours before anyone reported its location at the far end of the Averys' salvage yard. Interestingly, the license plates were not on the RAV4 when it was discovered by volunteer searchers. Nor were they found the following day, when hundreds of volunteers scoured nearly all four thousand vehicles in the yard looking for evidence of Teresa Halbach. In fact, the plates weren't discovered until another two days after that; volunteers eventually found them crumpled up in the rear of a junked vehicle closer to Steven Avery's residence. Both Lieutenant Lenk and Sergeant Colborn had been wandering around the vehicles in the yard the day before.

However, when it was finally submitted, Sergeant Colborn's official report on his involvement in the Halbach investigation consisted of just a few lines. At least he was getting faster; instead of waiting eight years to file a report, as he had during Avery's wrongful conviction, he'd managed to write this half page in just eight months. But it included no mention of his call to the dispatcher about the car license plate number. We stumbled onto that recording of Colborn's call almost by accident.

The pretrial discovery materials provided by the state did not initially include taped phone calls to and from the Manitowoc County Sheriff's Office. In criminal discovery proceedings, recordings of relevant 911 calls or law enforcement dispatch communications—such as assignments to go to a particular scene or an officer's calls back to the dispatcher from that scene—are released. Radio transmissions over public airwaves can be monitored by anyone with a police scanner, so radio dispatch calls often involve numeric codes that both officers and dispatchers understand. In Avery's case, however, we were not satisfied with the usual recordings because they did not appear to include complete instructions to and from the dispatcher to officers. So we made a more broadly worded discovery request for all recorded communications to or from the Manitowoc County Sheriff's Office during the investigation of Teresa Halbach as a missing person and throughout the week of their search of the Avery property. The request went unanswered until after one of my cross-examinations of a detective during a pretrial hearing.

One of the many pretrial motions we filed challenged the circumstances of Pamela Sturm's allegedly divinely inspired discovery of Halbach's RAV4 in the Avery salvage yard on November 5, and therefore the admissibility of the vehicle, and the bloodstains inside it, as evidence. Sturm, a private investigator by training, came to the scrap yard that morning and got permission to search, supposedly acting as a private citizen even though she had the direct phone number for Sheriff Pagel and was the only one among all the volunteer searchers who was outfitted with a camera. Then, within minutes of her arrival, she miraculously discovered the RAV4—a needle in a forty-four-acre haystack of thousands of junked vehicles. It seemed *more* likely that someone had illegally entered the Avery property on a prior day and either placed or discovered the vehicle there, and law enforcement officials with knowledge of this enlisted Sturm's help because they did not yet have a warrant. If, on November 5, Sturm was indeed acting on behalf of law enforcement rather than as a private citizen, her search would be illegal.

After Sturm called Sheriff Pagel, Manitowoc County investigators swarmed onto the property and Calumet County Sheriff's Office detective Mark Wiegert, one of the interrogators who would extract Brendan's various "admissions" the following year, began preparing a search warrant so investigators could seize the RAV4. In the warrant application, Wiegert referenced information that Manitowoc County Sheriff's Office detective Dave Remiker had given him—but it was different from what Remiker had written in his report, which was that Wiegert told him he was arranging some volunteer searchers that Saturday morning to "coordinate our efforts." However, *that* sounded a bit too much like the volunteers were acting as agents of law enforcement, which would have invalidated the entire search, and so it was omitted from Weigert's warrant application.

At a pretrial hearing on this motion, Detective Remiker backed away from that statement in his report, and in the process he dropped a bombshell. He testified that when he wrote his report he had misunderstood what Weigert had told him about law enforcement coordination of the volunteer searchers. How did he know this now? Because just before testifying at the hearing, he had gone back and listened to a recording of the phone conversation he'd had with Wiegert on the morning of Saturday, November 5. What recording was he referring to? The recording of the phone call he had made from an office telephone in the detective bureau of the Manitowoc County Sheriff's Office. You mean to say that there are tape recordings of phone calls, not just radio transmissions, by Manitowoc officials?

The prosecution told the judge presiding over the Avery trial, Manitowoc County Circuit Court judge Patrick Willis, that this was the first they'd heard that such recordings existed, a full ten months after the search. This was the first proof we had that the phone lines at the Manitowoc County Sheriff's Office were recorded, and it opened the floodgates for us to acquire not only that one phone recording but also many more. Judge Willis ordered the recordings turned over to the defense, and we received both incoming and outgoing calls from all of the telephone lines the department was using at the relevant times, including the phones in the detective bureau, the booking room, and the dispatcher's room. These tapes included calls the dispatcher had received on a phone line instead of via radio. Detectives and officers seemed to speak so freely in these phone calls that I had to wonder if even they knew they were being recorded. It was like listening to the Nixon Watergate tapes, only with slightly less profanity.

In this unexpected gold mine of detail was the call Colborn made to the dispatcher about the license plate on Teresa Halbach's car two days before the vehicle officially turned up. During Avery's trial, Dean established that the call transcript read similarly to what an officer might say if he came upon a vehicle while on patrol. After the dispatcher read off the plate numbers, Colborn asked, "A '99 Toyota?" This sounded suspiciously like Colborn had been looking at Teresa's 1999 Toyota RAV4 when he made that call. But how could this be, if Teresa's vehicle had not even been found yet? Unless, perhaps, Colborn really *had* found it but didn't for some reason report the discovery.

Also among these phone recordings were calls from the authorities that, we believed, showed just how determined they were to focus on Steven Avery—and only Steven Avery—as the suspect in Teresa's disappearance. When one officer learned that Teresa's RAV4 had been discovered on the Avery salvage yard property, he asked if a body had been recovered as well. When told no body was found, he asked, "Do we have Steven Avery in custody yet?" Steven Avery was one of several family members who had access to the property, and there were several public access roads into the yard as well. Yet, even at this early stage of the investigation, with no body and no proof even of a specific crime, the officer's suspicion fell straight onto Steven Avery.

Suppose you were never able to have a private word with anyone you loved or trusted or relied upon for nearly a year and a half, because every conversation you had was listened to, recorded, and then listened to again. That was the inhuman situation faced by Steven Avery and Brendan Dassey.

In the months before Avery's trial, we regularly received audio CDs of recordings of his and Brendan Dassey's calls from jail. They surely ran to more than a hundred hours, and it became obvious from the investigative reports produced in discovery that an officer was assigned to listen to all of the recordings every few days or so. If we had gotten our way, none of those jailhouse tapes would have been allowed as evidence. Before the trial, we filed a motion requesting that they be precluded as a matter of fairness. All phone calls and all visits from his family were recorded; even some visits with his pastor were being taped. (Visits from his counsel were not supposed to be recorded, and I have no evidence that they were—but, for some reason, the jailers always scheduled our meetings with him in a room that contained audiovisual gear, which they assured me was switched off.)

We were not objecting to the jail's practice of recording inmate contact, which is a security practice employed by most jails, but to their potential use as evidence in court; the possibility that Avery's conversations with his loved ones could be used against him in the trial was grotesque. His bail, set at $750,000 cash, would keep him behind bars at least through the trial. He was, in the eyes of the law, still an innocent man at that time, and it could not be said that he was a real flight risk. He had lived in Manitowoc County his entire life and was strongly asserting his innocence. If he had the resources to post bail, he would be free to enjoy the company of his family without worrying that his words were being turned into evidence of guilt. An affluent person could have avoided all that surveillance. In our brief to preclude the state from using the jailhouse recordings, we argued: "The wealthy man would enjoy no greater presumption of innocence on the same charges, facing the same evidence, than does Avery.

"Avery, like any human being, needs the support of loved ones. An innocent man in jail may need the support of his closest family."

We were also concerned that over the course of so many months, a casual remark made in conversation could be misconstrued or twisted into an apparent admission of guilt. Lawyers routinely remind their clients to be cautious about what they say on the phone, and not to reveal trial strategy; moreover, each call is preceded by a recorded warning that the conversation will be taped. Despite this advice, many clients forget, or a family member might innocently ask a question, like "What does your lawyer say about that?," thereby eliciting revealing comments from the defendant. In any event, our motion was denied. Judge Willis said that by going ahead with the phone calls after being given a clear warning, Avery had waived any privacy rights that he had.

As it happened, these recordings became far more important in telling Steven Avery's story in *Making a Murderer* than they were in the trial. Perhaps they are most revealing for what cannot be heard. There is no shortage of frustration and exasperation. But in the sixteen months that he was in custody before the trial, Steven Avery had countless opportunities to slip up, to say something truly or seemingly incriminating. He never did. All we could find out from listening to well over a hundred hours of his calls from jail was that he yearned to get out of there and that he believed the authorities were out to get him. From the recordings of phone calls made by law enforcement, we could see that he might be right.

19

The old courthouse in Manitowoc has been sitting on the southwest corner of Eighth and Washington Streets for a century, its stately domed presence like that of a monarch on his throne, gazing down at his subjects. Inside, grand staircases wrap around a central atrium as they lead upstairs to the courtrooms. Downstairs the Clerk of Circuit Court Office is on one side of the atrium, and across from it is the Manitowoc County Sheriff's Office. Many counties have moved their sheriff departments out of their old courthouses and into modern, less central office buildings. Not Manitowoc.

It was a warm afternoon near the end of July 2006 when I walked up the steps. Through the tumult of my first four months since joining the Avery defense, I had worked toward this moment: hunting down a vial of Steven Avery's blood that was accessible to people in the Manitowoc County Sheriff's Office. Even now, it seemed to be a long shot.

Once the authorities claimed that specks and smears of Steven Avery's blood had been found in the RAV4 of Teresa Halbach, he faced a steep climb. They also noted, pointedly, that he had a cut on a finger. Peculiarly, though, many sets of fingerprints had been recovered from the vehicle and yet none were Steven Avery's. There was also a clear palm print, right near the rear hatch door latch, but it was not Avery's (and, as of this writing, it has not been identified). Indeed, no trace of Steven Avery was found in that RAV4 other than the bloodstains. Presumably, the state could theorize that he'd worn gloves, thereby eliminating the chance of prints. How, then, could his blood be on the dashboard—especially if it had come from that cut on his finger? Had he taken *off* the gloves? If so, back to the original problem: Why weren't his prints found anywhere in or on the car? If he took the time to wipe off his fingerprints, why were other people's prints found? And how could he *not* wipe up his blood if he was wiping off his fingerprints? These questions troubled me. But there was no innocent explanation for the presence of Avery's blood. Either he had bled in the car or someone had planted his blood.

A frame-up was what Steven Avery had claimed from the very beginning, even before he was arrested. He'd told reporters that if his blood *was* found inside Teresa's vehicle, someone else had put it there.

"Absurd," Prosecutor Kratz scoffed. The Manitowoc County Sheriff's Office did not have access to Steven Avery's blood, he insisted.

I considered the possibilities. What sources of Avery's blood were available?

A few drops of blood, found on the bathroom floor in Avery's trailer, were later shown to have been his. There was nothing unusual about finding the blood of a man who worked in a junkyard, cutting up cars and wrenching out stuck parts, in his own bathroom; everyone who worked at the scrap yard inevitably got nicks and cuts. In a photograph of one of those drops in the bathroom, taken by investigators, it looked as if someone had removed part of the stain. The center was gone, and just an outer ring of blood remained. Perhaps, I considered, these spots of blood could have yielded enough to plant in Teresa's car. But not much blood was actually recovered from the floor, and it wasn't clear who'd had access to the blood in the bathroom.

Because DNA testing had eventually led to Avery's exoneration in 2003, maybe, I thought, blood had been collected at some point during the appeal process. However, I confirmed with the Wisconsin Innocence Project that the DNA sample taken in 2002 was obtained by rubbing his inner cheek—an abundant source of epithelial cells—with a cotton-topped stick called a buccal swab, which is much like a Q-tip. Epithelial cells can be planted, but they cannot be mistaken for blood.

Could his blood have been drawn under other circumstances somewhere along the line? I waded deeper into the records, and it turned out that the 2002 DNA tests were not the first. A review of the procedural history revealed that, back in 1996, Avery's DNA had been compared to scrapings from underneath Penny Beerntsen's fingernails. (It didn't match.) Had Avery's blood been collected for *that* series of tests?

On this the record was silent, so I called Rob Henak, one of the lawyers who'd represented Avery at the time. He told me that Avery's blood had been drawn in prison and then sent in an overnight package to a LabCorp testing facility in North Carolina. After the results came back, he didn't know what had become of the rest of the sample, but he gave me the name of his contact person at LabCorp. That was my next call. Did LabCorp use all of the blood in their testing process? Not even close; they took one milliliter, a fraction of the quantity in the vial. What did they do with the remainder?

"We usually ship it back to the person who gave it to us," the Lab-Corp worker told me.

That made perfect sense—unless the person who sent it to the laboratory in the first place was in prison. Prison mail is heavily restricted, and Avery wouldn't have been allowed to receive blood through the prison mail. So where could it have gone instead? My LabCorp contact wasn't sure but offered to root through their files to see if they could find out. The answer came back after some days: LabCorp had shipped the vial to the clerk of the court where the matter was heard. That would be the Manitowoc County court. I rang the Clerk of Circuit Court Office, explained that I was Steven Avery's attorney, and asked if the files from that old case were accessible. It was possible that, after all these years, they were now stored off-site.

"Avery?" the clerk said. "It's right here. We've had a lot of interest in it."

Of course. At the time that Avery was exonerated in 2003, reporters interested in the details of his conviction two decades earlier would have needed to go back into those files in order to untangle what had happened. It was a promising lead but not one to get *too* worked up about. Blood is considered a biohazard, and so the clerk's office might have destroyed the sample at some point. It was not a trial exhibit they'd be required to retain for any period of time. And, if the vial were still actually *in* the court files, what would the condition of its contents be ten years after it was taken?

With the storm of other motions and developments in the Halbach murder case, it had taken me a while to find the time to get up to Manitowoc's courthouse. But finally, at the end of July, I made it there with our investigator, Pete Baetz. This visit, our first, was not part of *Making a Murderer.*

At the clerk's office in the courthouse, we were led to a partitioned area that was accessible to anyone coming or going through it but not visible at all moments to the clerks who were at work in the office. Sitting atop a file cabinet was a battered, beaten-up cardboard box. The clerk set it down on a table for us. The box wasn't sealed; the flaps weren't even folded down. I had expected the judge's orders, legal briefs, and motions to be in it but not any actual trial exhibits; these are normally kept in a vault or some other secure area. But the first thing I saw, jutting out of the box, was an oversized trial exhibit—a foam-board chart, the kind of display sometimes used in trials as a visual aid for the jury. This is what was keeping the box from closing. Pete and I started digging through the piles of motion papers and transcripts that were stashed in no logical order. Then, toward the bottom of the box, we suddenly saw a white box, about eight inches by six.

"What's this?" I wondered.

It had little initials written all over it and had clearly once been sealed with red evidence tape. At one end, I could see that this original seal of evidence tape had been slit open and that the white box had been resealed with just a piece of ordinary clear Scotch tape. Writing on the outside of this box indicated that it had, at least at one point, contained a blood sample. We could not tell if there was still a vial in there, and, if there was, whether or not the sample had remained liquid or become a congealed mass. Pete took a bunch of pictures of the out-side of the box, and then we left without opening it. Doing otherwise might have jeopardized our position. But from that point, I proceeded on the assumption that the box may have held a vial of Steven Avery's blood—and that this blood could well have been the source of the bloodstains found in Teresa's RAV4. After all, the box was easily acces-sible and not secured.

If the blood in that vial was still liquid, it would presumably be due to a preservative called ethylenediaminetetraacetic acid, or EDTA. EDTA is not found naturally in human blood, but it is often added to blood samples to prevent them from clotting. When blood clots, its iron molecules bind with other substances that help with coagulation, and EDTA interrupts that process by attaching itself to these iron molecules, segregating them from other substances. Its effect is to keep the blood in liquid form. Purple tops are generally used to identify vials of blood samples that have been treated with EDTA.

Blood collected at a crime scene should typically not contain any EDTA. Its presence in such samples would strongly indicate that the blood had not come from someone actively bleeding but rather from blood that had been previously collected and treated with the preservative. What if there was no EDTA present in samples of Avery's blood taken from the RAV4? How long is EDTA even detectable in a sample? Would that prove anything one way or the other if the sample that may have been used was ten years old? And, in 2006, was it even possible to test for the presence of this chemical in a dried bloodstain found at a crime scene?

Back then, the Internet was only of limited help to me. What research I could even find online about EDTA was often incomplete, just short abstracts of this study or that one from scientific journals. Without purchasing expensive online subscriptions, I could not access the articles themselves. To read them, I had to go the old-fashioned way and find a library that stocked scientific journals. The Medical College of Wisconsin had been a rich source for me in the past during preparations for expert testimony, and also when I was trying to learn about my father's illness and my own. Such research takes time, but even though there was a lot of other pretrial work to do, I got down to it.

After weeks of digging in the library stacks and making phone calls, I still couldn't find any scientists to tell me what the chances were of detecting EDTA in a blood sample ten years after it had been taken and treated with the chemical, or whether it was even possible to test dried bloodstains for the presence of the preservative. Nobody could say; barely anybody had done a test like that, especially not in a forensic context. My research revealed that only one commercial lab had tried to do such testing, for a defendant who was arguing that he, too, had been framed. But the government had used the FBI lab to refute the evidence, and the commercial lab had stopped doing such tests altogether. In exploring the possibility of having a lab devise such a test, I learned that it would cost tens of thousands of dollars, well beyond our budget. The price tag was a moot point, however, as I was turned down flat not only by commercial labs but also by universities that might not have charged as much. In the end, I reluctantly concluded that no one had an answer on the stability of EDTA.

Of course, the whole thing could come to nothing anyway. All I knew was that inside an unsecured evidence box at the Manitowoc County Courthouse there was a smaller white box that presumably held a Styrofoam, clamshell-type container, but I did not know what was actually inside it. It was time to find out if there even was a test tube in the clerk's file, much less one that held still-liquid blood.

In the meantime, I'd learned that investigators from the Manitowoc County Sheriff's Office, which was right down the hall from the Clerk of Circuit Court Office, had been involved in handling the old Avery case file while he appealed his conviction—the same file that had, at least for a while, contained his blood sample. In fact, none other than James Lenk, then a detective sergeant, had been involved in transporting evidence from the files for testing during the wrongful conviction appeal. Now a lieutenant, Lenk had claimed to have found the ignition key for Teresa Halbach's RAV4 in plain view on the floor of Avery's bedroom, even though no one had noticed it during six previous searches. And, along with Sergeant Colborn, he was one of the Manitowoc law enforcement officers who especially should *not* have been involved whatsoever in the investigation of Teresa Halbach's disappearance because of his connection to Avery's civil lawsuit against the county and sheriff.

This complicated background became part of the motion we filed on Steven Avery's behalf asking the court not only to secure the old 1985 case file but also to allow us supervised access to the blood vial.

In addition to revealing the web of connections linking Steven Avery to Lenk and other law enforcement officers in the Manitowoc County Sheriff's Office, which showed that we had a good-faith basis for suspecting a frame-up, I described the dilapidated box I'd found holding everything, as well as the container inside with the slit evidence tape inside it that, at least back in 1996, had likely held Steven Avery's blood.

The court granted us permission, though not before Ken Kratz demanded that our papers be sealed from the public on the grounds that they contained information that was potentially prejudicial and "that would tend to influence or contaminate the possible jury pool in this case."

If unintended irony were a felony, Kratz would be serving twenty-five years without parole.

20

In December 2006, I arranged to open the small white box from the 1985 Avery case, in the Manitowoc County Clerk of Circuit Court Office. Also present were Norm Gahn, the special prosecutor from the Milwaukee District Attorney's Office who specialized in DNA evidence—and Calumet County Sheriff's Office detective Mark Wiegert.

When I entered the room, I was surprised to see that Wiegert only had the 8 x 6-inch white box. There was no sign of the bigger cardboard box into which everything had been thrown.

Gahn was puzzled, too. "Um," he said, looking at the small white box. "No, I thought there was a big box."

"I thought it was gonna be in the big box, too," I said.

Wiegert said, "My understanding is, that is it. The other items were fingernail scrapings and hair."

We donned green gloves before opening the white box. Inside, there was indeed a Styrofoam clam-shell container. For the first time we saw that it, too, had at one point been sealed with red evidence tape. And, just like on the white box holding it, this seal was at one point slit open.

"Want to spin it around?" I said to Norm. "It looks like it's cut through, doesn't it?"

Wiegert lifted the top off the container to reveal a tube of blood, labeled with Avery's name and the date it was drawn, nestled in the Styrofoam.

Norm rocked the vial back and forth. "It's still liquid," he said, surprised.

Three things about the vial struck me immediately. First, there was no seal on the vial. Second, in the center of the vial's rubber stopper was a visible hole. And third, around the sides of the vial, trapped between the stopper and the glass, was a coating of blood *above* the level of the bottom of the stopper.

We went on documenting the condition of the vial and the containers.

Norm plainly was taken aback. As we were finishing, he said to me, "Well, this is a game changer."

I said, "Look, we've been saying all along, if Avery's blood is in there, it was planted. Kratz was claiming that it was a preposterous allegation because you didn't have access to any of his blood. Here it is, right across the courthouse atrium from Lieutenant Lenk and Sergeant Colborn."

"You're right," Norm agreed. "This is a game changer."

As we left the Manitowoc County Sheriff's Office, he said that he was going to try to find explanations for this, and if there were any tests that could be done to determine if the blood collected from the RAV4 could be connected to the blood in the vial.

A couple of critical points about this vial were not mentioned in *Making a Murderer*. The Clerk of Circuit Court Office had no sign-in sheet to record the identity of people who inspected the file and its exhibits. And even if there *had* been some form of monitoring, the Manitowoc County Sheriff's Office had passkeys to all of the offices, including that of the Clerk of Circuit Court.

I was staying in Manitowoc that night, so I went back to my hotel room, eager to report back to Dean. After months of sleuthing, we had struck gold: conclusive evidence that, from the very beginning of the investigation into Teresa Halbach's disappearance, the Manitowoc County Sheriff's Office had essentially unfettered, unmonitored access to an ample supply of Steven Avery's blood. Not only that, but the Manitowoc detective at the center of the highly suspicious "discovery" of the victim's car key, James Lenk, had also been involved in handling material from the box that held the blood vial a few years earlier. Unlike others currently involved in the case against Avery, Lenk had a chance then to learn about this stash of Avery's blood.

Back in the hotel, the filmmakers had set themselves up in a corner of my room. Honestly, at that stage, they had been around so much that I barely noticed them anymore. When I called Dean, my discovery was bubbling out of me, and it was captured on film:

Let me tell you. This is a red-letter day for the defense. It could not have been better. The seal was clearly broken on the outside of the box and inside the box is a Styrofoam kit. The seal is broken on that. We pulled the Styrofoam halves apart and there, in all of its glory, was a test tube that said "Steven Avery," inmate number, everything on it. The blood is liquid. And get this. Right in the center of the top of the tube is a little tiny hole. Just about the size of a hypodermic needle. Yes. And I spoke with a LabCorp person already who told me they don't do that. You can. . . . Have you fallen on the floor yet or no? Think about it, Dean. If LabCorp didn't stick the needle through the top, then who did? Some officer went into that file, opened it up, took a sample of Steven Avery's blood, and planted it in the RAV4. Yeah, he knows where we're going.

Dean was back in Madison.

"Game on," he said.

"Game on, exactly. Game on," I replied.

When I hung up the phone, I realized the camera had been running the whole time and had captured my giddy, gloating account of the day. At that moment, I hoped they would not use the footage. It was too unguarded. This is about the only thing that ended up in the film that I wish had not.

Later that evening, when the cameras were gone, I got a call from Norm Gahn. It was the first of a few conversations we had about how the vial would fit into the trial of Steven Avery. Gahn is a good lawyer, and it was evident that he found the afternoon's revelations disturbing and had moved quickly to see if there were innocent explanations, and to see if the RAV4 bloodstains could be analyzed for the possible presence of EDTA—the same research I had conducted. Moreover, if any testing could be done to detect EDTA, Gahn had already thought about ways EDTA might innocently have come to be present.

I had done the same before we went to the courthouse: As it happens, EDTA has uses outside of blood laboratories, primarily as an ingredient in various cleaning products. For instance, it is a component in Armor All products, which are used to clean the interiors and exteriors of cars. It is also in some laundry soaps, which means it ends up in water treatment plants; this has led to a dispute about its persistence in the environment, between environmentalists, who argue that it is like a heavy metal that does not deteriorate, and the chemical industry, which says the evidence shows that EDTA breaks down into harmless molecules with exposure to sunlight.

Norm Gahn had also learned that EDTA is found in Armor All. The RAV4 was Teresa Halbach's first car, and she no doubt kept it spiffy. It was obvious that if any EDTA turned up in the blood samples taken from the vehicle, he would suggest that it was neither a surprise nor sinister, just the residue of a young woman's efforts to care for her most prized possession. I kept notes from one of our conversations: *FBI can do EDTA testing, but it would take them 3–4 months. They can do them on the stains and on the vial.*

As any diligent lawyer would, Gahn was already thinking ahead to how each side might present different views of the same facts. During the trial of O. J. Simpson, EDTA was found in a bloodstain on a sock of Simpson's, and his defense team argued that the EDTA showed that the blood had been planted. Over the years, a few other people had made similar claims. The FBI, which had been heavily criticized for using shoddy science to try to explain away the EDTA finding in the Simpson case, had stayed out of most of these other ones. Their position had been that the tests were too sensitive and could mistake chemicals normally found in the environment and the background for EDTA. Now, though—according to Gahn—the FBI believed it could devise a test that wouldn't be triggered by what they deemed irrelevant chemicals to give a false positive. That is, in my view, the FBI believed they could come up with a test that was *less* likely to suggest that blood had been planted.

Despite all my research, I had not read about any revised FBI test, so all I knew about it was what Gahn was telling me on the phone. He wanted an adjournment to do the testing, and if we wouldn't agree to one, he did not want us to be allowed to argue to the jury that the failure to test was intentional, or even to cross-examine on it.

At this point, Steven Avery had already been in jail for nearly fourteen months. To postpone the trial for another four was out of the question.

"No way," I told him.

In late December, after our meeting at the Clerk of Circuit Court Office to view the vial of Avery's blood, the state asked the court to release it to its investigators for chemical testing. Norm Gahn had neither a willing laboratory nor specific tests in mind. I objected to allowing the state carte blanche access to the blood and urged the court to seal it in a safe where it could not be tampered with by anyone. The court agreed to keep the blood secure until all parties had a chance to see if any lab could be found that would provide relevant chemical tests on the blood. The court also unsealed the motion we'd filed to allow the box in the clerk's office to be opened in the first place. This hearing was the first time the public, and the media, learned about the existence and the suspicious condition of the blood vial.

Remember that Steven Avery had maintained from the beginning of the investigation into Teresa's disappearance that the only way his blood would be in the victim's vehicle was if someone had planted it there, and that a year before this hearing, Kratz had publicly scoffed at this claim. He said that the Manitowoc authorities couldn't have planted Avery's blood because they didn't have access to any of it. Now, it was evident that Kratz was wrong. All along, a vial of Steven Avery's blood had been sitting in the old case file in the Clerk of Circuit Court Office, a short walk through the building from the Manitowoc County Sheriff Office—and the broken seal of evidence tape suggested the possibility of tampering. Naturally, the reporters present that day in court were astonished at this development. To date, the narrative had been dominated by the prosecution's depiction of Steven Avery as a monster, and this was the first detail to the contrary that they'd got their hands on. They asked me about it as we left. How had we found this? Speaking outside the courtroom, I basically repeated what I'd told Judge Willis in the motion we'd filed and during the arguments—all information that had just been discussed in the public forum of the courtroom. This did not please Ken Kratz, and he complained to Judge Willis.

Given the history of this case and the prosecution's previous use of publicity to prejudice Steven Avery's chance for a fair trial, this was indeed rich. Well before this, we'd actually moved the court to dismiss the case because the Kratz March 1 and 2, 2006, press conferences had irreparably damaged Avery's right to a fair trial. Kratz had spewed, as if they were proven facts, one poisonous utterance after another declaring that Teresa Halbach had been tortured, raped, stabbed, strangled, and shot. As we were learning through the discovery process, virtually all of these assertions were either uncorroborated or provably false. Judge Willis denied the motion to dismiss and he was reluctant to grant, as an alternative, a complete gag order out of concern that it would violate First Amendment protections meant to ensure that the press had access to information it needed to report fully on events in court. Instead, Judge Willis informally instructed us to limit our out-of-court comments to matters that had gone on during the hearings.

Now, after Kratz's complaint, I received a letter from Judge Willis not only scolding me but also suggesting that I had violated the code of ethics for lawyers in Wisconsin with my comments to reporters on the day of the hearing. This seemed to me to be untrue, and patently unfair, considering that he never made a similar threat to Kratz, whose press conferences violated clear ethical rules that a lawyer shall make no out-of-court statements about "the existence or contents of any confession admission or statement given by a defendant or suspect." Nor did Judge Willis castigate Kratz for stating "any opinion as to the guilt or innocence of a defendant or suspect in a criminal case or proceeding," another violation. The brief after-court comments I'd made that day were limited to matters of public record, in accordance with ethical rules and Judge Willis's guidelines, and they also easily qualified under Wisconsin's "safe harbor" rule, which allows statements that are "required to protect a client from the substantial likelihood of undue prejudicial effect of recent publicity not initiated by the lawyer or lawyer's client." That is, I could stick up for my client against the flood tide of prejudice that Kratz had triggered with his press conferences—not to mention that unleashed by the Manitowoc County sheriff, who declared over the course of a three-part news special that if Steven Avery was found not guilty of Teresa Halbach's murder, he would kill again. And speaking with a Green Bay television reporter, Sheriff Peterson had dismissed the notion that Avery had been framed by saying, "If we wanted to eliminate Steve, it would've been a whole lot easier to eliminate Steve than to frame Steve." The reporter apparently had a hard time believing what she was hearing and asked what he meant by "eliminate."

Sheriff Peterson obligingly explained. "If we wanted him killed, it would be much easier to kill him."

Judge Willis ultimately backed down from his threat of sanctions against me, but this incident embodied a double standard that would soon be applied to matters that were far more serious.

If not Steven Avery, then who had killed Teresa Halbach? Two months before Avery's trial began, in early January 2007, Dean and I submitted papers under seal that listed ten people who we believed had as much access and opportunity to kill her as Steven Avery did. Officially referred to as the "Defendant's Statement on Third-Party Responsibility," we explicitly stated that we were *not* accusing any of these ten people of killing her; we just wanted to show that it was possible that someone *other* than Steven Avery could have done it. It was important that the jury know about the existence of other potential suspects, despite the almost nonexistent official investigation of anyone else, even after investigators discovered what were apparently human female pelvic bones in a burn pit in a quarry owned by an Avery neighbor, Joshua Radandt.

Wisconsin, along with many other states, has a rule of evidence—clarified in *State v. Denny* (1984)—limiting the defense's ability to name alternative suspects to a jury. Based on the concept of "legitimate tendency," the purpose of this rule is to establish reasonable guidelines about when and why a third-party suspect might be introduced. To avoid diverting the trial to a discussion of collateral issues, and also to avoid unsupported jury speculation, there must be some evidence of a direct connection, or "legitimate tendency," between a third party and the crime with which the defendant has been charged. But the third-party liability rule is just a rule of evidence, which should not be permitted to trump a defendant's constitutional right to present a defense.

All of the people on our list, which included other members of the Avery family and friends, had been at the salvage yard on October 31, 2005, the day Teresa Halbach disappeared. One man was a frequent customer who had attacked his own girlfriend with a hatchet a few days afterward. When first questioned, he denied killing Halbach but later said he would take the blame because he was going to prison anyway. Despite this admission, law enforcement agents ignored him as a possible suspect.

On January 30, 2007, in perhaps the most unfair pretrial ruling we received, Judge Willis ruled that Steven Avery did *not* have the right to name any third parties with access and opportunity to kill Teresa Halbach—unless he could also provide a motive. This additional burden of proof did not apply to the state, which at trial provided no motive for Steven Avery to kill her. Indeed, we argued that he had none. We knew of no one who did. Ken Kratz's pretrial publicity effectively shut down defense investigation opportunities. Nobody in the local community was willing to cooperate with us. While this may have changed after *Making a Murderer*, a decade ago Dean and I were all too often stuck with the inadequate investigation of other suspects done by law enforcement agents. Without their essentially unlimited resources, not to mention their authority to compel people to cooperate, we could not explore other potential suspects among Teresa Halbach's circle of friends or romantic or sexual partners. A study by the Justice Department in the early 1990s found that 80 percent of murder victims were killed not by strangers but by people who they knew or were close to; that is even more true when women are the victims, and more recent

FBI data show similar patterns.* † Yet, those individuals were ignored as possible suspects in this case.

Judge Willis's decision also left us wide open to the prosecution's accusations that we were making law enforcement officers "the bad guys." Conveniently omitting we had been legally gagged from introducing suspects other than Steven Avery, Ken Kratz told the jury that we had offered only one alternative to Steven as the murderer—namely, law enforcement. This fabrication was possible because of Judge Willis's ruling. Certainly, we were arguing that evidence had been planted, but it was never our contention that the Manitowoc County Sheriff's Office investigators, or any other branches of law enforcement, had been involved in the killing of Teresa Halbach. We believed only that they had framed Steven Avery because they thought he was guilty, or wanted him to be guilty, so that his lawsuit would wither away, and that they felt justified in taking whatever steps necessary to nail him. He would not walk free a second time if they could help it.

* U.S. Department of Justice, Bureau of Justice Statistics, "Murder in Large Urban Counties, 1988," May 12, 1993. http://www.bjs.gov/content/pub/press/MILUC88 .PR.

† Federal Bureau of Investigation, Expanded Homicide Data Table 10: "Murder Circumstances by Relationship, 2011." https://ucr.fbi.gov/crime-in-the-u.s/2011/crime-in-the-u.s.-2011/tables/expanded-homicide-data-table-10.

21

"A defendant's confession is like no other evidence," U.S. Supreme Court justice Byron White wrote in 1991. "It is probably the most probative and damaging evidence that can be admitted against him, and, if it is a full confession, a jury may be tempted to rely on it alone in reaching its decision."

As hard as it may be to believe that innocent people would admit to committing a crime, it has happened consistently throughout history. Trying to reel back a confession is close to impossible. Take the case of Margaret Jacobs, who, like Brendan Dassey, was a teenager who accused a relative of joining her in a heinous crime.

After implicating herself and her grandfather, George Jacobs Sr., in various illicit actions, she tried to recant her confession. Why, she was asked on the witness stand, had she made the original, damning statements?

"They told me if I would not confess I should be put down into the dungeon and would be hanged, but if I would confess I should save my life," she told the court.

Despite Margaret's efforts, her grandfather was hanged. The trial of George Jacobs Sr. was held in the town of Salem, Massachusetts, in 1692, an era when Satan was believed to walk the earth. Her grandfather was one of twenty people executed for witchcraft, nearly all on the confessions of self-styled witches. (Margaret's own trial was delayed because, fortuitously, she came down with a boil on her head; before she recovered, the witch courts had been disbanded and a new court found her innocent.)*

More than two centuries later, in 1932, Edwin M. Borchard published

---

* Kelly McCandlish, "Salem Witch Trials Documentary Archive and Transcription Project: Margaret Jacobs," University of Virginia, 2001. http://salem.lib.virginia.edu /people?group.num=&mbio.num=mb18.

Convicting the Innocent: Sixty-Five Actual Errors of Criminal Justice, which cataloged wrongful convictions, including a number based on false confessions, going back to the eighteenth and nineteenth centuries. Back in those days before reliable mass communications or regular postal service, Borchard notes, it was not uncommon for people to wander off, not be heard from, and then be presumed dead. A suspect would be found, forced to confess, and then convicted of murder. How do we know these were false confessions? In eight cases, the supposed victim later turned up, "hale and hearty," as Borchard, a professor at Yale Law School, wrote.

Three hundred years after Margaret Jacobs succumbed to pressure from the adults who were questioning her, Brendan Dassey cowered, alone and afraid, in an interrogation room.

Because the act of speaking against one's own interests seems so counterintuitive, false confessions are extraordinarily dangerous evidence. Juries give confessions a great deal of credence, even when they show signs of being drastically unreliable—as Brendan Dassey's confession did. It revealed nothing trustworthy about the death of Teresa Halbach but was a living, breathing gauge of the great lengths to which the prosecution team and the Manitowoc County Sheriff's Office were willing to go in their pursuit of Steven Avery.

From the outset, Ken Kratz's description of Brendan Dassey's confession at that press conference on March 2, 2006, which was echoed in the details of the criminal complaint—that Teresa Halbach had first been stabbed, then her throat slit, then strangled, and finally shot—sounded ridiculous to me. And indeed, not long after Kratz so triumphantly declared, "We have now determined what occurred sometime between three forty-five p.m. and ten or eleven p.m. on the thirty-first of October," the wheels started to fly off. Contrary to Kratz's pronouncement, the prosecution did not know what happened on October 31, 2005, because Brendan *himself* didn't know. Reports from the forensic laboratory were coming in at a dizzying pace, and not one of them backed up his account. Included in the discovery materials were videos and transcripts of Brendan's "confession," which revealed that even with tireless coaching and cajoling from experienced investigators, Brendan could not provide a coherent account of the torture and murder in which he claimed to have participated.

In virtually every case where DNA has revealed the innocence of a person who had confessed, the suspect had offered specific details that only the real killer and investigators would know. How could this be? These innocent people were picking up the incriminating information from their interrogators. The tape and transcripts here unmistakably showed that this had been the case during the questioning of Brendan Dassey by Detective Mark Wiegert of the Calumet County Sheriff's Office and Special Agent Tom Fassbender of the Wisconsin Division of Criminal Investigation.

Brendan's story drifts around about what time he saw Steven Avery on October 31 and whether he saw Teresa Halbach with Avery. But how had she died? Brendan mentions stabbing her in the stomach.

"What else did he do to her? (pause) He did something else, we know that. (pause) What else?" asks Wiegert.

He tied her up, Brendan replies. This, apparently, is not the answer they were looking for, so Wiegert asks again. "We know he did something else to her. What else did he do to her?"

After a moment's pause, Brendan suggests: "He choked her."

Nope, still not correct. Wiegert gets more specific. "What else did he do to her? We know something else was done. Tell us, and what else did you do? Come on. Something with the head. Brendan?"

This time, Brendan pauses for a long while, unable to guess what they want him to say. Finally, he comes up with something that might have happened to her head.

"That he cut off her hair," he says.

No, not that. (There was none of Teresa Halbach's hair in the bedroom.) Both detectives begin to throw questions at him.

"What else was done to her head?" Fassbender says.

"That he punched her," Brendan says.

"What else?" Wiegert asks.

Brendan says nothing, so Wiegert asks again: "What else?"

No answer.

"He made you do somethin' to her, didn't he?" Fassbender asks. "So he—he would feel better about not bein' the only person, right?"

Brendan nods. "Yeah, mm huh," he mumbles.

"What did he make you do to her?" Fassbender continues.

No reply.

"What did he make you do, Brendan?" Wiegert asks.

No reply.

Wiegert repeats the question. "It's okay, what did he make you do?"

"Cut her," Brendan said at last.

"Cut her where?" Wiegert asked.

"On her throat," Brendan said.

So far, Brendan has described stabbing, choking, punching her, and slitting her throat. He is guessing but still has not landed on the single, solitary fact that can be corroborated with physical evidence, which the lab results had uncovered just a few days earlier. A fragment of a skull bone recovered from Avery's burn pit and examined by the state's anthropologist showed a small hole and minute traces of lead, both signs of a gunshot wound. This fact has not yet been made public, so if Wiegert and Fassbender can get Brendan to disclose a shooting, it will seem like information only the real killers could know—and thereby salvage Brendan's story, making him a believable participant in the murder and thus a star witness against Steven Avery.

"So Steve stabs her first, then you cut her neck?"

Brendan nods yes.

"What else happens to her head?" Wiegert continues.

"It's extremely important you tell us this, for us to believe you," Fassbender says.

"Come on, Brendan, what else?" Wiegert says.

No reply.

"We know, we just need you to tell us," Wiegert says.

Defeated, Brendan says, "That's all I can remember."

By now, Wiegert is clearly frustrated that Brendan won't give him what he wants: that one fact not yet released to the public. If the shooting of Teresa Halbach doesn't come from Brendan's statements, they cannot be corroborated as reliable. In his eagerness, Wiegert is about to contaminate the whole interrogation.

"All right, I'm just gonna come out and ask you," Wiegert says. "Who shot her in the head?"

"He did," Brendan says.

After he has finally confessed to their satisfaction, Fassbender demands Brendan provide an explanation for why it has taken so long.

"Then why didn't you tell us that?" he asks.

"'Cuz I couldn't think of it," Brendan replies.

And on it goes. But Brendan's continuing story—that Teresa Halbach was carried outside, and shot as she lay near the side of the garage, and then put into a roaring fire—has a significant problem. How was her blood found in the cargo area of her RAV4? Also, the detectives believed that she had been shot inside the garage, yet Brendan says that he had not been in there. So with more egging by Wiegert and Fassbender, he adapts his narrative to include the back of the RAV4 and the garage.

"That makes sense," Wiegert says with relief. "Now we believe you."

Fassbender also feeds Brendan an important fact, which the state later falsely claimed Brendan had come up with on his own. The prosecutor at Brendan Dassey's trial told the jury that Brendan volunteered that he had seen Steven Avery do something under the hood of Teresa Halbach's car, a detail that allegedly proved he had been present because, when the RAV4 was discovered, its battery cables were disconnected.

Actually, Fassbender suggests that fact to Brendan when he asks him what else he did to the car.

Brendan says he doesn't know.

Fassbender asked, "Okay. Did he, did he go back and look at the engine, did he raise the hood at all or anything like that? To do something to that car."

Brendan answers "yeah" but says he does not know what Avery did under the hood.

And he never says anything about the battery cables.

The interrogation techniques Wiegert and Fassbender employed were developed in the 1940s by John E. Reid, a former Chicago police officer and polygraph operator who became famous for being able to extract confessions without resorting to physical force. He founded a consulting firm, John E. Reid & Associates, Inc., in 1947, which still exists today, and his methods continue to be taught as standard practice in police departments across the United States (and today, almost nowhere else).

A central aim of the Reid technique is quite logical: Have the suspect provide details that would only be known to the actual criminal— where a weapon was discarded, for instance, or a specific description of a piece of jewelry that was stolen; any facts peculiar to the crime but not disclosed to the public. The point was to be sure that the person making the admissions really *had* committed the crime. (After the baby of Charles Lindbergh and Anne Morrow Lindbergh was kidnapped in 1932, a notorious crime that drew worldwide attention because of Charles Lindbergh's stature as a pioneering aviator, more than two hundred people came forward to claim responsibility.) Knowledge of secret details is highly incriminating and, more often than not, forecloses any realistic possibility of going to trial. To many defendants in those circumstances, it seems their best choice is to plead guilty.

Early in the twenty-first century, however, research by Brandon L. Garrett of the University of Virginia revealed the risk of blindly relying on such an authentication process. He looked at sixty-six recent cases in which a person had confessed but was later exonerated through DNA testing. Of those innocent people, sixty-two—that is, 94 percent— had provided insider information. "Confession contamination is overwhelmingly prevalent among persons exonerated by DNA tests," Garrett reported. "Almost without exception, these confession statements were contaminated with crime scene details which these innocent suspects, as we now know, could not have themselves been familiar with until they learned of them from law enforcement."[*]

---

[*] Brandon L. Garrett, "Contaminated Confessions Revisited," *Virginia Law Review*

The Reid techniques were part of a reform wave that swept through the justice system in the 1930s. Like J. Edgar Hoover's Technical Crime Laboratory, which fostered the growth of spurious forensic science disciplines, they reflect the desire to replace the crude processes of the past with scientific processes then modernizing everyday life. The use of brutal force, or the "third degree," was documented in 1931 by a commission chaired by George Wickersham, who had served as the attorney general for the Taft administration, in the commission's *Report on Lawlessness in Law Enforcement,* one of the first investigations into misconduct within the police force. Five years later, the U.S. Supreme Court weighed in. After hearing an appeal from three black tenant farmers who were tortured with whippings, beatings, and a partial hanging until they confessed to the killing of a white man, the court overturned their convictions and death sentence in *Brown v. Mississippi.* It was the first time the court ruled that a criminal conviction could not be based on a coerced confession. Under the Fourteenth Amendment to the Constitution, the court unanimously held, people were entitled to "due process" of law—and physically coerced confessions denied that right. The *Brown* ruling applied to police interrogations in every state. With its new limits on the threat or use of physical force, the Supreme Court ruling had opened an investigative void. Up stepped Reid, who developed psychological techniques that were portrayed as a "scientific" way to question suspects.

Under Reid's* procedures, investigators assure the suspect that they already know what has happened, and that if the suspect wants any help, he must come clean. Bluffs are a common tactic: Investigators can suggest that witnesses or other evidence incriminate the subject. At every turn, the suspect is assured that the interrogators

101 (2015): 395–454. http://www.virginialawreview.org/sites/virginialawreview.org/files/Garrett_101–395.pdf.

* Douglas Starr, "The Interview: Do Police Interrogation Techniques Produce False Confessions?," *The New Yorker,* December 9, 2013. http://www.newyorker.com/magazine/2013/12/09/the-interview-7.

know what happened and are only awaiting some explanation from the suspect as to how and why it happened. The rubber hose was gone. In its place was the cornered mind. Manhandling gave way to manipulation.

In another Reid technique, investigators invite versions of the crime that minimize the suspect's culpability. The Brendan Dassey interrogation is a textbook example.

Brendan: He said that it was a girl that he was kinda pee'd off at.

Wiegert: Did he say who, who it was?

Brendan: Teresa Halbach.

Wiegert: Why was he pee'd off at her?

Brendan: I don't know.

Wiegert: I think he probably told ya. So just be honest. We already know.

Fassbender: He's obviously not holding anything back from you. He had you come to see this.

Wiegert: We already know.

Fassbender: *He used you for this* [emphasis added]. So bring us into the garage again. You mentioned earlier that's when he threatened you. Tell us that.

Brendan: That he threatened me that if I would say anything that he would stab like she, he did ta her and that, um, he was pissed off at her because of he wanted to get his Blazer in the thing that like that last time she was there and he couldn't.

Reid interrogators also are taught to use the "false friend" approach, demonstrated in earlier interrogations of Brendan when Fassbender tells him he is not acting as a police officer at that moment but as the father of a sixteen-year-old boy like Brendan. He assures Brendan that he is not in trouble and that the officers will "go to bat" for him.

Even before we read the actual statements or saw the tapes, Avery was scoffing at their plausibility. At the end of March 2006, he gave an interview from the jail to Carrie Antflinger of the Associated Press in which he accurately anticipated the manipulation that had gone on during the interrogations. "He's sixteen years old and with the detective, it don't take much . . . to coerce him to say that stuff. You figure, he can't even cut deer up . . . he can't even do none of that."

Steven was alluding to a fact well known to the Avery family: Brendan was unable to dress a deer killed while hunting. He was repulsed by taking a knife to a deer that was already dead.

Len Kachinsky, meanwhile, was going through the motions of fighting the use of Brendan's statements, even though he assumed that the story attributed to Brendan was true. In reality, his strategy was to make Brendan a witness at his uncle's trial, and thus win a break. First, though, they had to go through a suppression hearing.

In general, courts want to know if a person who makes a statement to the police did so voluntarily—without coercion through physical or psychological threats—and with the knowledge of the rights to remain silent, and to have an attorney present during questioning. If a judge finds that a confession was not coerced, and that it was given after *Miranda* rights were read, it is admissible at trial. The *reliability* of the statement is left for the jury to decide. Built into that process is the assumption that a subject who speaks after being told of the right to a lawyer and to remain silent is doing so voluntarily. A number of legal scholars argue that *Miranda* is not an adequate safeguard of reliability. For one thing, there are more than eight hundred versions of the *Miranda* warnings used across the country. The problem becomes more acute when juveniles are being questioned. The vast majority of those

Miranda warnings were written by adults for other adults, and most require an eighth-grade reading level. Studies have shown that many of the warnings are couched in language beyond the comprehension level of juveniles, especially under the high stress of a custodial interrogation.

A related issue is the overall susceptibility of young adolescents and others to pressure. Perhaps it is no surprise that in Garrett's study of the sixty-six false confessions made by DNA exonerees, one-third of the innocent were juveniles at the time of their convictions, and at least one-third were mentally ill or had an intellectual disability. Garrett reports that others—without a formal diagnosis from an expert—were often described as having low intelligence and being highly suggestible.

Could Brendan's "confessions" be trusted? That question had been taken off the table by Kachinsky, who had implicitly endorsed their truthfulness before seeing the videotapes or speaking with Brendan, Understandably, Kachinsky wanted to find a way out of a life sentence for Brendan, and a deal with the prosecution was a path that any responsible lawyer might explore. But another way would be to fight to protect an innocent client from being convicted and serving any prison time at all. Kachinsky just assumed his client was guilty even before meeting with him for the first time. Given that assumption, it appears Kachinsky made only a halfhearted attempt at suppressing the confession. It was no surprise that on May 12, 2006, a judge in Manitowoc denied Kachinsky's motion and ruled that statements Brendan Dassey made to the investigators could be used as evidence against him.

We didn't realize it at that time, but a series of e-mails later emerged that showed Kachinsky had already been working with the state's investigators to strengthen their case—even though by then Brendan had been clear in telling him that he had *not* had any hand or part in the death of Teresa Halbach. Nevertheless, anticipating the judge would rule that the statements could be used at trial, Kachinsky e-mailed Wiegert a week beforehand and told him that the defense's private investigator might be able to help law enforcement find the van driven by Brendan's mom, "which may contain some evidence useful in this case." (There was no such evidence.) Kachinsky cautioned Wiegert that he was providing the information in confidence. "We would prefer to stay unnamed in any affidavit for a search warrant if at all possible," he wrote.

At the same time, Kachinsky and his investigator, Michael O'Kelly were plotting to get Brendan to talk as soon as he returned to jail after the May 12 hearing, likely expecting that he would have just lost the motion to block his earlier statements. He would be at an emotional low point and vulnerable, and perhaps could be persuaded to implicate himself in a credible way, which he had not done so far. Their reasoning appears to be that, by making him look *more* guilty, they could make him more attractive as a witness against his uncle and thus strengthen his hand in plea bargaining.

Unless you think it would be a bad idea, I was planning on going to Sheboygan on Wed afternoon for a general pep talk and talk to him about giving you a complete statement to you on Friday, Kachinsky e-mailed O'Kelly on Tuesday, May 9.

No, O'Kelly wrote in response, he did not want Kachinsky to visit Brendan just two days before O'Kelly's planned visit.

It could have Brendan digging his heels in further. He could become more entrenched in his illogical position and further distort the facts. He has been relying on a story that his family has told what to say about October 31, 2005 >> thus it will take me longer to undo if I can even without your visit.

We need to separate him from fantasy and bring him to see reality from our perspective. We need to separate him from the unrealistic world that his family resides within.

Brendan needs to be alone. When he sees me this Friday I will be a source of relief. He and I can begin to bond. He needs to trust me and the direction that I steer him into. Brendan needs to provide an explanation that coincides with the facts/evidence.

I would like to obtain his confession this Friday. Brendan should provide details of the crime scene and data that has been previously undisclosed that mirrors the crime scene data.

In the same e-mail, O'Kelly expressed utter contempt for the Avery family, stating, This is truly where the devil resides in comfort. I can find no good in any member. These people are pure evil.

Kachinsky's decision to hire O'Kelly was surprising, since Kachinsky had never worked with him before. Brendan, by that point, was adamant about his innocence; he wanted to take a polygraph to prove his truthfulness. O'Kelly was first hired for the limited purpose of administering a polygraph, which he told Kachinsky gave inconclusive results. O'Kelly then described Brendan as a kid with no conscience. Despite that opinion, Kachinsky then brought O'Kelly on board as the defense investigator for Brendan.

O'Kelly videotaped his jail confrontation of Brendan on May 12, portions of which were seen in *Making a Murderer*. Until I watched the documentary, I had never seen that video recording. I was shocked. I have never seen a defense investigator so clearly doing the prosecutor's work of extracting a confession from his client. And O'Kelly managed to be even more garishly coercive than Wiegert and Fassbender had been. He lied to Brendan, telling him that he failed the polygraph, even though he told Kachinsky that the results were actually inconclusive. "Why don't you draw another picture over here of him stabbing her?" he prompts Brendan at one point. "Why don't you draw a picture down here . . . of you having sex with her there."

And then, "Okay, why don't you do this," O'Kelly suggests. "Why don't you draw a picture of the bed and how she was tied down. But draw it big-sized so we can see it."

I was especially distressed to see that O'Kelly showed Brendan a pre-printed form—presumably meaning he had used it with other clients as well—that offered only two choices:

1. "I am sorry for what I did."
2. "I am not sorry for what I did."

"How about a third choice, 'I didn't do it'!" I practically yelled at the television.

The coaching of his client completed, Kachinsky invited Wiegert and Fassbender to come back the next day, May 13, and nail down Brendan's story. No consideration is being offered by the state for this additional information at this time, he wrote in an e-mail to the investigators and prosecutors that laid out the terms of his invitation.

In other words, a freebie.

Ahead of time, Kachinsky explained, O'Kelly would brief them on his discussions with Brendan. Ordinarily these would *never* be turned over, because O'Kelly's conversations with Brendan were covered under the umbrella of attorney-client privilege. It got worse: The interview may occur without my physical presence as I have some military duties to attend to on May 13, 2006, he continued. So without any promise whatsoever of leniency or immunity in hand, Kachinsky handed over his sixteen-year-old client with a 70-point IQ to investigators trying to solve a notorious murder. And Kachinsky left Brendan to face his accusers alone.

In his May 13 session with investigators, Brendan gave a new version of events that changed the time, location, and method of the killing. His updated story failed to mention the RAV4. When asked why he omitted that detail, he said he had not seen it that day. This did not work for the investigators because Teresa Halbach's blood was found in the cargo area. Wiegert became exasperated, saying: "Brendan, at some point, she's in that truck. We know that. Okay? Bleeding. So you can't say you didn't see the truck or know where the truck was because she has ta' be in that truck after she was bleeding. Okay? That's just the way it is. And I'm not gonna sit here and let ya lie to me. You need to be honest here."

Fassbender jumped in with the "false friend" angle again, emphasizing that they wanted to help him. Why, they had even come out there on a Saturday morning! "We know you were involved in this. There's no question about that, but we're looking for the detail so we can know, so we can match everything up with the evidence, and so we can believe what you say. Do you understand that?"

Brendan took the hint and changed his story. Yes, he had seen the RAV4 in Steven Avery's garage, and Teresa was put into it after she had been stabbed, and was bleeding. Why was his version this Saturday different than his March 1 statement? Brendan said some of those details were lies or guesses.

If somebody is making up a story, they don't have a memory of what really happened to draw on. It's just a story they've told and when they're asked to repeat it later, they cannot remember all the little details they may have previously included. That's the thing about lies.

Postmarked June 29, 2006:

> *Dear Judge Jerome Fox, Hello, I was going to write to you a while back, but I didn't have a pencil. All my statements that I gave to investigators are not true.*

The Dasseys quickly came to realize that Len Kachinsky, far from fighting to protect Brendan from an unjust prosecution, was trying to help the state win a conviction. They sought a new lawyer but were turned down by the judge, until he learned that Kachinsky had let Brendan be questioned out of his presence.

Would Brendan be a witness at Avery's trial? Kratz refused to rule it out, right through the following January, claiming there was a chance he would cut a deal. We could only hope it was true.

In anticipation of Brendan's testimony at Steven Avery's trial, Dean and I hired an expert who could explain to the jury how false confessions come about. We felt confident that we could convince the jury that this was a coerced confession, even if no rubber hoses had been involved. The state turned over this teenage boy as if he were a kebab on a barbecue, and even charged him with first-degree intentional homicide, all in order get to his uncle.

Rather than damn Steven Avery, we felt Brendan's testimony could actually help bolster the rest of our defense: that the few bits of physical evidence supposedly found at the crime scene had actually been planted; a spare ignition key to Teresa Halbach's RAV4, apparently found in plain sight on the floor of Steven Avery's bedroom after it had already been searched six times; Colborn's phone call about the license plates; all the other things that didn't add up. Put these together with the manufactured confession from Brendan, and we could argue— with reason—that the blood collected from the RAV4's dashboard, which came from Steven Avery, had been planted.

If investigators would go this far with Brendan, was it such a leap to think they would plant blood as well?

22

Charged with the heinous murder of his wife, a man named John Mc-Caffray from Kenosha, Wisconsin, appeared before a judge to plead that his trial be moved to another county. The local newspapers had all but convicted him before the trial even started, and public senti-ment was strongly against him. Under these circumstances, assembling a group of open-minded jurors seemed an all-but-impossible task. But the judge denied his request.

In 1851, after a Kenosha County jury found McCaffray guilty of murdering his wife, Bridget, by drowning her in a backyard cask, Judge E. V. Whiton sentenced him to death by hanging. Thousands gathered a half mile south of Kenosha on Thursday, August 21, to watch McCaf-fray's execution. What unfolded that day was a gruesome spectacle that would alter Wisconsin's history. The hanging was botched. McCaffray, his legs kicking in the air, dangled in the noose for twenty minutes as he slowly strangled. After this, Wisconsin changed its penal code to make life in prison the maximum penalty for first-degree murder. Mc-Caffaray's death sentence would be the last under Wisconsin state law.

In February 2005, more than a century and a half later—and less than three years after Steven Avery's exoneration—Wisconsin state senators Alan Lasee of De Pere, and Scott Fitzgerald of Juneau, proposed that an advisory referendum be held as a first step to restoring capital pun-ishment in Wisconsin. Although there had been multiple efforts to reinstate the death penalty throughout the twentieth century—such as the petition in the Oswalds' case—they had all failed. Under the Lasee-Fitzgerald proposal, death sentences would be reserved for people con-victed of multiple, intentional first-degree homicides, and only when those convictions were supported by DNA evidence. But the Avery Task Force hearings were well under way at this point, and Avery's exoneration had dampened the enthusiasm of an important senator,

David Zien of Eau Claire, who was the chairman of the state Senate committee on Judiciary, Corrections, and Privacy and had previously been one of the prime advocates for the death penalty. "I'm not soft on the death penalty," he said. "I'm just more conscientious about it."

The climate would change before the year was out. Five days after Steven Avery's arrest for Teresa Halbach's murder in November of that year, Senator Lasee announced that he was adding a new element to the referendum. He modified the proposal so that the death sentence could apply to someone convicted of one homicide, not just multiple. "It's sad that this murder occurred, but it brings the whole issue of the death penalty back in the news," he remarked. Meanwhile, another senator proposed that the death penalty also apply to people charged with murder, sexual assault, and mutilation of a corpse—effectively tailoring the new referendum measure to the charges leveled against Steven Avery. It was rushed through at the end of the spring 2006 legislative session, against the dramatic backdrop of Ken Kratz's prosecution-by-press-conference, and scheduled for the coming November.

In the 155 years since John McCaffray dangled from that rope for twenty minutes, Wisconsin had prosecuted numerous notorious criminals *without* resorting to the death penalty: anarchists who had killed nine police officers in a bombing, a serial killer and grave robber whose crimes were so deranged that he inspired Norman Bates in *Psycho* and James Gumb in *The Silence of the Lambs*, and the cannibalistic Jeffrey Dahmer, killer of seventeen men and boys. All of these defendants had faced a maximum sentence of life in prison. Even though twenty different death penalty bills were introduced after the stunning Dahmer case, none made it through the legislature.

That spring, Dean and I argued that the actions of law enforcement officials, as well as the looming vote on the death penalty referendum, made it impossible for Steven Avery to receive a fair trial and moved—earnestly but, we knew, hopelessly—for the charges to be dismissed. Beginning with his arrest, all seven of Wisconsin's media markets were swamped by Steven Avery coverage and commentary. Kratz's March 2, 2006, press conference was broadcast live on radio and TV throughout the state. At that point, the trial was then scheduled to begin in mid-October 2006, which meant the death penalty vote would happen just as the prosecution finished presenting its case against Avery. In an oral argument, Dean, the amateur legal history scholar, named some of Wisconsin's notorious crimes going back a century. "In a state with this history," he said, "Steven Avery now has become the poster boy for politicians pushing the death penalty referendum." And the trial, of course, would have to go into recess on Election Day. "His own jurors shouldn't be taking a day off to go vote on the death penalty referendum," he continued.

Needless to say, we lost our motion to dismiss the charges, and in November 2006, the death penalty referendum passed with 55 percent in favor of reinstatement; in Manitowoc, 61 percent voted for it. (The legislature ultimately did not adopt capital punishment.) Fortunately, Steven Avery's trial had been pushed back to the following February. But given the undeniable media bias against him, fueled in no small measure by the prosecution, what venue would give us our best shot at a fair jury? In his pretrial decisions, Judge Willis had not only banned us from introducing other possible suspects, he had also severely limited our ability to mention details of Avery's 1985 wrongful conviction. Probably more so than anywhere else, people in Manitowoc County would be familiar with that history and therefore perhaps skeptical of these new charges. We wondered if, in some kind of backhanded ploy, Ken Kratz was trying to provoke us into asking for the trial to be moved to a different county, where fewer potential jurors would have detailed knowledge of the tangled relationship between Avery and Manitowoc County law enforcement.

On the other hand, if we stayed in Manitowoc County and had a jury of Manitowoc County residents, the logistics of their meals, transport, and so forth would be handled by the very sheriff's department that we believed was out to get Avery. That department would have direct contact with Steven Avery's jurors, including feeding them and assuring their comfort. That was not acceptable. In the end, we worked out a compromise. Steven Avery's trial would take place in the Calumet

County Courthouse; he was being held in the Calumet jail, anyway. And Manitowoc County judge Patrick Willis would continue to preside. But we would have a jury of Manitowoc residents, who would be bused to the courthouse in Calumet every day by the Calumet County Sheriff's Department. Manitowoc County Sheriff's Office personnel would have no contact with the jurors. And so, on February 1, 2007, a pool of Manitowoc residents was summoned for jury duty.

Ask just about anyone if they know what happens during jury selection, and you are likely to hear that's when lawyers "pick" their jurors; in most cases, each side is looking for a particular type of juror. However, lawyers are not really *selecting* jurors, but rather *deselecting* unsuitable ones. The real goal of voir dire for the defense is to seek clues about which jurors might hurt the client and then try to get rid of them.

Going into voir dire for the Steven Avery case, Dean and I knew we had our work cut out for us. Each side could use seven peremptory challenges, but because of the high percentage of prospective jurors who came into court already believing Avery was probably or certainly guilty, these would have to be carefully marshaled. That made it especially important to persuade Judge Willis to remove as many biased jurors as possible, "for cause."

A common misconception is that jurors behave according to stereotypes of age, gender, race, ethnicity, socioeconomic class, education, hobbies, or reading materials. Most studies show that stereotyping actually doesn't work when selecting a jury. Demography is not destiny. On the other hand, there is no question that race is a strong factor in shaping people's experiences of law enforcement and influences whether they view the police as helpful and courteous or overbearing and dishonest. Similarly, in a case that's heavy on scientific evidence, jurors with more education—which can, but far from always does, reflect distinctions of age, gender, race, or class—are often better able to grasp the nuances and limitations of science and technology.

In the Steven Avery case, we wanted thoughtful jurors with higher education who could critically examine the state's case and understand the science that both sides would present. The higher-education component would be hard to come by in Manitowoc County because the county is largely rural with proportionately lower levels of higher education. Only 19 percent of the county population has college degrees, compared to 27 percent for the rest of Wisconsin and 29 percent nationally. Many manufacturers have pulled out of the county in recent years, most devastatingly Mirro Aluminum, a popular cookware manufacturer that had roots in the area for more than a hundred years. By the end of the twentieth century, nearly all of Mirro's Manitowoc-based operations had moved overseas, and its last Manitowoc factory closed down in 2003. In taking away the blue-collar factory jobs, these closures affected the county's entire economic ecosystem. Predictably, we had only a small group of college-educated jurors in the pool, and almost none made it on the final jury.

Our primary goal, however, was to find jurors who could faithfully apply the presumption of innocence to Steven Avery despite the onslaught of pretrial publicity, which we knew we could show in court was largely based on the false narrative supplied by Ken Kratz. But it's rare for people to directly express bias. Most jurors will say that they can set aside their bias or preconceived notions of guilt, even when they really cannot do so, because people like to think they are fair, and because of social pressure to "say the right thing." Ferreting these out is the central challenge for the defense during voir dire. By the time the defense gets up to probe possible areas of bias more carefully or subtly, many prospective jurors have already received the clear message that they should deny any difficulty they might have in setting aside opinions formed by things such as pretrial publicity. The judge and prosecutors often use leading phrasing that suggests to prospective jurors that there is a "right" answer to their questions (*"Can you follow the judge's instructions to keep an open mind . . ."*). And if a prospective juror *is* honest enough to admit to bias, everyone tries to rehabilitate them until they agree they will follow the court's instructions about the law. We also had to be suspicious about anyone who really wanted to be on this jury. Most people are not keen to set aside six weeks of their lives for a criminal trial, and those who are may well have hidden agendas driven by bias. So jury selection often comes down to a lawyer's judgment of how honest the prospective jurors are being about their ability to decide the case only on the evidence presented in court. This is an inexact method, to be sure.

Adding to the complexity of jury selection, especially for a long trial, is the question of interpersonal dynamics. Which jurors have the strongest and the weakest personalities? Who might potentially be selected the foreperson? Which ones will stick to their opinions, and which are more likely to cave under pressure? In the sterile setting of voir dire, it is very difficult to predict which jurors will bond with each other so that their votes dovetail in the end.

We considered hiring a jury consultant, someone who can strategize with counsel about what kinds of jurors to avoid. These consultants can be useful, but even before the trial began we faced a severe budget crunch. Because of the sheer volume of pages of material turned over by the prosecution in discovery—thousands of pages, as we mostly got only paper copies—we were having to pay a paralegal to scan and code them all. We also had to pay an investigator to interview witnesses, and the experts we consulted on DNA and cremains, and Brendan's confession, not to mention the travel costs for everyone we planned to have testify. A jury consultant falls in line behind all those other things in the list of budget priorities and becomes a real luxury. I've never seen one used in a case involving indigents. The Avery case was just a cut above that. On the other hand, the state was rumored to have used a jury consultant. They did not have one at the counsel table with the district attorneys, but some members of the media seemed to think the prosecution had a plant in the audience who would advise them out of the public eye. There were lots of people in the courtroom, so it would have been hard for us to tell if that was true. I believe reporters actually asked the prosecutors about this, and they were noncommittal. I never did find out.

Instead of a jury consultant, we ended up preparing a fifteen-page juror questionnaire that consisted of seventy-five questions intended to measure the impact of pretrial publicity. The prospective jurors were summoned to court on a Thursday, where they filled out the questionnaires on the spot so they couldn't be influenced by family or friends. Judge Willis sent them home with firm instructions not to read anything about the case or watch news segments on it, because they would return on Monday for formal questioning. That gave us the weekend to go over their written replies, but we were so tied up with other trial preparations that Kathy helped us out. She even brought the questionnaires with her while sitting and watching the children taking swimming lessons at the high school pool on Saturday morning, which I'm sure the other parents found strange. After reviewing every questionnaire, she would prepare a one-sheet summary of the highlights to shape our live questions in court. I had her summaries waiting for me by the end of the day. In 129 out of the first 130 questionnaires, prospective jurors expressed their belief that Avery was either probably or certainly guilty.

Starting that Monday, the prospective jurors were brought into court, one by one. Over the next five days, Dean and I would take turns asking them questions. We began poorly when Judge Willis denied our motion to strike an early juror whose husband was a former lawyer for Calumet County and who regularly sat with Ken Kratz at dinner functions. She denied discussing the case with him, but she also admitted meeting Tim Halbach, one of Teresa's brothers who was also a lawyer in the area, and felt very sympathetic to him. Moreover, she believed Steven Avery was probably guilty as charged. And yet, somehow, the court believed she could set aside those opinions and be fair. We would have to use our first peremptory challenge to remove her.

Another juror revealed knowledge that proved he had *already* violated the court's instructions not to read or watch anything in the media about the case: He knew about the court's last-minute ruling on the Friday afternoon before trial that allowed the state to send the blood evidence to the FBI for EDTA tests that would not be completed until the trial was nearly done. My motion to strike "for cause" was denied by Judge Willis, but we did not use one of our six remaining peremptory challenges on him because other jurors were even worse.

Just a few jurors later, another man admitted to violating the court's order not to read the newspaper or watch the news. This candidate told us that he'd read an article in the local paper about jury selection for the trial because he decided it didn't contain facts about Avery's case—a conclusion he could not have reached until after he'd read the entire article. Once again, Judge Willis denied our motion that this was cause to strike the man from the pool, deciding that the violation of the court's instruction order was "minor." We used a "peremptory challenge" on this juror, who also conceded that if he were backed into a corner, he would go along and vote the way the others did.

Our final five peremptory challenges were exhausted on jurors who struggled to explain how they would set aside their preconceived notions of guilt; who appeared to be deliberately minimizing their knowledge of the case facts and Kratz's press conferences; or who were tied to former Manitowoc County sheriff Tom Kocourek, whom Avery had sued as part of his civil lawsuit for wrongful conviction.

The panel of twelve jurors and four alternates, split evenly between men and women, had a heavy blue-collar bent. The nine who were employed outside the home included two laborers, a mechanic, a maintenance worker, a carpenter, a switchboard operator, and a waitress. Seven were either retired or homemakers. Included on the panel was a man whose son worked for the Manitowoc County Sheriff's Office as a low-level jailer, and another man whose wife worked at the Manitowoc County Clerk's Office. We would have preferred to have neither of those two jurors, but there were worse ones we'd had to remove with our peremptory challenges.

As I surveyed the final sixteen jurors, I was not pleased. But we had to play the cards we were dealt.

During the course of the trial, Judge Willis had to dismiss all but one alternate for conflicts or violations of the court's instructions. The sixteen jurors were not sequestered until deliberations began, meaning that they could go home at the end of each day as opposed to a hotel, where they would be under supervision and cloistered from news coverage. One of the sixteen jurors was reported to have been running her mouth about the case and Avery's guilt while drinking at a supper club on a Friday evening near the end of the trial. She denied the allegation, but the reporting witness was credible, so the judge dismissed her. Another juror was a homemaker whose husband watched the trial reports on TV and often told her what happened in court when the jury was sent out of the courtroom; he also repeatedly expressed his opinion that Avery was guilty. This juror was also dismissed. Still another juror was reported to have acted suspiciously while other jurors were talking about whether or not they could be found out if they searched the Internet for information about the case. This juror had confidently exclaimed that no one would ever know if they had done Internet searches but turned ashen when another said a computer search trail could still be found even if they tried to delete it. This juror was not dismissed. Judge Willis also refused to remove a juror who revealed halfway through the trial that, contrary to her sworn jury questionnaire, she really was acquainted with Manitowoc County Sheriff's Office detective David Remiker, a frequent partner of two central figures in the Avery evidence drama—James Lenk and Andrew Colborn, who were both at the scene when virtually every piece of incriminating evidence was "found." She admitted she'd previously sat on a jury that rendered a civil verdict for Remiker of more than $100,000, which clearly indicated that the jury had judged his credibility favorably.

In the end, perhaps it was a minor miracle that we had persuaded seven of the twelve jurors to vote "not guilty" in an early round of deliberations.

23

Just before the Avery trial began, in a private meeting in Judge Willis's chambers, Ken Kratz had a proposal to make. Reporters wanted to be able to speak with him at the end of each day of trial, but he told the judge that he did not intend to speak with them *every* day and instead planned to do so every other day. Although Dean and I had no plans for press conferences at that point, Kratz suggested that we could also meet the press at the same conferences he would be giving. And on the alternating days, the only person speaking to the press would be Mike Halbach, one of Teresa's brothers.

Wait a minute. We had no objection to Mike Halbach talking to reporters, but as far as we could tell, he saw things just as the district attorney did. The notion that we could not offer our comments alongside his was ridiculous; Ken Kratz's proposition essentially amounted to us getting one chance to tell our side of the story for every two that the prosecution did. As anyone who has seen *Making a Murderer* knows, this laughable scheme was not followed. The routine we eventually worked out was that Kratz and/or Mike Halbach would give their statements and then one or both of us would go to speak.

Having failed to get a gag order for the months leading up to the trial, the only proviso *we* requested was that at the daily news conference, the parties confine themselves to speaking only about that day's events. No comments about upcoming testimony or evidence were permitted. We sought this limit, which Judge Willis agreed to, in case the jury violated his instructions and watched TV news coverage. That seemed possible, considering what had already happened during the voir dire. If the jurors did look at news of the trial, at least they would only be hearing our takes on the same things they had already seen or heard.

Considering how much Ken Kratz seemed to crave the limelight, he took an interesting position on the documentary filmmakers before the trial.

By the fall of 2006, Laura Ricciardi and Moira Demos had been working on the Steven Avery story for the better part of a year. They had spoken with members of his family and with us and with anyone else who could help tell this story and its remarkable arc. Ricciardi had approached all of the principal players, including Kratz, to whom she wrote a detailed and thoughtful letter about the project. As a lawyer herself, she was aware of his responsibilities and limitations, and her letter suggested that any discussions would not go into forbidden areas. She got no reply. We knew none of this backstory at the time, but her letter would soon enter the case record.

That November, Ricciardi got a phone call from Detective Mark Wiegert. He was coming to serve her with a subpoena. The prosecution wanted all of their footage of interviews with members of the Avery and Dassey families, as well as with anyone else who might know anything about the death of Teresa Halbach and the guilt or innocence of Steven Avery and Brendan Dassey. At that point, the filmmakers had 255 hours of raw tape, most of it archived but very little of it indexed. To make copies would literally take 255 hours. For them to provide what the state demanded would mean that they would have to stop all other work and, for every hour of tape, spend another five hours to get it ready. Not only did they not have the time or the money to do this, they could not even afford to hire a lawyer to respond to the subpoena. While they eventually obtained counsel, Ricciardi herself made their initial reply asking the judge to quash the subpoena. In an affidavit, she said the prosecution's request would kill the project. She had no recollection of speaking with anyone about the facts of Teresa Halbach's death and had not provided any footage, or the content of any interviews, to the defense. This certainly was true, as I knew. Nevertheless, the prosecution came storming back. The Avery and Dassey families had stopped speaking to law enforcement and so, the prosecutors argued, these interviews were the only sources of information available to the state. Then they took the matter one absurd step farther. Kratz argued that the filmmakers were an "investigative arm" of the Avery defense, citing their presence at the Manitowoc County Clerk's Office to film the old Avery blood vial. Of course, the office was a public space, and they had every right to be there.

With the forensic evidence mostly coming up as blanks, this subpoena seemed like a desperate act. Plenty of other outlets had recorded interviews with the Averys, but the prosecutors did not subpoena that material from those corporate news organizations. Instead, they'd gone after two independent documentary filmmakers who did not have two nickels to rub together.

Judge Willis threw out the subpoena.

Ken Kratz was also refusing to say if the state would call Brendan Dassey as a witness—or if there was any evidence whatsoever to support the two counts of sexual assault and kidnapping that were added to the original murder charges brought against Steven Avery after Brendan Dassey's interrogation. With just days until the start of trial, we appeared in court before Judge Willis on January 29, 2007. The day was important on two fronts. First, it bared some of the fundamental weaknesses in the state's case. Second, the hearing was the occasion of a memorable comment Dean made in court that was captured by the *Making a Murderer* filmmakers, showing his gift for unrehearsed speech that was literate, spontaneous, and profound.

Without Brendan Dassey's testimony, Dean told Judge Willis, not a single iota of evidence existed to support the claim that Teresa Halbach had ever been in Avery's trailer, much less assaulted there. The state had known this for close to a year.

"And on March 10 [2006], when this Amended Information was filed, following eight and nine days after the successive live news conferences, the State had physical evidence, in its possession, making it impossible to believe that someone had been stabbed and slashed repeatedly in Steven Avery's bed," Dean said. "There was no blood in that bedroom. And when Brendan Dassey said that we cut off some of her hair, or I did, at Mr. Avery's request, with a large knife, the State knew, or should have known, that not one strand of Teresa Halbach's hair was found anywhere in Steven Avery's trailer; indeed, not one detectable trace of Teresa Halbach's DNA, hair, blood, anything else, anywhere in his trailer."

We believed that, even if the state were to dismiss those two charges ahead of the trial, the judge should give a "curative" instruction to the jury to help undo some of the damage caused by the unsupported but heavily publicized allegations.

"I think some further action will have to be taken by this Court to counteract the effect of allegations made against one young man, Defendant A [Brendan Dassey], in a separate case, that were imported, although inadmissible, imported in the public mind, to impugn the presumed innocence of Defendant B [Steven Avery], in an entirely separate case," Dean said.

This argument roused Ken Kratz to a state of high dudgeon. Such an instruction would be terribly unfair to the prosecution, he claimed, and, in fact, to prevent it, the state would not dismiss the rape and kidnapping counts.

"The prejudice to the State, Judge, should be obvious," Kratz said. "But if we have to start this case swimming upstream, if you will, in the face of some instruction given to the jury that they should be taking some negative view of the State, then we intend to proceed on all six counts."

He also complained that the jury pool had been contaminated by recent negative publicity about the state—namely, our discovery that the investigators did in fact have access to an ample supply of Steven Avery's blood that could have been used to plant evidence in Teresa's RAV4. Kratz was also unhappy that a plea bargain with Brendan Dassey had been thwarted the previous May and bemoaned the disqualification of Len Kachinsky, but insisted that Brendan might yet give evidence against Avery. It was, at a minimum, wish-driven thinking. Had Brendan ever been able to credibly testify that his uncle had killed Teresa Halbach, I have no doubt that the State would have figured out a way to make that happen. "The prejudice to the State, Judge, should be obvious," Kratz said. "But if we have to start this case swimming upstream, if you will, in the face of some instruction given to the jury that they should be taking some negative view of the State, then we intend to proceed on all six counts."

When Kratz finished, Dean calmly rose from his seat. Law students will no doubt be hearing what he said next for many, many years.

"All due respect to counsel," Dean began, "the state is supposed to start every criminal case 'swimming upstream.' And the strong current against which the state is supposed to be swimming is the presumption of innocence. That presumption of innocence has been eroded—if not eliminated—here by the specter of Brendan Dassey, and that's why the court needs to take further curative action."

Judge Willis said he didn't think that the State had engaged in any conduct that required him to give a special instruction to the jury, meaning the prosecutors could continue to reap the benefit of publicly painting Avery as a rapist without having to prove it. As Dean said:

Since March 10, up through the WFRV report last night, for example, Steven Avery has been presented as the man who allegedly *raped*, mutilated and murdered Teresa Halbach. Now, the first question, I guess in a bigger scale, this raises, is how many times will Steven Avery be charged in Manitowoc County with rapes he didn't commit. This makes *two*. And the public, for ten months, has been led to believe that he's a rapist, in addition to all else they might think about him. Where do we go, you know, forget getting the eighteen years back on the first one, where do we go to get the last ten months back? Where do we go to get our presumption of innocence back, from a public who believes and has heard time and again that he is an alleged rapist, even before murder?

Part VI

DÉJÀ VU

24

Complicated cases have the power of black holes, their gravity pulling in every bit of your energy. Ahead of Steven Avery's trial, which was expected to last four to six weeks, Dean and I knew that we would need to relocate temporarily to Appleton, about a hundred miles from where we each lived, to be nearer the location of the Calumet County Courthouse in the county seat of Chilton, Wisconsin. At the southeast end of Appleton, just beyond the edge of town, and closest to Chilton, we found two furnished apartments on Lake Park Road. This would mean a twenty- to thirty-minute drive to the courthouse each morning, but it would also leave us well clear of the Halbach family, who lived just outside Appleton. Apart from about six or seven hours of sleep each night, and breaks to eat, pretty much every minute not actually spent *in* that courthouse was dedicated to the trial, and there was no time for sidewalk or bar stool litigation. It was a grueling regimen, but not at all unusual for lawyers on trial.

Our mornings usually began at 6:00 a.m., although Dean got up earlier to work out at a gym where he had taken a membership. Huffing and puffing away on the treadmill or stationary bicycle, he could look up at the televisions—at least a few of which would usually be tuned to the morning news—and watch footage of himself or me in court the day before. It was surreal. Dean doesn't drink coffee, but I had two or three cups each morning over a quick bowl of cold cereal. Inevitably, though Dean had often squeezed in time at the gym, he was ready to leave the apartment complex for the courthouse before I was. We would drive together and get to the courthouse in Chilton at about 8:00, no later than 8:15. The Calumet County Courthouse was not at all like Manitowoc's. The old courthouse in tiny Chilton (population thirty-six hundred in 2007) was built of red sandstone with a copper dome in 1913. But now the courtrooms were in a modern addition, and the old building was relegated to county administrative offices.

As we arrived each day, a cluster of TV trucks with satellite dishes greeted us. Judge Willis had a custom of meeting privately with the defense and prosecution every morning to preview likely disputes over the evidence and testimony that were expected to arise during that day's session. If the dispute had to be argued, we'd go out into the courtroom and each side would put its issues on the record. This strategy helped curb—but did not eliminate—lengthy sidebars during the court day proper, which would burn up the jurors' time. But this wasn't its only, or perhaps even primary, purpose. On our very first visit to Judge Willis's chambers in March 2006, back in Manitowoc County, I spotted a book about managing high-publicity cases on his desk. He seemed keen to avoid being caught off guard by surprises in the courtroom that he would have to decide on the fly, on camera. Maybe he had learned from Judge Lance Ito's performance presiding over the O. J. Simpson case. The jurors would arrive by about eight thirty, having been picked up by bus in Manitowoc County and transported a half hour to Chilton. After we finished the morning arguments, testimony would then begin.

As soon as Judge Willis declared the lunch recess, we'd leave the building. Just down along Main Street from the courthouse was a mom-and-pop diner that had great soup. I once heard that President Obama used to keep only blue suits in his closet so that he didn't have to waste time in the morning figuring out what to wear; Dean's culinary version of the presidential blue suit is a grilled cheese sandwich. He ordered that every day at lunch, along with whatever soup the diner was serving that day. I had the daily special, period. This diner was the one place in town where no one bothered us, where we would be left alone by friends or supporters of the Halbach family. We did not at all consider ourselves to be their adversaries, but the antagonism was understandable. The proprietors and servers there treated us like family. Our lunch routine became a blessed break from the coiled tensions of that courthouse.

At the end of the court day, we'd return to our Appleton apartments on Lake Park Road by six, then head out for dinner. In Appleton, we had more choices for dinner than we had for lunch in Chilton, but wherever we went, Dean and I would be instantly recognized. The daily trial coverage on television had made our faces familiar, even if people could not immediately place us individually. Nearly everyone within a hundred miles of that courthouse considered us to be the bad guys in this fight; after all, we constantly appeared on the nightly news defending the man that most Wisconsinites now viewed as a monster. One Friday night, we went to a Red Robin chain restaurant for burgers. A woman spotted her young children straying a little too close to us and immediately ushered them away as though we might abduct them. We didn't take the community's antagonism personally. A career as a criminal defense lawyer is not a popularity contest. Most evenings saw us back at our apartments by 7:30 p.m., where we quickly reviewed e-mails—many from people following the live stream of the trial. Most of these were one-offs, and not much use.

One evening, though, after the first week of testimony, an e-mail landed that had enough gravitational force to tug me away from the Avery case for a few minutes.

The subject line read: POTENTIAL CLIENT INQUIRY. The author was Fawn Cave, a woman from Texas. I'd never heard of her, but she had found me because of the Avery trial live-stream.

In filling out the "comment" section in the online form on our law firm's website, Fawn Cave began:

Re: Ralph Dale Armstrong
To Whom It May Concern:
I would like to find out about Ralph Dale Armstrong and the Charise Kamp murder.

Actually, she had plenty to tell herself. Her mother was a cousin of Ralph's. Fawn's story was dense, but as I unraveled it I realized she was claiming to have had a horrifying encounter with Ralph's brother, Stephen.

Without going into too much detail unless it is requested of me, the night that I got to my mother's and saw him for the first time in 20 years or so, he proudly displayed his tattoo of the "scales of justice" that were tipped on his hand. For some reason that I didn't understand, he felt it necessary to tell me every single detail of this ladies rape and murder.

He told me that his brother, Ralph, was seeking a new trial for DNA and that he hoped that he never had to see him face to face again because Ralph Dale had a hate for him (Steve) because of the murder and that he was in prison for something that he and Steve Armstrong knew Ralph didn't do.

She recounted a wild tale of being so scared that she fled in the middle of the night, grabbing her child and a friend who had come along. This incident had taken place years earlier, but she had only recently had the time to look up details of the case online, and read the transcripts of the trial.

After all these years, please imagine my shock at reading the transcripts from the trial that convicted Ralph Dale. Steve Armstrong was there.

She pointed out that the brothers had a strong resemblance, and remarked, Maybe the individual that was hypnotized was accurate in the memory.

Within a day or so of Fawn and her friend driving off, she wrote, Stephen had stolen a car and hadn't been heard from since. The entire story seemed so crazy that it was beyond making up. This encounter had even taken place in Roswell, New Mexico, a venue held dear by fans of UFOs (unidentified flying objects), science fiction, and conspiracy theories.

I have no choice but to put forth what information that I have regarding this. It's not something I really want to do, but Ralph Dale is my family, whether or not we ever knew each other.

In closing, Fawn said she looked: forward to hearing from you very soon.

I read her message a few times. The Avery trial was in full bloom, so I passed it along to my assistant for safekeeping with a note. Surprising and interesting email from out of the blue on Ralph's case. Print out and keep in file for my return.

There was one man whom we heard from most nights. He was writing to us from the south of France, on the Mediterranean. In the relentless Wisconsin winter, with its short, frigid days and long, cold nights—on the first day of jury selection it was sixteen degrees below zero in Chilton, not including the gusty wind chill—just *hearing* from someone in a place where the temperature was in the sixties was a warming thought. However, our correspondent meant much more to us than just a sunny postmark. His name was Jim Shellow, a dean of the Wisconsin criminal defense bar and past president of the National Association of Criminal Defense Lawyers. When I was a young public defender in Madison, I'd sit in on Jim's trials to watch him pick juries or cross-examine the state's forensic chemists in narcotics trials. Unlike many lawyers, he was not cowed by the cloak of white-coat expertise. Jim was the one who had lured Dean away from his work as a civil practice attorney by persuading him to join Shellow, Shellow & Glynn. After this move into criminal defense work, Dean hadn't looked back. Jim now spent winters in the south of France, and he'd been following the trial over the Internet. Jim, of course, remembered Steven Avery well, because his law firm represented him on the appeal of his 1985 wrongful conviction. Often, Jim would write to Dean with his thoughts at the end of our day, which would be late at night in France. It was almost like having another member of the defense team present in court, watching out for us—though he had better weather.

Kathy and I also spoke in the evenings, of course. I would off-load some of the day's events from court. She'd also catch me up on whatever was happening at home. My routine was to leave Appleton at the end of the court day on Fridays and get home by about eight, when

Kathy and I would eat dinner. I'd conk out pretty quickly, and then on Saturday mornings I'd go to the kids' basketball games. Grace, then in seventh grade, was on a school team, and Stephen was playing in a league for older boys. By late afternoons most Saturdays, I'd be on U.S. Highway 41 back to Appleton—usually with a care package of a few cooked meals, often enough for Dean and me to share for a night or two before we had to return to Appleton's restaurant scene.

I didn't realize it at the time, but Dean and I were not the only ones catching grief for our defense of Steven Avery. Grace found herself under a minor siege one day in the school lunchroom. Another girl's parents had been following the trial, but anyone reading or watching most of the media coverage could be forgiven for not realizing that the truth was being contested. Grace's classmate had clearly picked up her parents' strong views on Steven Avery, the case, and, by extension, me. This girl declared that Avery was obviously guilty and demanded that Grace explain how her father could defend someone who had done such terrible things. Grace had not been following the case in the press—what kid her age would?—but she had picked up enough listening to my conversations with Kathy to realize that the defense had raised serious questions about the evidence, and a debate broke out at the cafeteria table. It wasn't quite that scene in *To Kill a Mockingbird* when Scout Finch fights a boy who insults her father, but Grace gave it back.

The trial was wearing on our whole household, in different ways. The kids and Kathy really had my back.

25

During the months leading up to the trial, Ken Kratz and I had been civil, even cordial, with each other. But once the jury was sworn in, his cordiality vanished.

Not a big deal. The mannerisms of another lawyer are usually not really of great moment for me, but I have to acknowledge that Ken Kratz's approach to questioning witnesses got under my skin. When any civilian witness testified, he would soften his voice and make a conspicuous effort to appear gentler, more tender, as if he were *so* sorry that the defense was making them suffer through a trial and the ordeal of testifying in court. Perhaps he thought this would make him seem like a good guy to the jury, but it struck me as smarmy and fake. A criminal investigation and prosecution is not a popularity contest. A professional approach to the circumstances is not demonstrating callousness to the survivors of a crime but rather the ethical duty of police and prosecutors. Not letting his manner bug me was part of my duty, I realized, so I did my best to filter him and concentrate on what the jury was hearing and seeing.

Perhaps the most important early witness from our perspective was Teresa Halbach's former boyfriend, Ryan Hillegas, who led the search party that formed during the first days after her disappearance. Although they were no longer romantic partners, Hillegas testified, they spoke in person or by phone about once a week. In fact, Teresa had been living with Hillegas's best friend, Scott Bloedorn. That most murder victims, especially female, are killed by people they know well does not seem to have ever crossed the investigative radar in Teresa's murder. From the outset, investigators had their eyes on one suspect only, Steven Avery, and our efforts to suggest other suspects had been denied by Judge Willis. I tried to highlight this law enforcement bias in my cross-examination of Hillegas.

Q. Did the police ever ask you for any kind of alibi for October 31?

A. No.

Q. They never asked your whereabouts whatsoever?

A. I don't believe so.

Q. Okay. Anybody, point blank, ever ask you if you had any knowledge about her disappearance or were involved in it?

A. I don't know if they did it like that, like they were accusing me but, of course, people asked me if I had talked to her or knew anything. And that's why I was there to help.

Q. Okay. And to your knowledge, did you ever hear the police ever ask Mr. Scott Bloedorn if he had an alibi for Monday, October 31, in the evening, late afternoon hours?

A. I don't know that.

Q. So it would be fair to say that you weren't in anyway treated like a suspect, that you could tell?

A. That's correct.

Right after Hillegas's testimony, we heard from Pamela Sturm, a second cousin of Teresa Halbach's who had found her RAV4 in a remote corner of the Avery scrap yard. She had been searching on foot for about thirty minutes with her daughter, Nicole, and somehow zoomed in on it at the far end of the property, among the four thousand other vehicles in the forty-four-acre yard. The vehicle was halfheartedly obscured by boards and branches, in a way that made it actually stand out from the vehicles nearby. It was double-parked along a single-file row of vehicles, sticking out noticeably in the lane. Significantly, it was not in the car crusher that sat idle just one hundred yards away, surrounded by stacks of other vehicles that had been crushed that very week. We, of course, knew from the phone tapes that Sergeant Colborn, of the Manitowoc County Sheriff's Department, had a conversation with a dispatcher two days earlier during which he'd read off the plate number and description of the RAV4 as though he were looking right at it. If Pamela Sturm *knew* where to look, her quick discovery of the RAV4 was not all that remarkable. But she and Ken Kratz tried to make sure that remarkable was exactly how it played to the jury:

Q. Ms. Sturm, do you know how many vehicles are on this property?

A. I didn't at that time. I had no idea.

Q. Looking at it now, do you think you got lucky?

A. Yeah. Well, not lucky, God showed us the way; I do believe that.

At the end of the day, the reporters asked me what I thought about God leading her to Teresa's car. I scoffed but hastened to explain that this was not because of any doubts of mine in divine power.

"Not that I don't believe that's not possible," I said. "I just don't believe her. She's too weird. They went right to that thing."

The following week, the state presented Manitowoc County Sheriff's Department deputies James Lenk and Andrew Colborn, who—in addition to their involvement in Steven Avery's 1985 wrongful conviction because of their failure to pursue the leads from another law enforcement agency that they had the wrong man imprisoned—seemed to be able to find what numerous other investigators could not. Both of them were present for the purported "discovery" of the RAV4's ignition key on the floor of Steven Avery's bedroom. Lenk had also been on hand when a bullet fragment was discovered in Avery's garage four months later, when there was no pretense of needing Manitowoc personnel for a large-scale search of the yard. Once again, he'd made a vital discovery—the garage—that had already been searched many times. And we suspected that Colborn had located the RAV4 before Pamela Sturm because of his mysterious call two days before its discovery was reported. On the day Sturm found it, Lenk signed out of the property on a log of all officers entering or leaving the area of that property where the RAV4 was located. But he had never signed in. This meant either he arrived at the salvage yard much earlier than he now claimed (i.e., before the log was begun) or that he somehow eluded the officer responsible for recording all law enforcement checking in and out of the access point nearest the RAV4. Later, under oath, Lenk would give irreconcilably different stories of when he had arrived to the area of the RAV4. This opened the possibility that Lenk could have planted blood in the RAV4 after it was officially discovered, but before custody had transferred to Calumet or state law enforcement officers.

You would be hard-pressed to find more tension in a courtroom than that day as Dean began his cross-examinations. Colborn went first, and the following day, Wednesday, Lenk and another Manitowoc County Sheriff's Department investigator, Detective David Remiker—who had been awarded $100,000 by a civil court jury that included a woman now sitting in the jury box across the room—took the stand. And the next day, I would be cross-examining Dan Kucharski, a deputy of the Calumet County Sheriff's Department, which was the agency supposedly in charge of the investigation into Teresa Halbach's murder. Kucharski was the only non-Manitowoc County officer present at the time that the "magic key" was discovered by Lenk.

On our way back to Lake Park Road after Lenk and Remiker had testified, it dawned on us that it was the first day of Lent: Ash Wednesday. Both of us are Catholic.

"Let's go to church," Dean suggested.

This seemed like the perfect way to reach inside for strength after the tough day behind us, and as a preparation for the one that was coming.

Although a break in our routine would be welcome, anytime we went out in public to a new place we had to map out the possibility of awkward encounters. The Halbachs were Catholic and might very well be going to services that evening. We knew which parish they belonged to and so we chose a church on the north end of town where we were unlikely to encounter them or their friends.

In the liturgical calendar, Ash Wednesday opens the forty days of preparation for Easter. A priest or deacon dabs the foreheads of congregants with a thumbful of ashes collected from the burned palms of the previous year's Palm Sunday, evoking human mortality, and adds a verbal reminder from Genesis: "Dust thou are, and unto dust shalt thou return."

As Dean and I made our way to the altar, I detected a slight stirring as we were spotted by the congregation, what seemed—at least to me—like waves of frowns and glares. *Come on people*, I thought, *we're all Catholics. Can't we have a little respite with the Lord as fellow pilgrims through life?* Later in the Mass, we received Communion. As a Catholic, I believe that it is a chance to taste the goodness of God. My walk down the aisle also gave me a taste of the condemnation of the community.

Afterward, we grabbed a quick bite to eat, so we didn't get back to our apartments until 9:00 p.m.

Almost as soon as we walked in, there was knock on my door. It was the filmmakers, who of course had realized how pivotal a moment we were at in the trial.

"Do you mind if we come in and do a quick shot?" Laura Ricciardi asked.

We started grumbling. *No. This is too much. We're tired, and we have another big day staring at us.*

"Come on," Moira Demos pleaded. "We'll just set up in the background. We won't say anything."

We agreed, reluctantly, and started our work.

By then, we were not exactly oblivious to them, but their filmmaking apparatus no longer distracted us. When the trial finally began, the filmmakers were so much part of the courthouse scene that the other daily media were happy to let them run the pool camera feeds from the courtroom. Most of the news organizations had little interest in the vast majority of the testimony, and really did not want to devote technicians and reporters to monitoring every moment. But the filmmakers, with their heavy stake in documenting the entire process, were there for keeps. Cameras were trained on us all day—one that looked toward the witness stand and Judge Willis, and another toward the counsel table, which, in addition to capturing Avery, also took in spectators—and then in the press conferences afterward. Now, in the apartment, when they were plugged in and about to turn on the camera, Laura Ricciardi said something that probably had been on her mind since she came in the door.

"Don't you want to clean up?" she asked.

Dean and I were puzzled. We never fussed or primped before their filming sessions. We were fine.

"Don't you want to wipe the ashes off?" Ricciardi prompted.

We laughed. I could see the big dark smudge on Dean's forehead, and he was looking at the one on mine.

"No," Dean said, "we don't want to clean it off. You can film us like this."

"You're sure?" she asked.

"This is who we are," I said.

From our perspective, the following day's star witness was Deputy Dan Kucharski, the Calumet Sheriff's Office deputy who had been in the room for Lieutenant Lenk's discovery of the ignition key for Teresa's RAV4. That was his first day inside Avery's home, but it was not Lenk and Colborn's. They had both previously searched Avery's bedroom and found no key. I wondered why, if they planted the key in the bedroom, they did not do so at their earliest opportunity. I got the answer earlier in the trial, when I cross-examined Calumet County sergeant William Tyson. He explained that he had been instructed by his superiors to act as a watchdog and accompany Lenk and Colborn wherever they went inside Avery's home to be sure they were not alone at any point. Why it wouldn't have been easier for Calumet County to just assign their *own* officers to search Avery's home was never explained. Tyson said he was watching Lenk and Colborn carefully enough that it would have been difficult for either of them to plant the RAV4 key on his watch. But Tyson was replaced by low-level deputy Dan Kucharski on the day the key was "discovered."

At first, during the direct examination by Ken Kratz, Kucharski said that it would have been impossible for the other investigators to have planted the key without him knowing. But as Kratz's questioning progressed, he backed away from that position.

"I would have to say that, that it could be possible, as in I was doing other things," Kucharski testified. "I was taking photographs. I was searching the nightstand. So, if we're just limiting it to if it was possible that they could do it without me seeing it, I would say, yes, I guess it is possible."

This was not the answer Kratz was looking for, and he moved quickly to take the sting out of it.

"All right," Kratz said. "And is that in the sense of, anything is possible?"

Kucharski ran with that.

"That's in the sense of it's possible aliens put it there, I guess," he replied.

This wasn't a star witness—this was a *galactic* witness, someone the prosecution had put on the stand in the hopes that he would vouch for the Manitowoc County investigators, and instead he did the opposite. Cross-examination was an opportunity for me to drive that message home, using Kucharski's own memorable language.

Almost as soon as I began, I went to the question of extraterrestrials.

"There weren't any aliens in the room, right?" I asked.

"Not that I know of," Kucharski said.

It seemed to me that believing Lenk and Colborn's story of how that key was found—in a really small trailer bedroom, after it had already been searched multiple times, with Kurcharski standing there—required a suspension of credulity. Had he even been watching Lenk and Colborn?

This was the first essential point I wanted to make. Now it was time for me to move on to the reality of the situation and see what burden that put on the plausibility of the key discovery tale.

Q. What we do know, is that when you came into that bedroom the first time, there was no key on the floor, was there?

A. That's correct.

Q. And you had been in that bedroom searching with Lenk and Colborn for about an hour, close to an hour, by the time that key was discovered, right?

A. Approximately, yes.

Q. Three people in that little bedroom, right?

A. Yes.

Yet, suddenly, that key magically appeared in plain view on the floor next to a nightstand. Colborn, in his testimony, tried to explain that the key may have fallen out of the back of the nightstand when he "roughly" shoved items back into it. However, the location and position of the key on the floor, attached to a cloth fob and plastic buckle, made that highly unlikely.

There had been no aliens in the room that day. Only Lenk and Colborn, and he conveniently distracted Kucharski. It felt like a good day for the defense.

26

The prosecution's star expert witness took the stand mid-morning on the tenth day of the trial. As soon as Sherry Culhane began her testimony, she turned away from Norm Gahn, the prosecutor who was questioning her, and faced slightly right toward the jury box. Her eyes fixed on the jurors, and she spoke directly to them.

"I work as a forensic scientist in the DNA unit," she said. "I'm primarily responsible for the examination of physical evidence for the presence of biological material."

Then in her mid-forties, Culhane had worked at the Wisconsin State Crime Laboratory in Madison for twenty-three years, making her senior in rank and experience to most of the other people in the lab.

Speaking straight to the jury was a bit of stagecraft that all the prosecution's witnesses used, and it was especially important for Culhane, who would need to be conscious that her audience were jurors, most of them unfamiliar with the jargon of her field. Of all of the state's witnesses, she would have to work the hardest to connect with them. The prosecution had no witnesses to testify that they had seen Steven Avery touch Teresa Halbach, much less *kill* her; whatever version of events Brendan Dassey might have offered, he was not going to be called. So Sherry Culhane's work was really the foundation of their case against Steven Avery.

Crime scene technicians had collected, cut, swabbed, and jackhammered 345 items of evidence from Steven Avery's trailer and nearby garage, the most taken in a single criminal case in Wisconsin's history: sheets and pillows, wood paneling and carpeting, sex toys like handcuffs, concrete from the floor of the garage; a .22 caliber rifle that hung in his bedroom; knives from the kitchen and elsewhere. Swabs had been taken from areas that showed no obvious traces of physical evidence but might still have formed part of the crime scene. It was a dragnet. From all of this, 180 individual items were identified as being suitable for DNA testing—also a record.

The state crime lab had been generating reports on the Halbach investigation for more than a year, and I had studied each one as it was delivered to us as part of the pretrial discovery. While the reports were summaries of the test findings, they were only a part of the picture. I also received the underlying notes made by the technician and other information about the lab's practices. Virtually none of what Sherry Culhane would say would be new to me, but based on her inflections—not just in her voice, but in what she and Gahn emphasized, and what they glossed over—I would adjust the cross-examination that I had already spent weeks preparing.

She told the jury that her department dealt with physical evidence.

"The word 'forensic' is simply applying science to matters of law," Culhane said. "So it's applying scientific principles to matters of law."

In criminal investigations, forensic scientists look for fifteen traits within a DNA sample. The number of variations for each of these particular traits was determined through a program of random sampling that was conducted globally. So scientists know how often a given variation of a trait is likely to appear, and this frequency is expressed as a fraction—one in seven, one in four, one in fifteen, and so on. A person who does not have all of the traits found in a genetic profile developed from a piece of biological evidence is excluded as the source of that DNA. If, however, the person has all the traits of that genetic profile, the laboratories then use formal probability—determined by multiplying those fractions out—to demonstrate the *extremely* low chance of the match being coincidental; that is, the odds of that person matching the genetic profile and *not* being the source of that evidence are incredibly small. Moreover, getting these results is not a matter of going to the right witch doctor; if done correctly, different labs can run tests on the same evidence and get the same results.

But as much as DNA testing illustrates the unreliability of much of what has for decades passed as "scientific" evidence, its results should still be scrutinized—not because of doubts about its fundamental reliability but to be sure that the people carrying out the testing process adhere to the scientifically accepted procedures and don't bend the rules. Yes, the scientific principles of DNA are sound; but their application through the actual testing also must be sound, or junk is the result.

Examining a witness—either your own or the other side's—requires planning not only of the individual queries but also the purposeful progression in the line of questions. The context for your inquiries should become apparent to the jurors. Norm Gahn is an experienced and capable lawyer, and his questions for Sherry Culhane clearly showed that he had carefully prepared for his direct examination.

He established Culhane's credentials—a college degree in biology and participation in various professional organizations—and then those of the Wisconsin State Crime Laboratory. It had written test protocols for all of its procedures, including DNA testing, and was regularly audited for compliance with them. There were also formal efforts to ensure that those procedures actually produced reliable results. Twice a year, an outside company provided dummy samples that were put through the same processes employed in real criminal cases. Each DNA analyst in the lab was required to show his or her proficiency in processing and interpreting these samples.

Q. Well, let me ask you this, what are the results of all the proficiency tests that you have taken?

A. They have all been correct.

Q. In other words, you've passed all of your proficiency tests?

A. Yes.

Gahn was establishing Culhane's expertise and the integrity of the lab to prove their ability to get it right. Further bolstering her authority, Culhane also served as a trainer for new DNA technicians and helped decide how work would be parceled out. In fact, some of the newer lab techs were in the courtroom for her testimony, and most of the

DNA lab techs back in Madison were watching via live stream. And there was more. This was not the first time Sherry Culhane had dealt with Steven Avery in the context of a criminal investigation. Just two years earlier, in 2003, Culhane had conducted DNA tests on thirteen pubic hairs that proved Steven Avery did not assault Penny Beerntsen. Culhane was able to collect cells from roots that were still attached to two strands. One was from a male whose DNA profile did not match Steven Avery's, so it was submitted to the Combined DNA Index System (CODIS) maintained by the Federal Bureau of Investigation, which contains DNA profiles of, among others, convicted felons.

"It hit on another individual," Culhane testified.

Q. When you say another individual, you mean someone other than Steven Avery?

A. That's correct.

Q. And you, yourself, performed this testing?

A. Yes, I did.

Q. And because of the testing that you performed, and because of the search of the CODIS data bank, what happened to Mr. Avery?

A. I believe he was freed from prison.

Q. And that was because of the testing that you did?

A. Correct.

Q. Basically, did you follow the same protocol that you did in testing that case, testing the 1985 case, that you followed in this case?

A. Yes, I did.

This demonstrated that Culhane was an impartial arbiter of the truth, someone who called the evidence as she saw it. She herself had cleared Steven Avery, hadn't she? Now, she was about give testimony on tests in another crime involving the same man. Could anyone possibly doubt her fairness?

Culhane had assigned herself to the Halbach murder investigation. With hundreds of pieces of evidence, it had essentially taken over the state's crime lab. In sifting through the avalanche of evidence, Culhane said, field investigators would tell her which items they most urgently wanted tested.

"Usually it's prioritized based on what is the most probative and what is most important to their investigation," she explained.

One of those priorities was a bullet fragment collected from Steven Avery's garage in mid-March of 2006.

"There was nothing visual on the fragment," Culhane testified. "There didn't appear to be any stain. So in order to remove any residual DNA that might have been on the bullet, I washed it. I put it in a test tube and washed it with some buffer that we use to extract the DNA. And the washing of that bullet, the washing liquid is what I performed the rest of my procedure on."

Q. And were you able to develop a DNA profile from that washing on Item FL, the bullet?

A. Yes.

She showed slides of the DNA profile developed from the bullet, and then from the victim.

"The profile from the bullet is consistent with all of the types from Teresa Halbach," Culhane said.

However, there was a major twist coming, and Gahn knew he would have to address it before I brought it out on cross-examination.

While testing this bullet, Culhane had contaminated a control sample. Control samples are run alongside the test of the evidence sample because the process is very sensitive, and contamination is a very serious possibility with DNA testing, for the same reason that the process is so powerful. A very small quantity of DNA is, in effect, photocopied over and over until it has a powerful chemical signature that can be easily read. It's why scientists are able to extract fragments of ancient DNA that have survived for thousands of years in mummies or bones. By amplifying those minuscule fragments, they can be seen. But that same amplification process can take contaminant DNA and magnify it, too. The control samples are, in essence, an alarm system that goes off when genetic material is present that should not be there. Negative control samples should not have any DNA in them when tested; if they do, it is a sign that contamination has occurred during the testing process. Earlier in Culhane's testimony, she had described a contamination log maintained by the laboratory. Over the previous five years, she said, during which the lab had tested about fifty thousand samples, only eighty-nine instances of contamination had been documented. The contamination log was primarily "a learning tool," she said.

That was the message she and Gahn emphasized when discussing the results of the tests on the bullet and the discovery of contamination in the process.

"That means that during the extraction procedure I inadvertently introduced my own DNA into the negative control," Culhane testified.

Q. Did that have any impact on your interpretation of your results?

A. It did not have any impact as far as the profile from the evidence sample. It's just the fact that I introduced my own DNA into the manipulation control.

No big deal. She had also figured out how the contamination had happened, she explained. She had been talking as she worked:

At the time when I was setting up these samples, I was training two analysts, newer analysts, in the lab. And they were watching me.

This sample was not an average sample, simply because we handled it a little different. It wasn't a swabbing, and it wasn't a cutting. The washing part of it was a little bit different than what we usually do. So I was explaining to them what I was doing and as I was setting it up. And apparently—I felt as if I was far enough away from my workbench not to introduce my DNA, but apparently I was incorrect.

In any case, she continued, her DNA only got into the control sample, not into the wash from the bullet.

They then moved on to the blood. Culhane said her initial tests detected blood in stains recovered from inside the Halbach RAV4. Teresa Halbach's blood was found in swabs collected from various spots in the cargo area of the RAV4. Culhane testified that Steven Avery's DNA was in bloodstains on the driver and passenger seats of the RAV4; on the center console; on a compact disc case that was near the console; and on the rear passenger door.

A bloodstain was also collected from near the ignition of the RAV4. The DNA in that stain, she said, was also consistent with Avery's DNA. And, Culhane testified, Steven Avery's DNA was found on the ignition key for the RAV4, which Lieutenant Lenk had discovered during the seventh search of his trailer.

Q. Did you arrive at a statistical number for this profile that would reflect how often, or how rare, or how common, this profile would be in the population?

A. Yes, I did.

Q. And could you explain to the jurors what that statistic is?

A. This number tells me that the probability of another unrelated, random person in the population, having the same profile as the evidence samples that we just talked about, is one person in four quintillion in the Caucasian population.

A quintillion is 1,000,000,000,000,000,000—more people than have been born since the beginning of the human race.

Q. Do you have an opinion, to a reasonable degree of scientific certainty, whether Steven Avery is the source of the bloodstain found on the dashboard by the ignition in Teresa Halbach's RAV4?

A. Yes.

Q. And what is that opinion?

A. My opinion is that Steven Avery is the source of that stain.

27

It was the middle of Friday afternoon when Sherry Culhane finished her direct testimony, and the judge and lawyers agreed that I should not begin the cross-examination without being able to conclude it on the same day. So we broke early, with Culhane's dramatic delivery of that damning statistic the final thing the jurors heard before the weekend.

I headed home to Brookfield. Grace had a basketball game the next morning, and I was looking forward to a roughly twenty-four-hour parole from my immersion in all things Avery. True, I did need to think about my cross-examination, but in anticipation of Culhane's testimony I had already spent sixty to seventy hours poring over the results and the notes from the tests in the Avery case. Lawyers, axiomatically, are never supposed to ask a witness a question to which they themselves don't know the answer. It would work out to ten hours or more of preparation for every hour of cross-examination.

Although it wasn't great for the defense that the prosecution got to have the last, strong word before the weekend, it at least gave me the chance to go through the pages of notes that I had taken during her testimony and to tweak my questions. I worked all that Sunday on refining my cross-examination, to be sure the jurors would understand the key points and why they were important. Often, the significance of testimony or a piece of evidence is not made explicit until closing arguments, and I could not afford to wait till then. The cross-examination had to be a closing argument in itself, so the jury would grasp that the peculiar circumstances surrounding the discovery of this DNA evidence, the contamination in the lab, and the absence of other physical evidence all raised serious doubts that a crime had occurred in Steven Avery's trailer or garage.

Already, I had structured my cross-examination into chunks, each addressing the principal elements of the narrative Culhane had provided on direct examination, but also things that we needed from her. Sometimes, it makes sense for a defense lawyer to go into a cross with guns blazing, immediately attacking the credibility of the witness with tough questions. In this case, though, we wanted Culhane to establish a few essential facts. Then the examination would, inevitably, get confrontational.

There had been a dusting of snow overnight, but all of the jurors were on time for the bus that would take them to the courthouse. It was a balmy thirty-two degrees when we arrived that morning in Chilton.

The spectator seating area was full. The reporters were all downstairs, watching the feeds from the courtroom. As soon as everyone was seated, I began.

"Good morning, ma'am," I said.

"Good morning," Culhane replied.

At the top of my list was the most damning evidence in the case: her testimony that the stains in Teresa Halbach's RAV4 contained Steven Avery's blood. Culhane had said over and over that it was her opinion, "to a reasonable degree of scientific certainty," that Avery was the source of the DNA in the stain.

But this did not mean that blood had been shed during a crime.

"What you are *not* saying is anything about how his DNA found its way inside the RAV4, are you?" I asked.

A. No.

Q. Your tests aren't designed to tell us how his DNA found its way into the location where you ultimately swabbed, are they?

A. No.

Q. What you are looking for is a DNA profile, and if you find it, then you compare it to a known reference sample, in this case, Mr. Avery, right?

A. Right.

Q. But if someone else planted Mr. Avery's DNA, or blood, or both, inside that vehicle, you wouldn't know that from these tests, would you?

A. No.

Q. So you cannot tell this jury, with any degree of certainty, scientific or otherwise, that Steven Avery was, himself, ever inside that vehicle, can you?

A. No.

Q. No meaning correct?

A. That's correct.

First mission accomplished: establishing that Sherry Culhane could not put Avery inside Teresa Halbach's vehicle.

Next on my agenda was challenging the posture of scientific impartiality, which Gahn had established when he'd asked about her role in exonerating Steven Avery in 2003. First, we reviewed her work in the exoneration—her testing of hairs that had been combed from the pubic area of the victim. It was her test, I noted in a question, that had absolutely cleared Avery and implicated a man who had committed similar crimes. I was merely retracing the steps of the prosecutor, crossing comfortable ground, and Culhane readily agreed. Each of my questions had been scripted in advance, keyed to the prosecution's narrative.

Then it was time to show why this pleasant story wasn't nearly as tidy as it had appeared during Gahn's direct examination.

Just as Culhane had during her direct testimony, I kept my eyes on the jurors as I put my questions to her, watching their faces to make sure that they remained engaged.

Q. Now, what Mr. Gahn didn't have you point out, though, let's get into a few other things; although you were the one who exoner-ated—or whose test exonerated Mr. Avery, the evidence sat at your lab for more than a year before you got around to doing the test that did exonerate him, right?

A. That's correct.

Q. And one of the things that you in fact said you do is control priorities and case flow of what gets tested when, right?

A. Correct.

Q. So, had you done that test as soon as it came in, the evidence being in September of 2002, I believe, Mr. Avery would have been exonerated then, wouldn't he?

A. Correct.

Q. So Mr. Avery sat for another year, in prison, because of the delays that resulted in your crime lab; isn't that right?

A. Correct.

And there was even more to the story of Steven Avery's wrongful conviction that began long before Culhane and the laboratory got around to processing the DNA tests that would clear him.

Q. Another thing Mr. Gahn didn't point out is another irony in this case. Not only were you involved in the 2003 exoneration of

Mr. Avery, but you were also involved in the 1985 conviction of Mr. Avery, weren't you?

A. I worked evidence on that case, yes.

Q. And you testified as a witness for the prosecution at trial in that case, didn't you?

A. Yes, I testified.

Q. In fact, the trial where he had sixteen alibi witnesses and was convicted included your expert opinion regarding some hairs that had been found and were offered by the prosecution to somehow link Mr. Avery to that crime; isn't that right?

A. To be perfectly honest, I do not remember my entire testimony from 1985.

After Steven Avery had been taken into custody as a suspect in the 1985 case, the police had collected a hair from his T-shirt. *Culhane* was the state crime lab technician who had testified that it was consistent with Penny Beerntsen's hair—bolstering her identification of him and undercutting his alibi witnesses.

When I began to question her about this, Norm Gahn stood up.

ATTORNEY GAHN: Your Honor, at this time I just question the relevancy of this to the testimony that Ms. Culhane gave in this case, the relevancy in this 1985 case.

THE COURT: Mr. Buting.

ATTORNEY BUTING: Mr. Gahn tried to present her as a totally unbiased witness for them, in the event that because she— her test in 2003 resulted in the exoneration, I think the jury needs to hear that she's also testified the other way for the prosecution at the beginning of the trial.

THE COURT: As I understand your line of questioning, it's an attack on the methodology that was used at the time, not on her credibility.

ATTORNEY BUTING: Also a question on her opinion and the validity of her opinions.

THE COURT: No, I'm going to sustain the objection.

I disagreed with the court's ruling, which cut off my line of questioning, but the point was less important than others, so I moved on. At least the issue had been raised, and the jury could do with it what they wished. Throughout the trial, Judge Willis tried to be evenhanded in the way he ruled on objections. For the most part I think he succeeded in that, but whenever it became clear that the prosecution was especially exercised about something, Judge Willis tended to rule in their favor. This was most evident whenever the state complained that our questions pushed the boundaries of his ruling precluding any evidence of third-party suspects. The state seemed very worried about any of that evidence coming in at trial.

Human beings have a powerful ability to kid themselves. More than two centuries ago, patients reported being cured of a variety of ailments through a regimen of magnetic adjustments made at the direction of a German physicist, Franz Anton Mesmer, who referred to the forces as "animal magnetism" (the verb "mesmerize" has its roots in his work). In France, a special commission, including Benjamin Franklin and noted chemist Antoine Lavoisier, concluded that patients had been cured because they believed they would be. It is one of the first documented episodes of the placebo effect. Today, investigators study the usefulness of drugs by testing them alongside placebos and observing the effects on patients. Technicians do not know which subjects have received the real drug and which have received the placebo. Neither do the patients. Vital signs, blood tests, and other relevant data are collected by people who do not know what the "right" or hoped-for response is supposed to be—sometimes they do not even know that research is being conducted. Conducting drug trials this way protects observation from the contamination of expectation and is referred to as blind testing. An important part of modern scientific investigation is taking precautions against "observation bias"—that is, seeing something just because you're looking for it.

Alas, the practice has not spread widely into the world of crime laboratories, and Steven Avery's case is a prime example of why this is problematic. I asked Culhane about the use of blind testing, in which the examiner does not know whose DNA is being profiled or what its relevancy to the investigation might be. First, she asked that it be defined. Then she acknowledged that it was not practiced in her lab.

Q. In your lab, when you get a reference sample, you know—in fact, you usually know the name of the person whose reference sample you are dealing with?

A. Yes.

Q. So when you tested Mr. Avery's DNA sample, you knew it was Mr. Avery who you were testing?

A. Yes.

And, yes, Culhane said, she knew that Steven Avery was the suspect and that the DNA of other family members was there for the purpose of "elimination"—that is, to rule them out. Fassbender, the special agent from the Wisconsin Division of Criminal Investigation who, alongside Sergeant Mark Wiegert, spearheaded the investigation into Teresa Halbach's disappearance, would regularly call Culhane to let her know when items would be delivered. He'd even told her that a number of items would be coming from Steven Avery's house and garage.

And he didn't hold back on what results he wanted.

Culhane had noted that in one of Fassbender's earliest calls to her, he'd said: "Try to put her [Teresa Halbach] in his house or garage."

Q. So you are being told, before you do any of these tests, that Mr. Fassbender wants you to come up with results that put Teresa Halbach in Mr. Avery's house or garage; isn't that right?

A. I had that information, but that had no bearing on my analysis at all.

Q. Of course not, but that's what you are being told to do?

A. That was information in the investigation.

Fassbender gave Culhane a list of items that he wanted her to test: handcuffs and leg irons (covered in fluffy pink fake fur) taken from Avery's trailer; the license plates from Teresa Halbach's car; the .22 caliber rifle from Steven Avery's bedroom, to see if traces of her blood were on the barrel and if Avery's DNA was on the trigger guard. There were pieces of carpet, and of wooden paneling that had been pried off the walls surrounding the bed in Avery's bedroom, and other items taken from the trailer.

Brendan Dassey was never physically in the courtroom during his uncle's trial, but his story loomed over the proceedings, a weather system that never cleared. Anyone who had followed the news from a year earlier would have at least a passing familiarity with his purported confession. I had to work on the assumption that jurors remembered, at least vaguely, the gore-ridden narrative that Kratz had recited in his press conferences. This was part of our shadow-boxing.

Q. You never found any DNA of Teresa Halbach's on any carpet in his house, did you?

A. No.

We turned to the trailer, which if Ken Kratz was to be believed, had been the scene of a throat-slashing and brutal stabbing.

Q. All the bathroom items, the floor, the vanity, the sink, whatever, right?

A. Mm-hmm.

Q. You tested all of those?

A. Correct.

Q. None of them had Teresa Halbach's blood on them, did they?

A. No.

Q. You also tested, there were some drops that were found on a molding of a door near the bathroom or bedroom, right?

A. Yes.

Q. No DNA of Teresa Halbach, right?

A. Correct.

It was a sprawling crime scene, but—at least as Kratz had told it—the central acts of violence were supposed to have been committed in Avery's bedroom. What about the headboard of the bed, its legs and spindles? The nightstand? Outlet covers and light switches?

Q. No DNA from Teresa Halbach?

A. That's correct.

On the handcuffs and leg irons she found a mixture of genetic profiles from several people, none of them Teresa Halbach. It was significant that DNA was recovered from those items, because it meant that they could not have been cleaned up with bleach, which would have destroyed the DNA.

"That's correct," Culhane said.

Then there were the knives.

Q. I see at least seven, just in the May eighth report, right?

A. Yes.

Q. No DNA of Teresa Halbach's?

A. Correct.

The absence of Teresa Halbach's DNA anywhere in Avery's trailer was, of course, terribly important. But it still left the urgent question of Steven Avery's DNA that was found in the RAV4. On direct examination, Culhane said that it had been found in two forms, and in two general locations: in bloodstains on and around the front seats and in a swab collected from the hood latch. There was a third place, as identified by Kratz in his opening statement. He had shown the jury a

PowerPoint slide with a picture of the RAV4's rear door, with a circle drawn around it, and said there would be evidence that Steven Avery's DNA would be on its handle.

I asked Culhane about this.

"Based on my results, I didn't find Steven Avery's DNA on that sample," Culhane testified, directly contradicting the special prosecutor's own claim.

Was it plausible that Steven Avery's blood in the RAV4 and the DNA on the ignition key had been planted?

As Culhane had confirmed, Steven Avery's blood had been collected from two areas in the car: on and around the front seats and a dab just inside the rear passenger door. Yet no blood of his, nor any of his DNA, was found in the rear cargo area or on the cargo door—though that was where a quantity of Teresa Halbach's blood was found. All of *his* was in the front.

Wasn't it possible for someone to have planted Steve Avery's blood only by opening two doors?

"I really can't comment on that," Culhane said.

Actually, she could.

Q. Okay. You have got—if someone was to plant Mr. Avery's blood in that vehicle, to get to those six stains, they would need to open the driver's door, right?

A. Yes.

Q. Likely, or the passenger door on the front?

A. Yes.

Q. From either one, but more likely the driver's door, you could reach the location where all of the stains were found in that front seat area?

A. Except for the rear passenger door.

Q. I'm getting to that. Okay? The first five that you found were all in that front compartment?

A. Yes.

Q. Front seat compartment?

A. Yes.

Q. Reachable by opening one door, right?

A. Yes.

Q. And, then, the only other stain that you found there was in the rear passenger door that could also be accessed simply by opening that one door?

A. Yes.

Q. So if somebody was to plant Mr. Avery's blood in that vehicle, before you got it on November—in November, all of those stains you found could have been done by simply opening two doors?

A. Yes.

For some reason, five months after Teresa's RAV4 had been discovered and Sherry Culhane had already taken dozens of swabs in the hunt for traces of DNA, someone had decided to take a swab of the hood latch. By that time, the RAV4 was back at the Calumet County Sheriff's Office. The swab was taken in April 2006 and later sent to the state crime lab, where Culhane conducted a DNA test on it. It yielded a very small quantity of human DNA that contained Steven Avery's genetic profile. After *Making a Murderer* came out, Kratz noted that the hood latch DNA was omitted from the documentary. He argued that this was powerful, damning evidence of Avery's guilt because it could not have been planted using the vial of blood at the clerk's office. He said that this was Avery's "sweat DNA."

However, there is *no such thing* as "sweat DNA." DNA is found in all nucleated cells, but it's not possible to identify from DNA alone what bodily fluid or tissue its source was. To determine the bodily source, the analyst must perform presumptive tests for specific proteins, such as those present in blood, semen, and saliva. There are no presumptive tests to identify sweat as a bodily fluid. Culhane testified that the hood latch swab was discolored and may have contained blood, but she did not perform the presumptive blood test. Instead, because it was such a small quantity, she went right to the DNA extraction.

Q. Now, many months later, April I believe it was, you got a swab that was told to you was a hood latch swab?

A. Correct.

Q. That was not tested, or did not come from your test in November?

A. Right.

Q. And you weren't present when it was taken, by whomever, sometime before it arrived at your lab?

A. No, I was not.

Q. And you didn't do a presumptive test for blood, right?

A. Correct.

Q. You didn't see any blood particularly visible on the swab, right?

A. Right.

Culhane admitted the swab was dirty and discolored and that it may have contained blood that wasn't visible to her eye. Only a presumptive test could have ruled out blood as the source of the DNA, but she never performed that test.

The testimony of the next witness, Nick Stahlke, a forensic scientist from the Wisconsin State Crime Laboratory in Madison, provided an innocent explanation for Avery's DNA on the hood latch. Stahlke testified that he had been inside the passenger compartment of the RAV4 performing examinations before getting out and opening the hood *without* changing gloves. That small quantity of DNA found on the hood latch could have been "touch DNA," innocently and inadvertently transferred by the crime lab's own analyst, which had nothing to do with Teresa Halbach's disappearance.

As I continued my cross-examination of Sherry Culhane, I turned to the ignition key that Manitowoc County Sheriff's Office lieutenant James Lenk reported finding on the floor of Steven Avery's bedroom during the seventh search of the room in November 2005. Culhane had swabbed the entire key and then put the whole swab into a buffer solution that would capture any DNA. Normally, half of that swab would be saved for possible retesting later—but not this time. She assumed right from the beginning that any "touch DNA" found on the key would only be present in a small amount, so she would need to use the entire swab to detect it. Indeed, the result obtained was only a small amount of DNA, about 30 microliters. Did she know that there were 20,000 microliters of DNA in a blood sample? Or 2,000 to 3,000 in a buccal swab? She did not, she said. But, she acknowledged, what she had found on the key was a low amount.

Could that small quantity of DNA have gotten on the key by rubbing a toothbrush or a buccal swab on it?

Yes, she said.

Q. Okay. And from looking at this key, and your swab, and the evidence you found, you cannot tell whether the DNA that was found on that key was planted there by somebody or not, can you?

A. No.

Q. And, indeed, if somebody did plant the DNA on that key that you determined—that you found in your tests, it would look much like what you found?

A. Yes.

Q. Okay. Now, you found no mixture of DNA on that key, right?

A. Right.

Q. You did not find any DNA of Teresa Halbach on that key, did you?

A. That's correct.

Q. A car key that presumably she handled and used daily, right?

A. Correct.

Q. And you did swab all the way around the key?

A. Yes.

At this point, we'd gone through Steven Avery's entire trailer and all the items taken from it that did not show any trace of Teresa Halbach's DNA.

"Would it be fair to say that you were not able to—as Mr. Fassbender requested—'put her in his house'?"

"That's correct," Culhane said.

There was no sign that Avery had touched the .22 caliber rifle collected from the trailer—as it emerged later, it was the property of the landlord—nor was there any sign of a back splatter of blood on the barrel, which often appears as residue in a close-range shooting. This was one of the things Fassbender had specifically requested Culhane test for. Investigators had jackhammered the concrete floor of Steven Avery's garage and swabbed stains on it, and once again there was no sign of Teresa Halbach's DNA. However, Steven Avery's *was* present. No cleanup operation could have removed hers while leaving his. The garage had not been sterilized.

We were about to turn to the contamination problems in the lab. But there was something else that Sherry Culhane could establish.

Q. By the way, in all of this evidence that you have tested, all of it, some of it we heard you found Mr. Avery's DNA, things in his own garage or his own house, right?

A. Yes.

Q. Did you ever find any DNA of a gentleman named Brendan Dassey, anywhere, in all of your tests?

A. No, I did not.

Q. Not one shred, right?

A. No, I did not find his DNA.

Q. And you had his profile?

A. Yes, I did.

Culhane had been on the stand for the entire morning and an hour or so after lunch. During the lunch break I checked with some of the reporters and other observers listening to my cross-examination, to be sure they were following what I was doing as well as why it was important to the case. This was something I did frequently throughout the trial whenever we had a break in the action. The reporters were educated, intelligent people, whereas some of our jurors were *not* highly educated; the state had struck most who had college educations, and there were not many to begin with. If the reporters couldn't understand my cross-examination, it was unlikely the jurors would, either.

On some days it seemed the points I was trying to make didn't sink in, so when we restarted the questioning of a witness I would go back and revisit a topic to clarify the points before moving on. But with Sherry Culhane, it seemed to me that the examination was going very well, and the reporters were all following the points I was trying to make. The time had come to start bringing it to a close. This evidence, which had seemed so potent and damning on Friday after Gahn's direct examination, turned out not to have been as carefully studied, not as precisely collected, not as reliable as he and Culhane had initially made out.

I began by addressing basic laboratory contamination prevention procedures.

Did the analysts in the DNA Unit of the Wisconsin State Crime Laboratory wear surgical masks? Did they use disposable lab coats? Did they change lab coats from one case to the next? Were their sensitive work areas equipped with hoods to create an air space that was protected from stray contaminants?

No, Culhane said of those precautions, they were not in place at her lab. I noticed that she had stopped looking directly at the jury when answering my questions.

I turned to the contamination log, which recorded the number of clear incidents of contamination discovered during testing at the Madison office of the state crime lab. I asked her to count the number of contamination reports between 2004 and 2006. There were fifty. Of those, she had filed seven. In a lab with ten to twelve analysts at any one time, that was well above average.

A. That depends on how many cases each analyst works.

Q. That's true. You, though, have seven out of fifty, which is more than the average, if you divide it evenly, correct?

A. But not all those analysts work the same number of cases.

Culhane had already testified that she spent about 70 percent of her time on DNA testing and the rest on supervision and training, while the rest of the analysts worked exclusively on DNA.

Q. Isn't it true that for this two-month—two-year period, you have one of the highest contamination records of anybody at the Wisconsin Crime Lab in Madison?

A. I don't know. I haven't counted up all the other instances of other people. So I really don't know how many each analyst has.

Q. Well, take a moment and look if you like.

A. Do you want me to count up for each analyst?

Q. I want you to see if there's anybody who has more errors in that twenty more—twenty-four-month period than you?

Culhane seemed distressed. Gahn interrupted with objections to the relevancy, perhaps relying more on principles of chivalry than of law, but Judge Willis let the line of questioning proceed.

Culhane did not dispute that she had the most contamination reports. "If you counted them up and your numbers are correct, then I agree with you," she said, barely looking up.

We turned to the kinds of contamination by her and other analysts. One time, DNA from one case had been mishandled so that it wound up in another case. In another instance, a sample had been mislabeled. In others, even after careful study, the lab was unable to explain how or when the samples became contaminated.

Then it emerged that Culhane had once contaminated actual crime scene evidence with her *own* DNA, and it had been sent into CODIS.

Q. But it wasn't even detected until you ran your own profile through CODIS, as if you were some suspect, right?

A. It was detected when we ran it through the system, yes.

Q. That's right. And so you had to then remove it from the whole CODIS system; otherwise you would look like you are some suspect?

A. That's correct.

In yet another incident, Culhane's DNA was found in the sample of another analyst's work, even though she had not worked that case.

Q. You ended up contaminating someone else's test?

A. That's correct.

This brought us to the contamination of the control sample during the testing of the bullet fragment.

The trickiest thing about contamination during DNA testing is that it is usually obvious only if DNA shows up in a sample where no DNA should be found at all, such as a negative control sample that is supposed to be free of *all* human DNA. But contamination in an evidence sample isn't so readily detected. DNA from a suspect or a victim could make its way into an evidence sample through cross-contamination within a crime lab and we'd never know it—Culhane had already admitted such cases occurred in her lab. The result would be reported as though the DNA was deposited at the crime scene rather than accidentally into the evidence sample in the crime lab itself. This is a big reason why test protocols do *not* allow an analyst to express an opinion about a DNA inclusion if the controls show contamination.

If contamination is detected, the laboratory protocols required either that the test be redone or that the results be reported as inconclusive. There was such a minute amount of DNA on the bullet fragment, however, that it had all been used in the initial, contaminated test, and so testing could not be repeated.

Culhane's solution? Waive the protocol and report the finding of Teresa Halbach's profile on the bullet.

Q. Out of all these tests that you have done—

A. Right.

Q. —not one single test put Teresa Halbach in Mr. Avery's garage?

A. That's correct.

Q. Except for this bullet.

A. That's correct.

Q. And this is the only one, right?

A. Yes.

Q. And you couldn't retest it, so you either had to call it inconclusive or else deviate from your protocol.

A. That's correct.

The lab's protocols allowed that certain situations call for deviations from the rules on interpreting results but that all deviations had to be documented in writing, peer-reviewed, and approved by two levels of supervisors. There was no signature by a supervisor on Culhane's deviation report.

"Apparently it was an oversight," Culhane said.

Over the previous decade, ever since DNA testing began in the state crime laboratory, Culhane testified that she had never sought a deviation from protocol.

"I have never had this situation before," she said.

Interestingly, Culhane's official report on the DNA results listed the profile of Teresa Halbach on the bullet fragment but did not disclose that in order to report that result she had to do something she had never before done in her career.

This was how I concluded my cross-examination:

Q. At no time, in this report, do you ever disclose, that in order to make that finding, you had to deviate from a protocol, did you?

A. No.

Q. Anyone reading this report would never know that, in order for you to make that call and say that that's Teresa Halbach's DNA, you had to do something you have never done in your career as a crime lab analyst, right?

A. Without discovery, no.

Q. So, if a defense attorney, or Court, didn't dig through all of those mass of papers that you have there and find this one-page [protocol deviation] report, no one would ever know that, in order for you to make that call in this case, you had to do something you have never done before?

A. The deviation that I requested was appropriate for this situation. And the results that I reported were correct. And that's why the deviation was requested. All my data supported the deviation, it was okayed—

Q. But—

A. —and it was reported.

Q. —ma'am, you did not disclose, in that report, that official report, that Courts, and juries, and judges, and lawyers, and everybody else relies on, that in order to make that call, you had to do something so rare you have never done it before, did you?

A. No, I did not.

Q. And you didn't put that in there because if you did, you wouldn't be able to satisfy Mr. Fassbender's request that you put Teresa Halbach in Steven Avery's garage, right?

A. That's not correct.

Q. Let's close with this. Other than that bullet, all your other tests, none of them put Teresa Halbach, ever, in his garage, or his house, or any of his vehicles, right?

A. Correct.

Q. Thank you.

Culhane's testimony proved to be much more helpful for us than it had appeared the prior Friday. She helped us prove to the jury the complete lack of *any* physical corroboration for the law enforcement–instigated Brendan Dassey confession. Even if it wasn't going to be used, we knew it was ever-present in the jurors' minds. Culhane, we hoped, had aided us in dispelling that myth. And she substantially undercut the import of the one piece of evidence that *did* appear incriminating—the "magic bullet" not discovered in Steven Avery's garage until four months after November's careful, weeklong searches, during which no bullet fragment had been found. Even if that bullet had not been planted in the garage later to incriminate Steven Avery, as we suspected the ignition key had been, the DNA test result now looked dubious because of the contamination, and then Culhane's unprecedented deviation from protocol when she made the call that Teresa Halbach's DNA was present on the bullet.

The forecast was brighter.

28

One evening well into our fourth week commuting to Chilton, as Dean and I were driving back to our apartments, I began musing aloud on the arc of the trial.

"Let see," I said. "We've had eighteen days of testimony."

Dean jumped in. "At least fifteen or sixteen of those days, we have been able to bring out a theme of our defense again and again. And that's remarkable," he said. "But it still all comes down to a key in his bedroom on the seventh search. Bones outside of his bedroom when there's a perfectly good working smelter that would be a much better place to burn a body. Blood in the RAV4 . . . His blood."

We had all but forgotten that the documentary camera was rolling, but neither of us was discussing privileged material. We were just candidly discussing the hills ahead of us in the courtroom.

"And," Dean continued, "a contaminated bullet in the garage. But even there, in describing these, you're already doing some of the explaining that we've gotta do and let me put it this way: If ever someone's bones are found twenty feet out my bedroom window in my backyard, I'm gonna be a worried guy."

The bones. In some ways, they were the most important evidence in the case, even more so for the defense than for the prosecution. It is a grim subject but, in the context of the case, cannot be avoided.

Teresa Halbach's body had been thoroughly burned, and only about 40 percent of her identified cremains—enough to fill a one-liter bottle—were recovered from two sites. In addition, what appeared to be burned human female bones were found at a third location. How they had been distributed was central to the defense and yet, to our surprise, not a single photograph was taken of any of these three places where cremains were discovered.

The first, and largest, source of the cremains was a burn pit behind

Steven Avery's trailer; the second was a burn barrel about 150 yards away, near the Dassey house; and the third was about a quarter mile away, in a gravel quarry owned by the Averys' neighbor, Joshua Radandt, where the last burned bone fragments were recovered. Although these last were never identified with certainty as human, the state's forensic anthropologist believed that two may have been from a female pelvis, and they were burned to the same degree as those cremains identified as Teresa Halbach's. It seemed unlikely—even in Manitowoc County—that there was some other similarly burned female body, so they were very likely Teresa's remains.

If Teresa Halbach's body had been burned somewhere else and the remains were moved to Steven Avery's burn pit, then he was clearly not guilty. *Nobody* would burn a body elsewhere and then bring the remains and put them into his own backyard. So the location of the original burn site was a critical question. It was not at all obvious, appearances to the contrary. In our quest for an answer, we ran head-on into one of the shoddiest aspects of the investigation—one that was a source of quiet embarrassment to the prosecution. Whether due to deliberate choice, unwarranted certainty, recklessness, incompetence, or indifference, none of the accepted scientific procedures for collecting burnt remains were followed. And once again, Manitowoc County Sheriff's Office deputies and officers were at the center of the action.

On Monday, November 7, 2005, a week after Teresa Halbach was last seen, a squad of nine deputies from the Manitowoc County Sheriff's Office showed up at the Avery salvage yard as if they belonged there; as if leading officials had *not* publicly promised they would have no role in the investigation; and as if there was not a strong contingent of law enforcement officers from other agencies, particularly the Calumet County Sheriff's Office, already on the scene.

One of the Manitowoc deputies looked in a burn barrel near Avery's trailer. Such barrels, typically fifty-five-gallon drums, are commonly used in rural Wisconsin for rubbish disposal. The deputy reported finding pieces of a melted cell phone and possibly a camera. Perhaps these were Teresa Halbach's? Steven Avery also had a burn pit close to his bedroom window, but the deputies did not go near it. Later, they would say that a barking German shepherd tied up nearby had discouraged them. The following day, a dozen officers from the Manitowoc County Sheriff's Office arrived at the yard. One of them, Sergeant Jason Jost, reported that near Steven Avery's burn pit he'd spotted a bone fragment that looked like a piece of a spinal column. Another gray fragment was nearby. In the space of twenty-four hours, the Manitowoc County Sheriff's Office had gone from finding possible property of Teresa Halbach's to possibly finding her bones.

This crime scene was handled in shockingly cavalier fashion. No one took any pictures or made videotape of the contents of the burn pit. Sergeant Jost never wrote a report on the circumstances of his discovery. The state forensic anthropologist, Dr. Leslie Eisenberg—who is specifically trained in the collection and analysis of burnt human remains for criminal cases—was not summoned before the scene was irretrievably altered and crucial evidence lost. Not even the crime lab was called until it was too late to properly document the scene. Thomas Sturdivant, a special agent with the Wisconsin Division of Criminal Investigation, oversaw the collection of the cremains.

"I observed what I thought were other bone fragments in and around the burn pit," he testified. "I picked up a twig. I moved some leaves and other things, and I could see the other bone fragments within that— within the charred debris. I noticed what I believed to be, uh, skull fragments."

At this point, the position of the bone fragments could have been critically important. By examining the cremains exactly as they were initially discovered, anthropologists could have analyzed their alignment. Had the body been burned at that location? Then the remains, even charred, desiccated, and crumbling, should have retained traces of the skeletal form. Instead, the cremains were shoveled into a sifter.

When John Ertl, a forensic scientist with the crime lab and a member of its field response team, arrived at the Avery property, he decided that there was no point in taking photographs.

"The scene had obviously been altered at that point," Ertl wrote in an e-mail that was read at the trial. "Had we been working any of these scenes from start to finish, there would likely have been more thorough photo record done by us."

After the cremains had been put through a sifter and shaken, witnesses testified that any pieces large enough to be of interest were jumbled together and loaded in a big box.

Agent Sturdivant testified that he rushed through the collection process because of uncertainty about the status of the missing young woman. "At this point in time, quite frankly, we don't know if Teresa Halbach is alive or dead. So I had made the decision that we need to get these bones, um, off to the crime lab to determine whether or not these bones were human bones and belonged to Teresa Halbach."

That made no sense as a rationale for so thoroughly destroying the crime scene. Dozens of officers were available, and experts like the anthropologist should have been recovering the bone fragments anyway. Asked about documenting the conditions, Sturdivant was unapologetic. "I did not take any photos," he testified. "I'll take responsibility for that and I'll take the criticism that comes along with it. No."

That evening, Debra Kakatsch, the coroner for Manitowoc County who had legal responsibility for the investigation of the cause and manner of a death that occurred there, was watching the television news when she saw a report that suspected human remains had been found at the Avery salvage yard. She and her deputies began calling one another to discuss what steps they would take. They marshaled experts such as a forensic pathologist and a forensic anthropologist. Then she contacted law enforcement agents to ask why she had not been summoned and to tell them that she planned to come out there the following day. But in a number of conversations with Mark Wiegert, she was put off—and eventually told that her services were not needed. This message was reinforced by the Manitowoc County Executive and the county's lawyer, who called to tell her that she had to back off. Because of Steven Avery's civil lawsuit for his false arrest and wrongful conviction, county officials had a conflict of interest in the investigation.

Finally, the Manitowoc County Sheriff's Office had found someone they didn't want on the crime scene: an individual who had *absolutely nothing* to do with the lawsuit. Meanwhile, the people at the heart of the suit were crawling all over the grounds and searching Steven Avery's trailer and garage, day after day, for more than a week. The hypocrisy was astounding.

Was Coroner Kakatsch excluded for some reason? We tried to present testimony from her at the trial, but Judge Willis ruled that whatever she had to say would not be relevant to the question of Steven Avery's guilt or innocence.

As a result of these maneuvers, whether deliberately calculated or the result of simple ineptitude, no one with the competence to determine how and where the remains had been burned was involved in their removal from the three locations. Dr. Eisenberg found a box of them on her desk later that week when she returned from a conference.

"Unfortunately, I know little or nothing about how the recovery was undertaken," Eisenberg testified.

To show how important and damning that was, we consulted the most impressive expert we could find: Dr. Scott Fairgrieve, a Canadian forensic anthropologist who is an international authority on thermal injuries to human bodies, and author of the seminal book on the recovery of cremains from a crime scene, *Forensic Cremation Recovery and Analysis*.

"One of the things context can tell you, if it's well done, is to approach the question of where the body was burned," Dr. Fairgrieve testified. "Was it moved? Was this the actual location or not?"

Figuring this out demands a meticulous mapping of the ground where the remains are found, he explained, and an exacting process of excavation. Wooden tools are best, because they have approximately the same density as bone or even cremated bone and are thus less likely to damage the fragile evidence.

"If you take a cremated bone and pick up one bone, you end up putting down ten," he testified.

Undisturbed, even crumbling cremated bones in place can show what happened during the burn.

"It's akin to taking a piece of glass and putting it on the floor and stepping on it," he said. "Well, you can see the outline of the glass and the size of the piece of glass, but you will also see all the cracks. So if you move it, you are not going to be able to see that outline anymore in its original form."

It was impossible to say, Dr. Fairgrieve continued, where the body had actually been burned: Steven Avery's burn pit, the burn barrel behind the Dassey house, the quarry, or some other location? But what about the volume of the cremains found at each site? Wasn't that the most important factor in determining the burn location? Most of them had been found in the burn pit nearest Steven Avery's house, and Dr. Eisenberg had said that the quantity of cremains and the presence of certain little bones suggested to her that the burn pit was the primary site of cremation.

Not necessarily so, Dr. Fairgrieve testified. He had taken part in cases where burnt remains had been found in two places and in which the investigators had been able to determine with certainty where the primary burn had taken place. In those cases, most of the cremains wound up at the place they were moved *to*. He also said that he'd found very small bones, such as the one-millimeter bones of the inner ear, at the secondary site where the majority of cremains were discovered. So if history were a guide, Steven Avery's backyard was *not* where Teresa Halbach was cremated. Someone had to have gone to the trouble of moving her ashes and bones to Avery's burn pit.

When, then, did that happen? Most of the Averys had been away since the Thursday of the week Teresa Halbach disappeared. Steven had left on Friday, the day before her RAV4 was discovered and the salvage yard was subsequently locked down by law enforcement.

The state noted that articles from Teresa Halbach's clothing, such as a zipper and grommets from Daisy Fuentes–brand jeans she owned, were discovered in Steven Avery's burn pit. This, the prosecution argued, was proof she was burned at that location. But not all of the grommets from that pair of jeans were discovered there, including the largest metal object—the top button clasp of the waistband—despite careful sifting and searches with magnets.

Frustratingly, the question of where Teresa's body was burned remained unanswered. No one, it seemed to Dean and me, could find beyond a reasonable doubt that it had happened in Steven Avery's burn pit. The state never offered any explanation to the jury, through testimony or in closing argument, why some of her bones had been found in the burn barrel and other suspected human cremains in that quarry a quarter mile away. To us, it seemed much more likely that her body was burned elsewhere, and then, to incriminate Avery, the cremains were scooped into the burn barrel and dumped in his burn pit, with some becoming entrapped in the muck at the bottom of the barrel.

One other thing about Dr. Fairgrieve: At the time he testified in Steven Avery's trial, he had been an expert consultant to the chief coroner in Ontario, Canada, for at least fifteen years. On many occasions, he had been called as an expert witness but always by the Crown—that is, Canadian prosecutors.

Never before had he testified for the defense.

29

Late on a Friday afternoon toward the end of the trial, Norm Gahn handed me an eight-inch stack of paper. Working at a sprint, the FBI laboratory in Quantico, Virginia, had invented a new testing protocol for EDTA and decided that the three bloodstains they tested, which were collected from Teresa's RAV4, did not contain the preservative.

This meant, in the FBI's opinion, that the stains came from Steven Avery actively bleeding in the RAV4 and were not planted using the vial of his blood from the Manitowoc County Clerk of Court's Office, which did contain the preservative. Moreover, the FBI was sending one of its top chemists to Wisconsin to testify that it was his scientific opinion that even though he had tested only three of six stains, none of the untested stains in the RAV4 contained the preservative, either. All things considered, this was both a remarkably agile piece of work by the FBI laboratory and a classic misuse of scientific procedures to prop up a prosecution. The state was desperate to show that the stains in the RAV4 had not been planted.

In fact, around the beginning of the year, FBI officials had told prosecutors that they did not ordinarily do this kind of testing and would have to do a major recalibration of their equipment to even attempt it. Even then, the testing could take three or four months. Given this forecast, the prosecutors asked Judge Willis to delay the start of the trial or to altogether exclude evidence about the availability of the blood vial in the Manitowoc County Clerk's Office. When he ruled he would do neither, federal prosecutors intervened on behalf of their state colleagues. They "offered their services, shall we say, their pull, or whatever, to expedite testing," Gahn told the judge.

Thus nudged, the FBI lab came up with results with only days to go before the end of the trial. Its report on the results was a very brief and conclusory summary that was misleading in crucial ways. (Most of those eight inches of paper were printouts of computer graphs from the gas chromatograph–mass spectrometer at the lab.) We argued to Judge Willis that this report should not be presented to the jury until we'd had the chance to hire our own experts and that it wasn't reliable. The judge said he would have a hearing on Monday about the evidence, and he gave us—meaning me, since I was handling the FBI science testimony—the weekend to get ready.

My father and mother may have had graduate degrees in chemistry, but I hate the subject. The weekend proved to be the low point of the trial for me. The first thing I had to do was get a complete copy of the eight-inch paper pile to an expert who could help me interpret what the documents said—and what they didn't say. With Kathy's help, I located Dr. Frederic Whitehurst, a former special supervisory agent of the FBI forensic lab who, a few years earlier, had gone public with concerns about its inadequacies. Dr. Whitehurst had worked at the lab from 1986 to 1998, and he was intimately familiar with the lab's practices and the culture that hid most of its procedural errors from public view. His public disclosure of problems in its explosives section forced him to defend himself from apparent retaliation by the FBI, although his revelations ultimately led to reforms.

Dr. Whitehurst agreed to review the EDTA test documents over the weekend, and so I rushed off to a copy center at the end of the day and hand-delivered a set to the UPS office at the Appleton airport for overnight delivery to his home in North Carolina, beating the 7:00 p.m. deadline for last shipment of the day by less than five minutes. He called me on Sunday with his thoughts, but it turned out he was not available to testify for the defense that week, the last days of the trial. He said he'd be willing to ship his copy directly to Janine Arvizu, a colleague in New Mexico who worked as a consulting lab auditor. But first I needed to find out if she was available to testify. I reached her at home on Sunday evening, and she agreed to clear her Thursday to come to Wisconsin—assuming that when she received the documents she found anything useful.

The next day, Monday, the court was back in session but the jury had been told to stay home. The entire day would be devoted to a hearing on the admissibility of the FBI's EDTA report, with testimony from Marc LeBeau, the chief of the chemistry unit at the laboratory. At the time, Wisconsin was the only state not to use the strict standards laid out by the United States Supreme Court to decide if so-called forensic evidence could be presented to juries. Every other state in the nation barred testimony that did not conform to the acceptable scientific practices as defined by the court. Wisconsin, on the other hand, essentially let in virtually any relevant evidence from expert witnesses and then left it up to each jury to decide how much weight to give it. Even though I was able to expose significant holes and flaws in both LeBeau's opinion and the newly created FBI testing protocol, Judge Willis denied our motion to exclude LeBeau's testimony and ruled that all of it could be presented to the jury. (Wisconsin's law changed a few years later and the FBI test may not have been admissible under current requirements.)

In front of the jury the following day, LeBeau was assured and conclusive when he was being questioned by the prosecution, and then contentious, even argumentative, when I was examining him. He claimed that the machinery used by the FBI could find even minute quantities of EDTA, but the machinery had proven the limits of its power only with laboratory samples—pure quantities of EDTA, precisely known and fed into the device—and not with bloodstains first dabbed up from the dashboard of a RAV4 by a wet cotton swab and then diluted further in a solution before being run through the machine, all after an unknown period in her car, exposed to the elements of late October and early November Wisconsin weather. Some years earlier, LeBeau had been involved in another case that relied on a novel testing process, which he'd hurriedly devised after being told that the United States attorney general personally wanted it done. That time, LeBeau found a chemical in the embalmed tissues of a woman that he said showed she had been administered a poison. Later, the conviction was overturned; that chemical was also found in the tissues of people who definitely had not been administered the poison.

Even though we were able to neutralize much of the FBI lab's testimony, it seemed clear to Dean and me that this had been a deflating moment for the defense. However, we secured one important, long-term result. After the judge admitted the FBI evidence, we asked for the indefinite preservation of all of the remaining blood evidence, along with the samples used by the FBI lab. Our position was that the current state of testing for EDTA was unreliable. One day, it might be.

"I would like the ability to do that testing when it reasonably becomes available to Mr. Avery to do it, as a matter of science and finances, regardless of when that may happen," Dean said. "It won't happen during the trial, so I'm just looking ahead."

The prosecution consented. Now, ten years later, science indeed has advanced, and this evidence may yet help reverse Avery's conviction.

By the time LeBeau testified in the Avery case, the independent lab auditor, Janine Arvizu, had reviewed the FBI's report. Later that week, she flew to Wisconsin and testified that the FBI procedures were unable to determine that the preservative was definitively not *present*, only that it had not been *detected* by use of their protocol.

I asked her what she thought about LeBeau's opinion that, by testing three stains, he could determine with confidence whether any of the other stains in the RAV4 did or did not have the preservative.

Her commonsense answer rang true with many people who watched *Making a Murderer*.

"I'm in the business of analytical chemistry, and we're not in the business of just making guesses about what might be in samples," Arvizu replied. "We have instrumentation to test samples and that's how we determine results.

"There's no way for an analytical chemist to know what's in a sample unless we test it."

Part VII

CAUGHT IN A FIVE-HUNDRED-YEAR RAIN

30

Kathy pulled Stephen and Grace out of school for the day, and the three of them drove two hours north to Chilton to hear the closing arguments. By the time they arrived there were no seats in the courtroom, so Kathy took them downstairs to the basement where the press was watching the live feed. One of the reporters let Grace sit in front of her monitor. Seeing the tangle of technology, how the reporters worked, was probably more exciting for them than having to sit quietly in the courtroom.

The custom is for the prosecution to speak first, then the defense, and the prosecution gets a rebuttal. This means the state has last licks. The logic is that the state has the exclusive burden of proof. Ken Kratz marshaled the state's evidence effectively enough but in the process went on at what seemed to be excruciating length about the meaning of DNA statistics. Since we never disputed that the DNA results were accurate in identifying the source of various stains, it was—for me, anyway—an essentially pointless exercise.

Dean and I split the closing for the defense, with each of us taking on the witnesses and evidence that we had handled. I began. A key point we needed to make was that we were *not* accusing the police of killing Teresa Halbach but of planting evidence that would make Steven Avery look guilty. Both Dean and I covered this ground. This was my pass: "We do not and have never claimed that the police killed Teresa Halbach. In that respect, they have that in common with Steven Avery. However, the person or persons who did kill Teresa knew exactly who the police would really want to blame for this crime."

This, I said, fed directly into the investigative bias that the Manitowoc officers held against Steven Avery over his lawsuit.

In the back of my mind throughout my closing argument was an incident that had occurred far from the courtroom, on the weekend after I'd cross-examined Sherry Culhane about the mishandling of

DNA samples in the Wisconsin Crime Laboratory. Kathy had organized a party for the families of Grace's and Stephen's basketball teammates at our house, and everyone had questions about what they had been watching on TV. One of the moms, though, had a comment. She worked in a laboratory herself and let me know in no uncertain terms how she felt about that examination.

"You were too hard on that poor tech," she'd said.

I was taken aback. It was a good reminder that impeaching a witness is not a clinical process. To me, that had been a technically and substantively successful cross-examination. On a human level, however, this woman from my own neighborhood had felt empathy for Sherry Culhane. I filed that admonishment away, as a powerful reminder not to sprain my arm patting myself on the back, and it shaped a segment of my closing.

> Now, you know, one of the odd things about trying a case with this kind of publicity, where other people can watch at home, or wherever, is that you get some feedback about how you do. Some of it not so good. And some people told me maybe I was a little hard on Sherry Culhane.
>
> And if you think that, you know, I apologize if I offended anybody with my cross-examination of her, but I ask you not to hold it against Mr. Avery. Because I have a job to do and as an advocate, I need to point out, if someone goes over the line and goes too far, you have to understand it.

One of Judge Willis's toughest pretrial rulings against the defense was that Dean and I could not bring evidence of third-party liability against anyone. That is, we could not try to specifically prove someone else killed Teresa Halbach or at least was a plausible alternative to Steven Avery who deserved consideration. However, that did not mean we couldn't argue in the closings that other people were around the Avery property that day or that other people had dealings of a personal or business nature with Teresa Halbach, and therefore they should have been looked at as closely as Steven Avery by the authorities. A biased police investigation that ignored other suspects was fair game for argument.

A Cingular Wireless expert had testified during the trial about evidence that pointed to someone erasing messages in Teresa Halbach's voice mail before she was reported missing. No investigative effort was made to explain who may have done so or whether this fact could be a lead to the real killer. By drawing attention to this in our closing arguments, Dean and I were not slinging charges against any individual but rather illustrating how many people were bypassed in the rush to pin the crime on Steven Avery. Two of these people were Bobby Dassey, Brendan's older brother, and his friend Scott Tadych, each of whom provided an alibi for the other.

"So when the state tells you that Bobby Dassey is this credible witness, who's the last person to see Teresa Halbach alive, maybe he's right, if he's the killer. Or Scott Tadych, his only alibi," I said.

Kratz leapt up with an objection, but Judge Willis told him he would hear it after I was finished speaking. I also alluded to—without specifically mentioning Kratz's multiple press conferences on Brendan— pretrial publicity that should not be taken by the jurors as evidence.

When I was done, the jury was sent out of the courtroom for a break. Kratz was in rare form. He accused me of willfully violating the court order and demanded that Judge Willis admonish me in front of the jury by telling them I had disobeyed one of his rulings. To me, in a closing argument a lawyer is supposed to pull the evidence together and show how it stands or falls, and address the lingering questions that the jury will inevitably have.

"Well, Judge, as the court I think has made clear, Mr. Avery, by his not guilty plea, means he isn't the killer, so somebody else has to be," I said. "What I was trying to do was simply point out all of the other avenues that the police could have examined and didn't."

Judge Willis took a look at his fourteen-page decision and said I had not tried to introduce evidence but simply made argument. His order had not forbidden that. Kratz was cranky. He had also taken exception to my allusion to pretrial publicity, of which he of course was the maestro.

"So to highlight something they may have heard on the news, or something earlier, is absolutely improper and I'm suggesting that Mr. Buting knows that," he fumed.

"I disagree," I replied. "This jury was exposed to false, misleading information for fourteen months. And it's not until they came into this courtroom that they heard the other side."

I assured the judge that my remarks would not go into the substance of the publicity but underscore the need for the jurors to decide the case based only on evidence in court.

"That's fine," Judge Willis said. "Anything else, Mr. Kratz?"

"I'm not sure how to unring that bell, Judge," Kratz said.

"Well, I wish I could unring it, too," I said, thinking back to Kratz's own press conferences.

In his summation, Dean spoke of how poor an instrument courts were for bringing "closure" to people who were suffering, speaking with empathy for the Halbach family and the loss of Teresa at twenty-five years old. But, he said, a trial could be an opening into the closure that could come in church, community, in a family's home.

He also spoke of Steven Avery's losses: "The 1985 case won't matter so much anymore, if justice is done this time. Will that ever go away? No, but it just won't matter so much anymore, the injustice that was done to Steven then, because there is—there is something redemptive in human beings going back, and trying again, and getting it right eventually."

We had to win over all twelve jurors to get an acquittal for Steven Avery, and we were concerned that some of them might not believe that Lenk and Colborn had acted maliciously to frame him. We needed to give those jurors a way to conclude that evidence had been planted to make them believe Avery was guilty, without requiring them to also believe that the cops were deliberately trying to frame a man they knew to be innocent.

"And what you critically, I think, need to understand, that if and when police officers plant evidence, they are not doing it to frame an innocent man," Dean said. "They are doing it because they believe the man guilty. They are doing it to ensure the conviction of someone they have decided is guilty. That's why you plant evidence."

Why Steven Avery's civil lawsuit would ignite such a response, he said, is not because it exposes bad cops but that it touches good cops.

"It erodes, fundamentally, the sense of identity, 'We get the bad guys, we don't get the good guys.' And here it is, they got it wrong, that department got it wrong. Not only do they get it wrong, but the right guy is still out there and he commits another rape."

Kratz, in his final minutes, spent less time rebutting the evidentiary arguments than he did putting words in our mouths that were the opposite of what we had said. He insisted that for our defense to be true, the police officers had to be the killers. And he claimed that I had smeared the victim by saying that no one had been found who could say where Teresa Halbach had been, or who she was with, for most of the weekend before her death. My point, of course, had been that this was yet another investigative angle that the police simply had not given sufficient attention to, but Kratz twisted my words until my original thought was deformed beyond recognition.

"And when you suggest that that victim had some responsibility, or something to do with her own demise, you need to be held accountable for that," Kratz said. "You need to be taken to task for that. And, again, as the prosecutor, I'm expressing my indignance about that."

His "indignance" expressed, he told the jurors that "everything in this case pointed toward one person, toward one defendant."

In a few weeks, when Brendan Dassey went on trial, Kratz would be saying that everything in the case pointed not to one person but to two.

31

The end of any trial, when the jury gets their final instructions and the bailiffs lead them out of the courtroom to begin their deliberations, brings about conflicting emotions.

On the one hand, the lawyer's work is largely over. There are no more witnesses to present or cross-examine. The closing arguments are done and it's now out of our hands and in the jury's. This brings about a partial sense of relief. A march that started many months earlier, that had taken over almost every waking hour of my life, was close to its end.

On the other hand, waiting for a verdict is one of the most wearing periods of the trial. The relief of having finished can be undone by anxiety about whether you might have done something better: an argument that could have been addressed more strongly in closings; a witness who perhaps shouldn't have been called by the defense; or one who wasn't called but who maybe should have been. In nearly every trial, this includes the defendants themselves, because defendants are not required to testify and rarely do. Many times when they do testify, it doesn't go well, no matter how much preparation their lawyers may have done with them for the state's cross-examination. Defendants are not professional witnesses. Witnesses for the prosecution, like Sherry Culhane and the members of law enforcement, have often testified many times and are polished from practice. For instance, they will turn to the jury while answering virtually every question. Most defendants have never testified in any court before. But when a defendant exercises his right not to testify, it does make the jury focus more on whether the state has met its burden of proof, instead of weighing the polished performances of the state's witnesses against that of a defendant's. Despite the judge's instruction that a defendant has no duty whatsoever to testify, and indeed an absolute constitutional right not to, might a jury feel the defendant is hiding something by not testifying? All of these thoughts churn through your mind during deliberations. Add to this the client's nervousness and that of his or her family and friends, and you have a time of real anxiety.

Dean and I had a small windowless room, almost directly below the courtroom, where we stored some of our files rather than wheel them back and forth to the courthouse every day. It was a soulless refuge, but that's where we spent our time while waiting for the verdict, trying to catch up on e-mails. When it got too claustrophobic, we wandered the halls and shot the breeze with the reporters who had covered the case for weeks.

The longer deliberations go, the more the stress builds on both sides. I often speculate about whether a long deliberation is good or bad for the defense, and the answer varies from one case to the next. In some cases I've had a gut feeling that if they do not come back with a quick verdict, it's a good sign for the defense. Perhaps they are harboring serious reasonable doubts and do not believe the prosecution's case. But the reality is that you cannot predict the outcome just from the length of deliberations. It may be that eleven of the twelve have no doubt of a defendant's guilt, but there is one juror holding out. Or it could be the reverse—eleven jurors who want to acquit and one holding out for a guilty verdict. I've seen both circumstances. Sometimes a long deliberation does raise the prospect of a hung jury, which can be a defense "win"—but only if the state isn't hell-bent on getting a conviction, meaning that they would be willing to plea-bargain or dismiss the case if the jury is stalemated. In a first-degree intentional homicide, a hung jury almost always means the case will have to be tried again. And the state will have had the first trial as a dry run of the defense's presentation.

That first evening, after the jury had quit for the night and the judge had given the lawyers an all-clear, as Dean and I were enjoying a dinner of Mexican food and Modelo beers—the first alcohol I'd consumed since the trial started—we got word from the judge's chambers that one of the jurors had a family medical emergency and could not continue. Judge Willis offered several options: Have the case decided by eleven jurors, bring back an alternate who had just been excused but was still sequestered, or go for a mistrial. After consulting with Steven Avery the next morning, we decided to have the alternate join the eleven. This meant, as Judge Willis told the panel the following day, that they would have to start their deliberations from scratch with the new member.

After doing our best to try to shape and curate every word that jurors hear during trials, along with the judge, lawyers lose control during deliberations. Behind closed doors, the discussion between twelve people takes on its own dynamic. The only time we get an insight is when they send out notes. What are they asking for? A piece of evidence, a section of testimony, a review of the instructions on the law? Is that good for the other side and, if so, can my side argue that the judge ought *not* to give them what they're asking for? Trying to read the tea leaves like this can get a little crazy. For instance, at one point the jurors in the Steven Avery trial asked for a whiteboard. Hmm. What did that mean? Obviously, that they were trying to sort through complicated evidence, which was really not a big deal, but everyone integrated this factoid into their own mental narratives. On the third day of deliberations, March 17, the jury sent a note asking to hear a portion of the testimony read back. Anyone sitting in the courtroom would have seen nothing amiss.

"Anything else before we bring the jurors in?" Judge Willis asked. "We'll bring the jurors in at this time."

A door to the side of the judge's bench opened, and the jurors strode in, the familiar line of faces. Then Judge Willis began to read the testimony. It was serious business, routinely carried out.

An hour earlier, it had been anything but.

When the note came from the jury, Dean and I had been waiting outside the courtroom.

As he had done throughout the trial with issues that were contentious or potentially contentious, Judge Willis called us into chambers for an off-the-record discussion. We were all on edge, of course, but perhaps Kratz and the prosecution more so. Their hopes for a quick verdict had been dashed.

I was pacing nervously. Kratz and Dean were seated, with Dean between us. By that point, any veneer of politeness between Kratz and me had vanished. I envied Dean's equanimity about Kratz and so many other things.

This request was obviously from a juror leaning toward the defense. It asked for testimony to be read back that was favorable to us: my examination of Sherry Culhane, the state's witness, on the subject of the .22 caliber rifle belonging to Steven Avery's landlord that was found in his bedroom. I had questioned her about her examination of the barrel, trigger, and trigger guard of the rifle. She acknowledged that she had found no trace of Steven Avery or Teresa Halbach on any of them, which was not at all helpful to the prosecution's trial theory that the gun had been used to kill Teresa.

Standing behind his desk, Judge Willis asked our positions on how we should respond to the request for that portion of Culhane's testimony.

I said that he should grant their request and read it back. Kratz leapt out of his chair and started toward me, his face red, teeth clenched, and the veins in his neck bulging.

"Of course you think so," he nearly yelled.

I moved toward him, on the verge of popping him, when Dean jumped up between us and pushed us apart. I'm pretty sure my teeth were clenched and my veins were bulging as well, because we got within a couple of feet of each other before Dean intervened. Judge Willis was behind the desk and couldn't have physically pushed us apart, but he did raise his voice as he told us both to knock it off. I turned around and took a few paces to cool off, surprised at my reaction. The last time I had been mad enough to fight someone I had been a teenager.

Calm restored, Judge Willis decided that he *would* read back that part of the testimony. We returned to the courtroom as if nothing had happened.

Later, when we were on our own, Zen-master Strang had a comment about the confrontation in chambers.

"I'm sorry I didn't let you get at least one punch in," Dean said.

32

Near the end of the fourth day of deliberations, Sunday, the jury reached a verdict. The foreman signed separate sheets for each of the three counts at 4:22, 4:23, and 4:24 p.m. It would be more than an hour before Judge Willis returned to the bench and brought in the jury, just in time for the evening newscast. Every television station in the state covered it live.

Along with the prosecutors and the Halbach and Avery families and their friends and supporters, Dean and I took our places. As many reporters as could get seats in the audience were there; the bulk were down in the basement media room watching the live feed. I stood anxiously near the defense counsel's table, waiting for our client to be brought out of the secure jail access door to my left. Finally, it swung open and Steven came out, dressed in a blue-and-black plaid shirt, nodding to his family before sitting at the table. He looked nervous. I sat next to him, with Dean to my right.

After a few moments, Judge Willis came out of chambers and we all stood. He called the jury in and we sat back down.

I studied the twelve jurors as they filed in. None of them looked toward the defense table, although, for that matter, I did not see any of them look toward the opposite side of the courtroom where the prosecutors stood with the Halbach family behind them. For the first time, the jury foreman's identity became evident; the foreman always enters last and takes the seat in the front row closest to the judge. I was not pleased. The foreman was not someone I had felt good about at jury selection or during the trial.

He handed the verdict sheet to the bailiff, who gave it to Judge Willis. He glanced at it.

"At this time the court will read the verdicts," he said.

I noticed Avery look over to the jury. He was gazing at them as Judge Willis read each verdict.

"On count one, the verdict reads as follows: 'We, the jury, find the defendant, Steven A. Avery, guilty of first-degree intentional homicide as charged in the first count of the Information.'"

Avery shook his head and glanced away from the jury for the first time. I could not see his face because I was to his side, but I instinctively put my hand on his back. It flashed through my mind that he must be reliving the verdict delivered in 1985. I barely heard Judge Willis read the other verdicts. The first one, which carried a mandatory life prison sentence, was all that mattered. Avery was looking at the jury again as Judge Willis continued to read each sheet.

"On count two, the verdict reads: 'We, the jury, find the defendant, Steven A. Avery, not guilty of mutilating a corpse as charged in the second count of the Information.'"

It was incomprehensible. Guilty of murder but not of mutilating the corpse? Again, Avery shook his head slightly and turned away.

Later, watching a televised playback of the verdict, I saw that Avery's eyes had welled up at this point. The first verdict was still sinking in. The jury found him guilty of count three, possession of a firearm by a felon, for the rifle found in his room—even though it belonged to his landlord. I did not care about that charge. If he'd been found not guilty of the first two counts, he probably would have been released on that one with time served.

Before Avery was led away through the security door, I leaned over and told him we would be back to see him in the jail as soon as we could. The security bailiffs made the two families leave the courtroom separately. Dean and I met with the Averys in a conference room for a few moments, feeling awful that we had lost and puzzled at how the jury could find him guilty of the homicide but not guilty of the mutilation of a corpse. Steven Avery's parents, Allan and Dolores, were devastated. They had hoped so much to avoid a repeat of the injustice they had suffered twenty years earlier, and I felt terrible that they were reliving that nightmare now. It was clearly a compromise verdict; some jurors must have felt he was innocent of the homicide as well but compromised on a not-guilty on count two. Meaningless, in the end.

Dean and I then hurried over to the Calumet County Jail to see Avery, but we were told he was not there.

"What do you mean he's not there?" I asked. "He came back from court ten minutes ago. He should be in the jail by now."

He had already been taken away to Manitowoc County Jail. I was shocked.

Steven Avery had been held in the Calumet County Jail from the very beginning of the prosecution, sixteen months ago, for safekeeping. I couldn't believe they'd had a car waiting, ready to transport him to the Manitowoc County Jail immediately. It was as though they'd known what the verdict would be before it was read in court.

Then a terrifying thought occurred to me as I considered another possibility. Perhaps they would see to it that Avery was "eliminated" that very night, just as Manitowoc County sheriff Kenneth Petersen had said, on TV, it would be so "easy" to do—easier than framing him—if they wanted him out of the way. They knew he would appeal and fight the case, just as he had done the last time, so wouldn't it be better to end it all right then? My paranoia went on a rampage. They would stage it and say Avery took his own life in despair after losing the trial. It might sound far-fetched, but after everything that had already happened it did not seem too far outside the realm of reality. I decided I had to try to forestall that possibility.

We were expected back in the courthouse media room shortly to make a statement. Ken Kratz was finishing his victory lap when we arrived, which he ended with a little smile and a conspicuous thank-you to the media for allowing him to "host" them in Calumet County. I don't know if he got the irony in that, but it had to have been obvious to him by then that most of the media did not like him personally or respect him professionally; we had been told as much by some of the reporters. After my kids had watched part of his closing in the media room, they reported that there had been some derisive hooting at his sanctimony.

As we moved to the podium, I was seething. The first thing I did was tell the press that Manitowoc County officials had already whisked Steven Avery away to their jail—so quickly, in fact, that they'd denied us a chance to meet with him after the verdict had been read. Nevertheless, I continued, I'd spoken with him before we left the courtroom and he was not despondent. He intended to appeal and fight to prove his innocence once again. I also openly warned Manitowoc County that his safety was their responsibility and that if anything happened to Steven Avery that night, they would be held responsible. The media seemed taken aback, so I clarified that he was *not* suicidal—and Manitowoc better not try to claim that he was if something did happen to him.

One of the reporters, citing Dean's remarks in the closing about the process holding redemptive possibilities, asked him about it.

"I mean, now you've been through this process," she said. "Was it the redemption you'd hoped for?"

"No. Redemption will have to wait, as it so often does in human affairs," he said. "It just will have to wait. Our criminal justice system failed Steven Avery badly in 1985. It failed him time and time again after 1985."

In one sentence, he summed up nearly two decades of appellate courts rejecting the pleas of an innocent man.

"I fear this is one more failure, in spite of everyone's best efforts, and honest efforts. So I'm very sad at a personal level because I've lost a case," Dean said. "I'm sad at a broader level, um, that we, you know, in human life, we just haven't mastered justice any better than we have."

Another reporter: "So do you think that there's a killer out there that the police have not caught?"

"Absolutely. I mean, that's been our position all along," I said

A *Milwaukee Journal Sentinel* reporter asked, "Do you think the guilty verdict on the homicide makes it more likely or less likely that Brendan Dassey would be found guilty of that?"

"We're not gonna comment on Brendan Dassey's case at all," I said.

"Neither should you," Dean snapped at the reporters. "How's that for being judgmental on a day of judgments? This is a kid who has a trial upcoming, and I'd like to see him start with a stronger presumption of innocence than his adult uncle was able to."

We kept the rest of our comments brief and ended the press conference as cordially as we could. I was still so disappointed and angry at what Manitowoc had done, denying us even the courtesy of waiting a few moments before taking Avery away so that we could visit him—our client—after he'd received a devastating verdict. To me, it is ironic that nine years later, when the sensation of *Making a Murderer* was at its height, some viewer took a screenshot of Dean and me standing at that podium during the post-verdict press conference and surrounded the image with clip art hearts and "girl crush" sayings. That moment when Dean and I were most disappointed and angry became an Internet heartthrob meme that went viral and found its way onto Valentine's Day cards and T-shirts.

After the press conference, I called Kathy. She, of course, had watched it live, and she consoled me—she knew just how bad I felt. I told her more about how angry I was and how worried I was about Avery's safety that night, even though I was powerless to do anything more than pointedly and publicly put Manitowoc County on notice at the press conference.

Dean and I then packed up our laptops in that basement courthouse room where we'd stored our gear and waited for the verdict, and left. We parted ways that night despondent but grateful that we'd had the chance to work together on such a difficult case. We would talk again soon, but now it was time for us to return home. I didn't feel like spending another night alone in the Appleton apartment, so I just gathered a few belongings and drove home through the darkness to Brookfield. I would return a few days later with a van to pack up the apartment for good, but that Sunday night I just wanted to go home as soon as I could. I have no memory of even seeing the road signs or billboards on the way. I left the radio off and drove in silence, my mind swirling, already second-guessing everything I had done for the last six weeks. It was bittersweet knowing that tonight I would sleep in my own bed while Steven Avery would, yet again, lie down in a jail cell. I slept poorly that night, and I'm sure he did, too.

As soon as I woke up the next day, I called the Manitowoc County Jail. When they said Steven Avery was fine, I exhaled.

33

I had lost cases before, but this one felt different. I walked through a fog during the days that followed. Most attorneys feel a letdown after a long trial, win or lose. The sudden decrease in adrenaline probably drives most of it. In those first few days, it is hard to move on to other tasks. I expected it to be the same in this case, but I found it very hard to disengage at all. I had many other clients whom I'd had to put on the back burner for months, including Ralph Armstrong, and they deserved my attention now. He was awaiting a new trial, but we had filed motions asking for the charges to be dismissed. There would be a hearing in a week or so, and in the meantime I had to ponder that intriguing e-mail from Fawn Cave I'd received during the middle of the Avery trial. But still, I just couldn't stop thinking about this trial. I was like one of those bitter-end Japanese soldiers, found on remote Pacific islands in late 1945, who did not realize that World War II had ended six months earlier.

For weeks I tormented myself by second-guessing everything I had done before and during the trial. *If only I had done this or that, maybe the outcome would have been different.* I received calls and e-mails from other defense attorneys expressing their support, but, as generous and well-meaning as everyone was, I took no comfort from them. Looking back, I was probably clinically depressed. Trial lawyers come out on the short end all the time, and if you cannot handle losing, then you've got to get out of the business. It's not that you brush off a loss; I'm always disappointed when my clients do not prevail. But somehow, the disappointment of the Avery verdict landed harder, and weighed on me longer, than any other in my career.

I also thought about the Halbach family and whether the verdict in the Steven Avery case would bring them any solace after their unfathomable loss. They did not ask to be placed in this position, but they carried themselves with dignity throughout what must have been some very difficult testimony to hear. I wondered if they had any doubts after hearing about the suspicious circumstances in which much of the evidence was discovered. If Steven Avery was not the perpetrator, then a terrible injustice had been done to the Halbach family as well because Teresa's real killer got off free. How would they feel if, years later, forensic tests exonerated Avery and perhaps implicated another person, as happened to Penny Beerntsen in 2003?

I had very little direct communication with the Halbach family, although they were in the courtroom with me every day. That's just the way it is in a homicide trial; defense attorneys are always in an uncomfortable position with victims' families. We are there to defend the person accused of killing their loved one, and it is rare that a case comes to trial with any doubt in the minds of the victim's family members about whether the defendant is guilty as charged. Victims' rights advocates from the prosecutor's office are with the family constantly, in and outside the courtroom, so the families naturally bond with the prosecution—and trust that the prosecutors are going after the true perpetrator. This is one reason why prosecutors can be so stubborn about reopening a case even after DNA tests of critical evidence have excluded the original defendant. How do prosecutors explain to a victim, or a victim's family, that they imprisoned the wrong person and, in doing so, allowed the guilty party to escape justice? Good prosecutors with integrity somehow summon the courage to have that conversation when it's appropriate, but I don't envy them.

Then Ken Kratz, of all people, provided me with the purpose I needed. In an interview after the verdict in the Dassey case, Kratz said Brendan's trial and confessions demonstrated how truly evil Steven Avery was. This really riled me up. Kratz opened a door that allowed me to do what Brendan's own attorneys had failed to do, which was show the world that his confession was false. This would prove that Steven Avery was wrongly accused of not only Teresa Halbach's murder but also of roping his nephew in as an accomplice.

Almost ten years would pass before my last surge of effort on behalf of Steven Avery and Brendan Dassey would be vindicated.

The trial of Brendan Dassey started just a few weeks after Steven Avery's verdict was delivered, and in my obsessive fugue, I followed the live stream on my office computer. His trial featured many of the same witnesses as his uncle's had, except that there was no physical evidence whatsoever implicating Brendan. The only evidence against him were his own words.

Viewers of *Making a Murderer*, who saw the travesty of Brendan's interrogations—first by Fassbender and Wiegert and then by defense investigator Mike O'Kelly—might well have been perplexed as to how Brendan could ever be convicted on such evidence. The answer is simple, and shocking. People who have watched the documentary know far more about those interrogations than the jurors who sat in judgment of Brendan in 2007 did.

Remarkably, across two entire trials, the three full, recorded interrogations of Brendan were not made public. Because Brendan Dassey did not testify against Steven Avery, to our disappointment, those tapes had not come into evidence. And in Brendan's own trial, only part of one had been used. I was shocked and mystified when his lawyers allowed the prosecution to cut off the last twenty minutes of that March 1, 2006, interrogation. I also could not understand why they never called Dr. Lawrence T. White, an expert on false and unreliable confessions, whom we had engaged to review Brendan's statements in the event that he was called as a witness at the Steven Avery trial. Dr. White was fully prepared (and paid for) by us already, and he would have been an entirely logical—and vital—expert witness at Brendan's trial, given that the entire defense was built around the claim that he had falsely confessed. We had offered Dr. White to Brendan's lawyers, at no expense. Instead, they had a psychologist who only spoke about Brendan's cognitive limitations. The judge presiding over Brendan's trial, Manitowoc County Circuit Court judge Jerome Fox, ruled that this witness was not competent to discuss how the detectives' interrogation technique was coercive and leading; many courts had already ruled that Dr. White *was* qualified to provide exactly such testimony.

The questioning of Brendan on March 1, 2006, made it painfully clear how little he understood the implications of a police interrogation. He thought he could simply go back to class after admitting that he'd raped and killed Teresa Halbach and mutilated her remains. Brendan's interrogators left him alone in the room while they went to tell his mother that he had confessed. The tape recording continued while Brendan was alone in the room, making for a stretch of dead footage about fifteen minutes long. Ostensibly to save the jury from sitting through that period of silence, the prosecutors proposed to cut off the remainder of that interview. Brendan's lawyers agreed, for reasons I still do not understand.

This meant that the jurors did not see or hear Brendan's mother, Barb Janda, coming into the interrogation room after that fifteen-minute dead spell. She was Brendan's first contact with someone other than a police officer.

Almost immediately, he tells her, "They got to my head."

Dassey's lawyers tried to introduce tapes of the two other interrogations from the day before, which showed in detail how investigators had pushed Brendan, assuring him falsely that they knew what had actually happened and that if he were honest with them, they would help him out. This was right out of the Reid technique interrogation playbook. But Ken Kratz and the prosecution team were able to block the introduction of these tapes, arguing that those taped recordings were hearsay and inadmissible when offered by a defendant. Prosecutor Tom Fallon, who had the lead role in Brendan's trial, was clearly a better attorney than Kratz, and I respected his talent and skill, but I was disappointed when he told the jury in his closing argument that "innocent people don't confess." Almost certainly, he knew that was not true. It is a phenomenon beyond debate.

Most troubling of all, the prosecution told different stories about the same murder to the two different juries. In Steven Avery's trial, Kratz had argued that a bullet fragment recovered from Avery's garage showed that Teresa Halbach was killed there and that "only one man" was responsible for her death. That man was Steven Avery. Kratz also said that it wasn't surprising that there was no blood evidence in Avery's bedroom because she was killed in the garage, not the bedroom. But to Brendan's jury, the prosecutors delivered another version of events entirely, relying on part of Brendan's March 1, 2006, statement. Just a few weeks after telling the Steven Avery jurors that Teresa Halbach had been murdered in his garage, they claimed that she was stabbed and killed in the bedroom of Steven Avery's trailer—and two people, he and Brendan Dassey, were responsible.

This was duplicitous and, in my view, a violation of the due process rights of Steven Avery and Brendan Dassey. In an earlier case, a federal court of appeals had ruled that the use of such a tactic was a "foul blow," and he said that the state's "duty to its citizens does not allow it to pursue as many convictions as possible without regard to fairness or the search for the truth."

However, almost none of this was appreciated by the public, or in our case, by Judge Willis, who had not seen the Brendan Dassey interrogation tape recordings. Those statements were not, after all, evidence in the case that had been before Judge Willis, and in Brendan's trial, Judge Fox excluded the two interrogations of Brendan's that would have shown the arm-twisting. Hardly anyone knew the whole story. That was going to change. After Brendan's conviction, a triumphant Kratz publicly declared that Brendan Dassey's statements showed what a terrible person Steven Avery was and that Judge Willis should take that into account in sentencing Avery. But Kratz gave no indication that he would actually give those statements to the judge. Everyone already knew what he was talking about, or *thought* they did.

This gave me an opening. For the next two weeks, I worked night and day to assemble a full picture of the Brendan Dassey interrogations: the goading, leading, trickery, and pushing of a hapless sixteen-year-old. I went through all of the tapes again, then wrote a fifty-eight-page sentencing memorandum that could function as a road map for Judge Willis as he navigated through hours of excruciating conversation between an intellectually and emotionally stunted teenager and experienced adult interrogators hell-bent on getting that young man to implicate his uncle and himself. It cataloged how and when the investigators fed answers to Brendan, and showed that he knew nothing significant that was not told to him by the interrogators. Included in our filing was Dr. White's report, which we had been unable to use at Steven Avery's trial; now, at least, it would be in the record. I also provided the court with complete transcripts of Brendan's interrogations, which ran to over four hundred pages. And for good measure, I filed DVDs with the video of his statements, and burned eight additional sets to provide to the press. Almost *none* of these things had yet seen the light of day.

Preparing all of this was an arduous task. But we could not have been more emphatic about the import of these materials for both Steven Avery and Brendan Dassey. In our brief, we said:

> The Brendan Dassey jury not only did not hear all of the statements that Brendan made to the police so it could judge fully what he said and how they came about, but they also were deprived of the kind of expert testimony necessary to assist them in understanding how certain police questionings may have affected the reliability of what Brendan told police. . . .
>
> A complete review of all the taped interrogations reveals . . . much more that explains why Brendan confessed to something he did not do. Because the jury in Brendan's trial did not hear most of Brendan's statements, or the full context of how they came about, this Court cannot simply rely on that jury's conviction to conclude at Avery's sentencing that he did any of the things Brendan described.

In the end, Judge Willis said he would *not* rely on Brendan's statements when sentencing Avery and, at our urging, even went a step further. A presentencing investigation of Steven Avery included a great deal of material attributed to Brendan Dassey, and if this was taken as

a legitimate finding, it could have a significant impact on the circumstances of Avery's incarceration. Prodded by us, Judge Willis wrote a
letter for the record on June 6, 2007, stating that there had been no
determination of Brendan's credibility by him or the jury in Steven
Avery's case. Indeed, two of the charges added because of Brendan's
account—sexual assault and kidnapping—were dropped by the state
before the Avery trial.

Judge Willis also made two findings that infuriated Kratz.

"The physical and forensic evidence introduced at Mr. Avery's trial
failed to provide corroborating support for a number of the allegations
attributed to Mr. Dassey," he wrote. "As one significant example, there
was no physical or scientific evidence demonstrating that Teresa Halbach was ever present in Mr. Avery's trailer."

In conclusion, Judge Willis also noted that two expert witnesses
"both called into question much of the information provided by Brendan Dassey because of his intellectual limitations, his susceptibility to
suggested answers, and the nature of the investigative techniques used."

Although these statements came close to a complete repudiation
of the entire Brendan Dassey narrative, they had little practical effect
on Steven Avery's fate. Brendan had not physically been present during
Steven Avery's trial, but his words had still haunted the courtroom.

Steven Avery did not say much at his sentencing, other than to reiterate
his insistence that he'd had nothing to do with the crime. "Well, your
Honor, I'm sorry for the Halbach family, Teresa Halbach's family, what
they are going through, the pain, the hate they got. There's nothing
else going to bring her back, you know. And my family, what they
are going through, and everybody's friends, and the community, it's
hurting everybody. And for myself, Teresa Halbach I didn't kill. I am
innocent of what all of this. And I figure later on, I will prove myself
innocent. I will take it from there. That's all I got. Thank you."

Unsurprisingly, Judge Willis gave him life without a possibility of
parole.

Few reporters paid more than glancing attention to my public filing on the unreliability of Brendan's story. One television journalist did a story, but other than that, the entire subject dropped from sight; it would not then cause any public soul-searching about what had gone wrong.

Not only had the prosecutors, the defense lawyers, and the judicial system failed Brendan. The press had, too.

34

After our shared eighteen-month immersion in the world of Steven Avery, Dean and I were eager to return to our own separate practices. We would work on a couple of matters together, neither of which even made it to court as the prosecutor decided not to issue charges, but otherwise we did not see that much of each other.

When Steven Avery's trial concluded, I received another e-mail about Ralph Armstrong from Fawn Cave. She was frustrated that I had not responded to her yet, so I apologized and asked her to be patient. Then I got in touch with Ralph. He faintly remembered Fawn and was dumbfounded by her story. His brother, Stephen, had left Madison soon after his arrest, and Ralph had not heard from him since. He agreed that we should follow up. My investigator contacted Fawn, and also her former friend, Debbie Holsomback, who had been with her when Stephen Armstrong told them *he* had really killed Charise; the two had fled in fear with their children that same night. As it turned out, they had *both* called John Norsetter at the prosecutor's office in 1995 to tell him this. That was ten years earlier!

Norsetter had never told us.

The Madison prosecutor may not have cared about Fawn Cave and Debbie Holsomback's story, but we did. Ralph's retrial was already pending, and we had brought motions to dismiss for misconduct involving the destruction of exculpatory evidence—a semen stain found in new testing of the bathrobe belt. While that was in front of the Wisconsin Court of Appeals, we informed the court of this astounding new information from, and it ordered a hearing. A new judge was assigned, and the case inched along as appeal cases are wont to do. It would be nearly two years before a hearing was held, in April 2009.

All courtrooms see their share of drama, but the testimony at that hearing was rare and vivid. The star witness turned out not to be Cave but her friend Holsomback. As the judge noted, she was a manager with IBM—a credible, responsible person who had only fleeting, but indelible, contact with the Armstrong clan. Attorney Keith Belzer, who had come aboard to help me with Ralph's case, took her testimony.

"How old are you, ma'am?" Belzer asked.

"Forty-four, fixin' to be forty-five," Holsomback replied.

She had first met Fawn Cave around 1994, when they were both living on the same street in a suburb of Fort Worth, Texas. They had children the same age who played together, and so were friendly but not terribly close. One day in the spring or fall of 1995, Holsomback explained, Cave had asked her for a ride to Roswell, New Mexico. Cave's mother lived there, and one of her sons, along with a niece and nephew, had been staying with their grandmother. It was time for them to come home, but Cave did not have enough space for everyone in her car. Debbie Holsomback had a truck—a Ford Limited-Edition Dallas Cowboys F-150, "Number 998 out of 1,000," she testified—with an extended cab. The kids and their things would all fit. It was a full day's drive from Fort Worth, but on the way back they'd make a stop at Carlsbad Caverns National Park.

A few minutes after they'd arrived at Cave's mother's house, a man came into the kitchen and put his arm around Fawn. The man was Stephen Armstrong; Holsomback did not know who he was, nor did she know who Ralph Armstrong was.

"What happened after he put his around Fawn and said something in her ear?" Belzer asked.

"He looked at Fawn and he said, 'You remember my brother Ralph?' Fawn nodded in compliance, yes, and he said, 'You know he's in prison in Madison, Wisconsin?' And she said, 'Okay.' And he said, 'He's looking for me and he wants me dead.'"

Holsomback said she'd began to wonder what she had gotten herself into. "And Fawn looks at Steve and says, 'Why would he want you dead? And he said, Steve says, 'Because I was supposed to show up at trial, and I didn't, to testify.'"

She continued, "And he says, 'You know that new DNA testing

that they're doing?' And we both, you know, nodded, and he said, 'It's gonna come back that Ralph didn't do it because I did.'"

Q. Okay. He indicated to you and Fawn that he had did it?

A. Yes.

Q. At this point did you even know exactly what, when he said he did it, what he was referring to?

A. No, not at that time. I thought, "He did it—did what?"

She would soon find out.

Q. What else did he say?

A. Steve was in Madison the weekend that this occurred.

Q. Okay. Go ahead.

A. He talked about how—that he had taken a bus into Madison, Wisconsin, and that he didn't have any luggage. He had to give Ralph all of his money to purchase clothes, toiletries, and such, and that they had partied all, you know, day with Ralph's friends, and that he was asked to take—to be taken back to Ralph's apartment prior to anybody else. And then he went into detail about the victim and called her names and said she got what she deserved, and it just escalated from there.

Q. Okay. Did he indicate that he had assaulted her in any way?

A. He didn't call it an assault.

Q. Okay.

A. He called it—he said that she enjoyed it and that he would have continued if the bitch hadn't died.

Q. At this point what did you understand him to be saying when he said that?

A. I understood him to say that he was the murderer.

Q. Okay. And that she enjoyed it, what did you understand him to be saying by that?

A. That she enjoyed everything that he did to her. What we would call, you know, violating her in every fashion and manner, he put it as if it was just a pleasurable thing.

Q. Okay. How did listening to Steve Armstrong say these things make you feel?

A. Well, I don't have a poker face, obviously, so I was scared. I wanted to get out of there, but I didn't want to alarm him because I could not imagine, for the life of me, why this person would be telling us these things unless there was some—he had no intention of letting us go, and so I just tried to remain calm, act like anything he said wasn't shocking, and try to figure out a way where I could get Fawn and the kids and myself out of there and we would just go to a hotel.

Q. When he was saying these things to you, can you describe for us what his demeanor was? I mean, how was he acting?

A. He was—you know, to be able to gauge it would be difficult because I did not know this person other than this being my first meeting, so to speak. He didn't seem agitated. He seemed pretty calm. He was clear in his description. It was just like, you know, water cooler talk. I mean that's the only way I know in how to describe it because I can't compare it to anything because I didn't know him prior to this.

Q. When Steve Armstrong stated to you and Ms. Cave that he had committed this murder, did you believe him?

A. Yes.

Holsomback and Cave went into the bathroom together, but Stephen Armstrong knocked on the door to ask them what we were doing. They opened the door and told him that girls always go to bathrooms in pairs.

"That was the only excuse we could think of, but we were talking about how we were going to get out of there."

Cave and her mother also conferred.

"I had brought with me a crossword puzzle book, so while Fawn was trying to get her mother's attention, I was sitting in the eating area, and in the crossword puzzles, the little squares, I wrote the things that Steve had said in the squares," Holsomback testified. All of the other adults had gone outside, leaving her with Armstrong in the eating area, which at that time had two mattresses in it.

"He went from one mattress over to the mattress I was sitting on and started stroking my hair and complimenting me and such and wanted to know if he could help me with my crossword puzzle," she said.

Q. Okay. And this is the crossword puzzle where you were writing down what he said?

A. Writing down what he was saying, and I kept flipping pages thinking please don't let him see what I'm writing.

Q. Why were you writing down what he was saying in a cross-word puzzle book?

A. For one, it reinforces my memory, and with me, writing it down, I couldn't forget. Not that I would ever forget what he had said, but it was just something to be able to remember the words that he chose, how he did it, and things of that nature.

Q. So he came over to you where you were sitting now and started playing with your hair?

A. Yes.

Q. Okay, what did you do?

A. I tried to remain calm, and I told him to please excuse me while I went to the little girl's room, and I got up and took my purse along with my crossword puzzle book to the bathroom.

She moved into the living room with the kids, and a few minutes later heard a scream. Cave, her mother, and her mother's boyfriend ran in from the backyard and went into the mother's bedroom.

"I go into the bedroom. Fawn is so upset, she's crying, she's hysterical, she's saying how he's going to get her, 'he's going to get me.' I'm trying to get her to calm down."

Q. At that time did you know who she was talking about?

A. Yes.

Q. Who?

A. Steve.

Holsomback recalled that Cave had become so rattled that she'd stopped making sense.

"It's dark outside and she was gonna raise the window, push the screen out, and go out into the dark, and she was doing this because she wasn't thinking clearly, so I stopped her and said, 'What are you doing? You can't go out into the dark. First off, we're not from here.' And she wouldn't settle down, so I slapped her, told her to take a deep breath and we'd figure it out."

Eventually, they worked out an exit. "The plan was as each person ran out, grab a kid and head to my truck," she said.

The four adults and three children made a break for it.

"Once I got the truck started, everyone except for myself, because I laugh when I'm nervous, were screaming, 'Get out! Here he comes! Here he comes!' When I threw the truck in reverse and hit the gas, you heard this loud"—here Holsomback smacked her hand against the witness stand, making a loud thump—"up against my truck, and I'm thinking oh, good, I ran over him, thinking that's what I did."

Then, she "threw it in drive, hit the gas pedal, and asked them in the backseat to please look in the bed of the truck to make sure that one person, Steve, is not in the truck bed."

They drove to a motel in Roswell and took a room for the night. The following morning, they returned to the house to pick up the children's clothing, bicycles, and other belongings.

"Being daylight, we figured surely to goodness nothing can happen to us," Holsomback testified.

They packed up, but, "as the truck was about to back up out of the driveway, here comes Steve from the street, comes up to the window, knocks on the window. I rolled the window down about that much." She showed a space of about two inches with her fingers.

Armstrong spoke into the truck, she said. "'Where y'all going?' And we said, 'Home.' And that's when he said, 'Well, I know where you live Fawn, and I'll be seeing you,' and he put his hand in a gun position like this and winked at her."

She backed out and they returned to Fort Worth. On the following Tuesday, Debbie Holsomback called the District Attorney's Office in Madison. Fawn was also on the line.

"I told him who I was, who Fawn was, and that we were calling and we wanted to speak to somebody who was involved with the prosecution of Ralph Armstrong. The gentleman who replied said, 'I am. You've got him. I'm John. I'm the one who's personally responsible for getting the conviction against Ralph Armstrong.'"

Q. Okay. At this point then what information did you share with the person who identified himself as John the prosecutor?

A. I had told him that we had met Ralph's brother Steve over the weekend, and that we believe that Steve is actual—the actual murderer. Steve told us that he was there, that he did it. He said that the DNA is going to come back as not being Ralph's, it wouldn't come back as Ralph's because Steve did the murder. I gave him details about what Steve said he did to this woman, and this man John said that he had the right man, that Ralph did this alone.

Q. When he said that he already had the right guy, did you continue to try to talk to him about this?

A. Yes. I asked him if he wouldn't even concede that it could be possible that Steve had done it. After all, this is a man who came into town, to Madison, gave his brother all of his money, had no money, no luggage, but yet the following day he has—when his brother's arrested, in his most time of need, Steve gets the hell out of Dodge? Why would he get, quote/unquote, the hell out of Dodge?

Q. All right. How did you know all that information?

A. Steve had told us this.

Q. He told you that, too, when you were in Roswell?

A. Yes. He told us everything about this weekend in Roswell, about how he had got there, what he did, what he did to this poor girl, and then how he got out once Ralph was arrested.

Q. Do you recall anything else that you said to the person who identified himself as John?

A. There was so many things I had said. I asked him if it would be possible that he had the wrong man in prison. I asked him wouldn't there be a warrant for Steve's arrest since Steve was supposed to testify and didn't, wouldn't there be a bench warrant for him? John said no, there was no bench warrant for him.

Q. Did you, in fact, ask if maybe possibly two people could have done it?

A. Yes, I did. I asked him could it be possible that if he's convinced that Ralph did it by himself, wouldn't it be possible that Steve was there? And he said unequivocally, no, that Ralph did this alone.

Holsomback had not yet started working at IBM in 1995, but the attention to detail and record keeping that would make her so good at that job were already evident.

"When we got back, I had a notebook, a spiral notebook. I had put this crossword puzzle book as well as the phone number that I had called of the Wisconsin District Attorney's Office—Madison, Wisconsin's District Attorney's Office, the date, the time, the person who answered the phone originally, the person who came to the phone and identified himself as the, quote/unquote, person responsible for the conviction, and then when the bill, the phone bill came in, I took the phone bill and put the detail with that notebook."

At the time, Holsomback and her husband were running a business out of their home, and so she put these materials into a box labeled

"1995" and stored it along with the other annual records in their attic. In 2000, she and her husband separated.

"I don't believe in saving a bunch of stuff, but for this one thing, this was very important to me. Because of that, Billy, that was—that would be my ex-husband—took it upon himself to empty the attic without my being there and threw all of this stuff in the garbage," she testified.

By then she had lost touch with Cave, who was no longer living on their block. Holsomback heard nothing from her for eight years, until she called out of the blue to ask if Holsomback remembered what happened in Roswell.

Before the hearing began, I mentioned around the courthouse that we were in the process of obtaining telephone records from 1995 that would show that Cave and Holsomback had indeed called the Madison District Attorney's Office to express their concern about Stephen Armstrong. This wasn't *entirely* true, but even though we were not able to get the records, no one from the prosecutor's office was prepared to testify fourteen years later, under oath, that the call had *not* taken place and risk being confronted with proof that it had. In fact, John Norsetter conceded that he remembered the phone call but decided that he did not have to tell the defense about it because it was not, in his view, credible information. Ralph Armstrong was the murderer. What would change his mind? Only a videotape of Stephen Armstrong committing the murder, he testified.

There were also two other interesting revelations. Stephen Armstrong had been found dead in his home by his landlord in July 2005, just two weeks after the Wisconsin Supreme Court vacated his brother's conviction, and his remains had been cremated. No autopsy was done to determine the cause of death, which was ruled to be by natural causes. I had been suspicious about Ralph Armstrong's brother even before then because he had seemed to just disappear twenty-five years ago. But the timing of Stephen's death was especially peculiar, and I wondered if he had learned about the reversal of his brother's conviction before he died. After I learned he was cremated, I even tracked down his landlord to see if any of his personal effects remained—a hairbrush, toothbrush, envelopes he might have licked, *anything* that might yield his DNA if we needed it in the future. But Stephen's residence had been cleared out, and nothing remained.

The following year, as the Dane County District Attorney's Office got ready to retry Ralph Armstrong, Norsetter ran a "Lexis-Nexis People Search" in May, a few weeks after the April 2006 DNA test excluded both Ralph Armstrong and Brian Dillman as the source of the newly discovered semen stain on the bathrobe belt. I later discovered in the police file a printout of the computer search showing that Stephen Armstrong was deceased, and there were little ink pen check marks next to all of the other paternal relatives of Ralph Armstrong who were listed as deceased. I was then in my early weeks on the Steven Avery case and had not yet been contacted by Fawn Cave. But having received that phone call from two frightened women in 1995, and now the new DNA exclusion of Ralph Armstrong and Brian Dillman, I believe Norsetter had reason to know that Stephen Armstrong should have been a suspect in the murder. Moreover, Norsetter testified that he *knew* Stephen Armstrong had no alibi for the time of the murder. There was more. The police had evidence from at least one of Charise Kamps's friends that she had confided that she'd recently been "stepping out on her boyfriend," and she'd told another friend that she was "going out on a date with Ralph's brother" the night that she died.

After reviewing the DNA tests that John Norsetter had secretly ordered in 2006, Oneida County Circuit Court reserve judge Robert E. Kinney, who had been assigned to the Armstrong case in Dane County, issued a twenty-nine-page decision declaring that the prosecution had acted in bad faith, violated court orders, and failed to carry out its duties to disclose exculpatory information to the defense. Judge Kinney was meticulous in his reading of the record and admirable for his ability to see behind the prosecution's blustering. The secret communications with the crime laboratory, after what Judge Kinney called my "hypervigilance" about the evidence, seemed to particularly offend him. Norsetter had said he just forgot to tell me about the additional lab testing he ordered.

The judge ruled that, "in light of Buting's constant letters and e-mails on this very subject, it is unreasonable to believe that Norsetter simply forgot about the requirement of notice to Buting."

Judge Kinney wrote, "The prosecution, by having private dealings with [the crime lab analysts], treated them like partisan witnesses. When results unfavorable to the State came in and the prosecutor directed more testing, what message was communicated?"

In the end, that newfound semen stain was sufficiently degraded that the unauthorized Y-DNA tests Norsetter ordered did not yield a full DNA profile. Still, I argued that it was highly suspicious that the tests Norsetter ordered would have produced a Y-DNA profile that could not distinguish between Stephen and Ralph Armstrong, who shared the same father, since paternally related individuals have the same Y-DNA. This would have effectively framed Ralph Armstrong with his brother's Y-DNA, and because, as Norsetter knew, Stephen Armstrong had been cremated, Ralph Armstrong could not obtain a nuclear DNA test to distinguish himself from his brother. But Judge Kinney would not go that far. He said he was not ruling that Norsetter had chosen the particular Y-DNA tests for the purpose of thwarting Ralph in clearing himself or, possibly, pinning the crime on Stephen. Nevertheless, he found the behavior of the prosecution was in "bad faith," and that the state's "misconduct" seriously prejudiced the defense.

Could Stephen Armstrong have been the real killer of Charise Kamps? Judge Kinney reviewed the record:

> The record here clearly raises many questions. The jury heard evidence that Stephen Armstrong arrived by bus in Madison on Sunday, June 22, 1980; the victim told a friend she was going on a date with "Ralph's brother;" pubic hairs were found at the scene that appeared to have been pulled out that did not match either the defendant or the victim's boyfriend; no blood or any physical evidence of any kind was found in the defendant's car, although the State's eyewitness said the perpetrator had made several trips back and forth from the victim's apartment to his car; there were

no traces of blood on the boots worn by the defendant. New DNA testing about which the jury did not hear showed that the defendant was excluded as the source of a semen stain on the robe as well as hairs found on the robe belt which was draped over the victim's body; the defendant was excluded from being the source of DNA on many separate items tested by the State as reported in its April 2006 lab report. So, if a new jury heard all of the above, along with evidence of a confession made by Stephen Armstrong, would it have made a difference? Our Supreme Court has already ruled that, even without evidence of a Stephen Armstrong confession, "the real controversy was not tried." While Norsetter could not have known, in 1995, about the Supreme Court's ruling or all of the parts of the State's case that DNA testing would later unravel, some of the DNA test results had come in by then and they were exculpatory. Significantly, what Norsetter unquestionably did know in 1995 was that the defendant was represented by lawyers who were pursuing a claim of actual innocence. According to [the United States Supreme Court],[*] "the prudent prosecutor will resolve doubtful questions in favor of disclosure."

John Norsetter chose not to disclose the confession of a third party, and that—along with the state's destruction of evidence—irreparably compromised Armstrong's ability to establish a viable third-party defense to the crime. "The failure of the prosecutor to disclose Stephen Armstrong's confession, coupled with his death and cremation, leaves the defense without a reference DNA sample with which to establish the veracity of the confession."

In light of the prosecution's actions resulting in the destruction of exculpatory evidence, and its suppression of the confession of a viable third-party suspect, Judge Kinney concluded:

The facts of this case are as unusual as a five-hundred-year rain. But

---

[*] *United States v. Agurs,* 427 U.S. 97, 108, 96 S. Ct. 2392, 2399–400 (1976).

the prejudice to the defense was not an act of nature. It stemmed from a series of conscious decisions that had very adverse consequences.

Because the defendant's due process right to a fair trial has been irreparably compromised, the defense motion is granted and the case is dismissed.

This order was dated July 30, 2009, by which time Ralph Armstrong had been in prison for twenty-nine years for a murder he did not commit. And the prosecution was still not finished.

At the time Charise Kamps was killed, Armstrong had been on parole from a conviction in New Mexico when he was a teenager. He'd admitted to drinking and taking drugs on the night of the killing, which was a violation of the terms of his parole. Although that drinking and carousing had happened three decades earlier, when he had been a graduate student, the authorities in Wisconsin urged the New Mexico parole officials to revoke his status, which had been in abeyance all those years of his incarceration. Instead of being released from prison in Wisconsin, Ralph was shipped to one in New Mexico.

If the State of Wisconsin was not done tormenting Ralph Armstrong, I was not done defending him. I flew to New Mexico and filed a writ of habeas corpus, demanding his release—which would take another year.

Part VIII

THINKING OUT LOUD

35

Laura Ricciardi and Moira Demos returned to Wisconsin to cover post-conviction hearings for both Steven Avery and Brendan Dassey, the last of which ended in December 2010. By then they had shot hundreds of hours of film, and it was obvious that they had way too much material for a standard-length documentary. We heard that they had hopes of making a four-hour film that would air over two nights, in the style of what used to be a called a miniseries. I saw them both after one of Brendan's hearings and learned that they'd finished a portion of the film to use in pitches to buyers and broadcast outlets. But it was a long, complex story of a crime in rural Wisconsin that had no famous people involved and no satisfying conclusion, and, so far, no one had bought it.

Netflix, meanwhile, was realizing that it needed original productions to provide to its subscribers. When the company had started, few of the major studios expected that streaming would become such a powerful way to distribute movies, and so the studios had liberally—that is, cheaply—licensed rights to films and television shows that they controlled. As those rights expired, however, the price to renew them was rising, and the Netflix library started losing valuable titles. To supplement what it could offer, Netflix had to source its own content, made by other creators: *House of Cards*, starring Kevin Spacey and Robin Wright, a remake of the BBC political melodrama series based on the Michael Dobbs novel, and *Orange Is the New Black*, a comedy-drama series adapted from Piper Kerman's memoir about her time in a women's prison. The Steven Avery story would be one of their earliest ventures into a nonfiction, dramatic true crime series, and the filmmakers called me one day to film an epilogue with commentary from several of Avery's past lawyers.

In October 2015, word came that Netflix would release the series on December 18. To me, this seemed terrible timing. Steven Avery's saga was compelling on many levels, but it most assuredly was not feel-good holiday fare. Then I heard that it was going to be ten episodes long, all of them released at once. *Bad marketing*, I thought; they ought to string out the story, build up drama, reveal developments from one episode to the next. That was how the radio podcast, *Serial*, had unfolded, and a huge audience followed it for months. However, no one was asking my opinion on the scheduling.

Just before it aired, Dean and I visited Steven Avery in prison. We wanted to prepare him for the show and its aftermath. Of course, he knew all about the project. I had seen a preview the week before it streamed. (Dean couldn't bring himself to watch.) I knew it was very well done and would make for gripping viewing.

By evening on December 18, both Dean and I were already getting e-mails from people who had watched all ten episodes of *Making a Murderer* that very day. Viewers wrote from all over the United States and from other English-speaking places like the United Kingdom, Ireland, Canada, Australia, New Zealand, and South Africa. But they also e-mailed from Scandinavia, Israel, and much of Europe. Soon, as though *Making a Murderer* was a virus spreading around the globe, I heard from viewers in Brazil, Argentina, Chile, and then the rest of South America. Africa followed, with Côte d'Ivoire and Madagascar, and then the Saharan and sub-Saharan countries. Asia came in the next wave, eventually followed by the Mideast Arabic countries, and finally we began hearing from viewers in Russia, Eastern Europe, China, and Central and South Asia. So much for my opinion that Netflix was making a terrible mistake by dumping ten episodes one week before Christmas. Tens of millions of people have now seen *Making a Murderer*, which received four Emmy Awards, including Best Documentary.

That December would also mark the first time that we would not spend Christmas all together as a family. Our son, Stephen, was at the Pontifical North American College in Rome studying to be a Catholic priest, and he was not able to come home to celebrate. So Kathy, Grace, and I planned to spend two weeks with him in Rome and Sicily, leaving Wisconsin on December 28. By the time our plane took off that evening, it had become obvious that *Making a Murderer* was turning into a huge international phenomenon.

Suddenly, I had over a thousand "friend" requests on Facebook and LinkedIn, nearly all from complete strangers. As for Twitter, my account had been the digital equivalent of a weedy, vacant lot. Two years earlier, I had gone on a mission trip with my church to rehabilitate houses, and some of the younger members in the group opened a Twitter account for me as way for us to keep in touch when we got back. (Now it would probably be Snapchat, or some other new thing that will be created by the time this book is published.) Between then and December 2015, I'd gathered a grand total of eight followers and had posted only a few tweets. Suddenly, *Making a Murderer* viewers started following me in droves, as many as a thousand a day, the number ticking up like a natural gas meter running nonstop in the dead of a Wisconsin winter. I soon had over twenty-five thousand, and as I write this it stands at more than sixty-four thousand.

Dean and I did not agree to be filmed because we wanted fame; for almost everyone who suddenly encounters it, fame is a currency that only plunges in value. Far more important than Twitter followers is the crowdsourced information the series has generated. By the time I was packing for Rome, I was already receiving tips from viewers about facts or scientific advances that might be helpful to Steven Avery's effort to reverse his wrongful conviction. I wanted to fulfill my obligations to protect Steven Avery's interest in obtaining a new trial, so I was careful to collect any information that could help him. Worried about missing something important in the flood of information coming my way, I hired my summer law clerk just before we left for Italy and gave her the passwords to my Facebook, Twitter, and e-mail accounts and asked her to monitor all of it, as well as Google for media reports and Reddit for theories and discussions. She harvested and organized the data into a Word document with links out to the sources, a rich compilation of theories, and possibly useful information. I passed it along to Steven Avery's current lawyer.

Because I was in Italy and inaccessible to American media during the first two weeks of January 2016, Dean's life was completely disrupted by media requests—but he did a yeoman's job with all of it. I did a few American and European newspaper and radio interviews. The one television interview I did while on vacation was a fluke. A college friend of Grace's had spent the fall semester studying in Rome, and we made plans to have dinner with him. Earlier that day, his mother—a local television reporter in Milwaukee—had texted him to see what he was up to. He was winding down in Rome, he said. She did not know that he knew Grace.

Oh!, his mother said, *there is a lawyer from Milwaukee who's become a huge sensation from* Making a Murderer *and he's hiding out in Rome and nobody is able to reach him.* She told her son that if he could, by any chance, locate him, it would be amazing. "I'm having dinner with him tonight," her son responded by text. I laughed so hard when I heard the story that I agreed to a short remote interview via Skype.

I tried not to let the buzz disrupt our family vacation, but it was a challenge. E-mails came in every day, most of them written and sent in the evening from the United States, which was midnight in Italy. Almost every night I spent two to three hours reading through them, until 2:00 a.m. So many people took the time to write such nice things about Dean and me and our advocacy on Steven Avery's behalf, and I am still humbled to this day. It was a stark contrast from the hate mail I received during and after the trial. I did my best to respond to every e-mail, however briefly. If someone took time out of their busy life to locate and write to me, at least I could acknowledge and thank them.

On one evening in Italy, Grace angrily slammed her laptop closed and said she was going to shut down her Facebook account. Since this was her only free method of contact with friends for those two weeks, this made no sense. *Why?* I asked.

"Because all my friends keep talking about 'sexy Jerry Buting'!" she said.

At the end of our trip, Netflix's public relations team was pleading with me to return to America via New York so I could do some quick media appearances. I had not brought appropriate clothing for television on vacation, so I enjoyed shopping for new Italian suits in a few after-Christmas sales. They had told me to expect vast public recognition when I arrived, but I was skeptical; after all, I had been walking around Rome for two weeks and no one had given me a second look.

Once again, Netflix was right and I was wrong. I got no farther than the gate at the airport in Philadelphia, walking to my connecting flight to New York, before people came up to talk and snap selfies. It was surreal.

36

With the spotlights shining straight in my eyes, it was hard to make out the faces of the audience at the Royal Oak Music Theatre in Detroit, but I knew every seat was filled. Dean and I had just been introduced to thunderous applause. Backstage, we had looked at the questions the crowd had written on index cards and submitted ahead of time, and picked out a good cross-section. The public appetite for serious discussion of criminal justice reforms was astounding.

Now the moderator was asking the first question. It was a surprise, one that we had not screened ahead of time. After all of these years in courtrooms, I'm pretty nimble on my feet. But no judge had ever thrown a question like this at me.

"Maria from Detroit asks," the moderator said, "'Jerry, what color boxers or briefs are you wearing right now?'"

Did my jaw drop? Possibly. I definitely could feel myself blushing. The audience tittered. Dean jumped in with a classic lawyer's objection.

"Assumes facts not in evidence," Dean said, "that he's wearing anything!"

The audience roared. I laughed. My glow of happiness about the serious dialogue about criminal justice was just a bit dimmed.

After my family and I returned to America from Italy, I tried to relieve Dean of some of the publicity load and so I gave a number of media interviews. Both of us think that *Making a Murderer* provides an unprecedented look at this country's broken criminal justice system, and we were pleased people were keen to know more. This was especially clear in the many questions we were receiving via e-mail. But as we saw lengthy media interviews compressed to just a few minutes, it became evident that sound bites from us would not be enough.

Dean and I talked one day about how great it would be if we could hold a public forum for ninety minutes or so and answer questions from the audience about the strengths and weaknesses of criminal justice in America. We test-drove our idea at an event in Milwaukee, and it was successful. Soon other cities were interested, and eventually a national tour, "A Conversation on Justice," brought us to twenty cities in North America, and then on to Scandinavia, Ireland, and the Netherlands. The United Kingdom, Australia, and New Zealand have been completed. Everywhere we've gone, we were impressed with the thoughtful questions people have. (Okay, not counting the one about my boxers.)

This tour gave Dean and me the chance to work together again, a blessing that renewed our friendship and allowed me to experience again all those qualities of his that I admire so much. It was not just getting the band together again, though. We got insightful questions at every stop, inspiring me to think deeply about reforms for America's criminal justice system. The first step is calling out the system's flaws as we see them. Next is figuring out what we can do to fix them. Here is a selection of those questions and my replies.

I'm not a lawyer or a police officer or a judge. What can I do to make the system better?

First, start voting.

Local sheriffs and prosecutors have enormous power. They can foster justice, or they can corrupt it. Yet, few Americans bother to vote when these positions are up for election. Often these contests are not scheduled in election cycles for major offices, when voter turnout is highest. When only 15–20 percent of citizens come to the polls to choose who will hold these powerful positions, the winner is "I don't give a damn."

Voter apathy makes it easy for a candidate to stroll into local office, because low-turnout races are easy to exploit. It takes less money and time get a small group of courthouse insiders to vote. A campaign can line up a few powerful local politicians in support of a candidate, often with tacit promises of favors or reciprocation. Lock up the early endorsements of a few insiders, and you can scare off any opponents.

The large number of sheriffs and prosecutors who run unopposed is a testament to the effectiveness of this strategy. One recent study of the ten-year period 1996–2006 found that 80 percent of chief prosecutor incumbents ran unopposed in both general elections and primaries. Incumbent chief prosecutors were reelected 95 percent of the time.[*]

Once elected to the position, incumbents can often stay in power as long as they want; this makes it possible for them to handpick successors and stack the deck to ensure their election. For many positions in the criminal justice system, dynastic inertia carries the day and creates an unbroken chain of insiders who hold these offices—particularly in smaller counties. There is also the argument that entrenched sheriffs and prosecutors have greatly contributed to the problem of mass incarceration in America. Other elected local officials, such as mayors and county managers, have to balance their taxpayer resources among many competing interests, such as police and fire departments, parks, waste management, and streets and utilities. But sheriffs and prosecutors have a singular focus: law enforcement. Voters can only evaluate their performance by how "tough on crime" they appear, often quantified as how many people they lock up in jails and prisons. They don't need to worry about balancing the cost of prosecuting and incarceration against other municipal needs. And once a defendant is sent to prison, the state incurs the cost of incarceration, not the local sheriff or prosecutor. The power of these law enforcement positions is especially evident in how their endorsements are coveted and championed by other candidates who run for office, such as governors and judges.[†]

We need to encourage and support candidates to run for office against entrenched incumbents. This means voting, getting friends to vote, and paying attention to local government. It works. Driven by a greater awareness of criminal justice and the limits of its tra-

---

[*] Ronald F. Wright, "How Prosecutor Elections Fail Us," *Ohio State Journal of Criminal Law* 6, no. 581 (2009): 592.

[†] J. Hoeffel and S. Singer, "Elections, Power, and Local Control: Reining in Chief Prosecutors and Sheriffs." *University of Maryland Law Journal: Race, Religion, Gender & Class* 15, no. 2 (2015): 319.

ditional approaches, voters in some larger cities are rejecting hackneyed promises to "lock 'em up and throw away the key." Veteran prosecutors in Chicago, Cleveland, and Jacksonville, Florida, all lost primaries in 2016.

But as important as elections are, they have proven to be a poor way to pick judges. Some favor judicial elections over judicial appointments by their governor because they fear political partisanship or corruption. However, the practice of judicial elections exposes candidates to the pressures of fund-raising, pandering, and other perils of political campaigns. These races are becoming saturated with money from special interest groups, particularly at the appellate level. One alternative is to select judges using a merit panel system, and then requiring that they stand for a retention vote after they have served a term on the bench. About twenty states employ this approach today, and most believe it preserves judicial independence more than elections do.

Second, embrace jury service.

Serving on a jury is the most direct way an ordinary citizen can have an impact on our criminal justice system. Indeed, it's the only opportunity to participate in the judicial branch of our government. But so many people dread receiving a jury summons in the mail almost as much as a root canal. It doesn't pay enough money; the selection process is tedious; and responsibilities such as young children or a small business are incompatible with jury service, particularly for a lengthy trial. This leaves only a small pool of potential jurors who may not be representative of the community, much less of the defendant's peers.

Before you immediately start brainstorming about how you can get out of jury service, it's important to understand that honestly performing your civic responsibility of jury service defends the same constitution that many men and women have lost their lives fighting for. And nobody gets shot at during jury duty. Doing your part doesn't mean that you must actually sit on a jury. You can serve equally well by being honest with the judge and lawyers if you cannot be impartial in a particular case because of pretrial publicity or personal experiences in your life.

Third, be a discerning, critical consumer of media.

Next time you see pictures in the newspaper or television footage showing people in handcuffs being led out of a police stationhouse by detectives, remember that those people most likely have been alone with the police for hours. They may not have had a lawyer present. No one has yet examined the evidence on *their* behalf. These "perp walks" are strutting pieces of theater that subvert the presumption of innocence and the due process to which all of us are entitled.

And remember that the full story does not get told at events staged by law enforcement and prosecution for the media. Just think back to those press conferences held by Ken Kratz.

What can be done to stop the coercive questioning of vulnerable people like Brendan?

We need statutes that bar the custodial interrogation of young people without counsel. Teenagers are particularly vulnerable to pressure from adults. One study of 340 exonerations found that juveniles under the age of eighteen were three times as likely to falsely confess as adults.[*] Time and again we've seen ghastly mistakes come out of sessions where detectives assume that a minor has committed a terrible crime and won't relent until the young person has admitted to it. The California Supreme Court accepted that a ten-year-old boy could waive his *Miranda* rights and admit to killing his abusive, neo-Nazi father.[†]

---

[*] Bluhm Legal Clinic, "Wrongful Convictions of Youth: Understand the Problem," Northwestern Pritzker School of Law. http://www.law.northwestern.edu/legalclinic /wrongfulconvictionsyouth/.

[†] M. Levick and S. Drizin, "Letting a Ten-Year-Old Waive His *Miranda* Rights? There Oughtta Be a Law," *Huffington Post*, October 21, 2015. http://www.huffingtonpost .com/marsha-levick/letting-a-ten-year-old-wa_b_8342988.html.

In Virginia, Robert Davis, an eighteen-year old man, falsely implicated by a high school classmate in the murder of a woman and her child, was interrogated for five hours while shackled in a cold room. Finally, he asked, "What can I say to get me out of this?" and said he was involved in the crime. The Virginia governor granted him a full pardon in 2015 after he had served thirteen years.[*] There have been multiple, infamous cases in Chicago. In New York, the interrogation of five young teens resulted in their wrongful conviction for violently assaulting a jogger in Central Park. Meanwhile, the real culprit continued a rampage of rape, maiming, and murder.

Illinois recently passed a variation of a bill colloquially referred to in social media as "Brendan's Law," which limits police interrogation of juveniles in custody. Under the new law, no one under the age of fifteen can be interrogated on a sex or murder case without a lawyer present, a compromise when juvenile justice advocates lobbied for anyone under age seventeen. Unfortunately, such a law would not have protected sixteen-year-old Brendan Dassey, but it's a good first step. The law also requires mandatory recording of juvenile felony interrogations of anyone under age eighteen.

Similar legislation was introduced in Tennessee after *Making a Murderer* was released.[†] It was not enacted, but the sponsor intends to reintroduce it next year.

It's also time for American law enforcement to end use of the Reid technique for interrogation, which is largely based on outmoded psychological assumptions that have never been supported by empirical evidence. These include the belief that police are good human lie detectors when multiple studies have shown otherwise. The Reid technique has been implicated in many false confessions, particularly those

---

[*] Lisa Provence, "Robert Davies Receives Pardon," *C-Ville,* December 21, 2015. http://www.c-ville.com/robert-davis-receives-pardon/#.V_VwTZMrIW2.

[†] Scott Broden, "Bill Addressing Child Interrogation May Get New Life," *Daily News Journal,* April 19, 2016. http://www.dnj.com/story/news/2016/04/19/bill-addressing-child-interrogation-may-get-new-life/83229008/.

involving young or mentally challenged suspects. The company that trains the technique to law enforcement contends that false confessions are caused by officers who apply inappropriate methods not endorsed by the company. That's a convenient excuse for a company with a significant profit motive.

Much of the rest of the English-speaking world has abandoned the Reid technique already. Some use a less confrontational method known by the acronym PEACE (preparation and planning, engage and explain, account, closure, and evaluate). Following this approach, officers allow a suspect to tell his story without interruption, and only later go back to get more detailed facts and present the suspect with any inconsistencies between the story and other evidence. Importantly, the police are prohibited from deceiving suspects during an interview, such as falsely claiming there is DNA or fingerprint evidence or a nonexistent claim by an accomplice linking them to the crime.

We were fortunate that Wisconsin law required a full recording of Brendan Dassey's multiple interrogations, even though his jury did not get to hear most of them. They were so appalling that I fought to make them public record. Later, a federal magistrate reviewed them all and found them to be impermissibly coercive; the federal magistrate overturned Brendan's conviction.

So-called videotaped confessions often amount to little more than a few minutes of recordings that are the result of a much longer—and, most importantly, unseen—process of cajoling, pressuring, and promising suspects. We know that innocent people confessed in between 20 and 25 percent of all the DNA exoneration cases. Why? What happened before that camera was turned on? Some police departments and prosecutors still resist recording the interrogation process out of vague concerns that the public will overreact to tactics that law enforcement see as necessary, if not pleasing to watch. But many agencies that do fully record such sessions emphatically endorse it. If the process is clean, the video will show that, and the odds are high that the case will result in a plea bargain without a trial. If it's not, the Brendan Dasseys of the world should be able to bring the recordings before a jury and show why they should not be believed.

Recording technology is ubiquitous and inexpensive. The United States Department of Justice in 2014 announced a presumption that agents (FBI, DEA [Drug Enforcement Administration], ATF [Bureau of Alcohol, Tobacco, Firearms and Explosives]) must record full and complete interrogations in any place of detention. This completely flipped prior policy that discouraged recording. Yet, as I write in 2016, only half the states require by statute or court rule that all parts of a custodial interrogation must be recorded.* State citizens should lobby for mandatory recordings if they do not currently enjoy that protection.

What about crime laboratories?

Crime laboratories, and the technicians who work there, are routinely treated as just another arm of law enforcement during investigations. But when these technicians come into court they are presented as "objective" experts rather than partisan witnesses. The leaders of these laboratories should build walls that prevent law enforcement and prosecution involvement in evidence testing, which is what so clearly occurred during the cases of Steven Avery and Ralph Armstrong. This process should include requirements that all tests should be confirmed by a separate team of lab technicians who do not know the identity of the suspect or what the "right" answer should be.

Lab results must be replicable by others. That is the foundation of the scientific process. The history of DNA exonerations is instructive: About *half* of all innocence cases involved invalidated or improper

---

* See Thomas P. Sullivan, National Association of Criminal Defense Lawyers, *Compendium: Electronic Recording of Custodial Interrogations* (2014), https://www.nacdl.org/WorkArea/DownloadAsset.aspx?id=33287&libID=33256 (including Alaska, Arkansas, California, Illinois, Indiana, Maine, Maryland, Michigan, Minnesota, Missouri, Montana, Nebraska, New Jersey, North Carolina, Ohio, Oregon, Texas, Vermont, Wisconsin, and the District of Columbia).

forensic "science." In 2010, the National Academy of Sciences issued a report, *Strengthening Forensic Science in the United States,*[*] which was critical of the current state of many of the various fields of forensic science in America:

> The simple reality is that the interpretation of forensic evidence is not always based on scientific studies to determine its validity. This is a serious problem. Although research has been done in some disciplines, there is a notable dearth of peer-reviewed, published studies establishing the scientific bases and validity of many forensic methods. . . .
>
> A body of research is required to establish the limits and measures of performance and to address the impact of sources of variability and potential bias. Such research is sorely needed, but it seems to be lacking in most of the forensic disciplines that rely on subjective assessments of matching characteristics. These disciplines need to develop rigorous protocols to guide these subjective interpretations and pursue equally rigorous research and evaluation programs. The development of such research programs can benefit significantly from other areas, notably from the large body of research on the evaluation of observer performance in diagnostic medicine and from the findings of cognitive psychology on the potential for bias and error in human observers.

Microscopic hair comparison analysis, bite-mark opinion evidence, tool-mark comparison opinion evidence, and other subjective pattern-based types of forensic "science" should be abandoned and prior cases that rest on such evidence should be investigated for possible wrongful convictions. In 2015, the FBI admitted that almost every examiner in its elite hair comparison unit gave flawed testimony in almost every

---

[*] National Research Council, *Strengthening Forensic Science in the United States: A Path Forward*, National Academy of Sciences, 2009. https://www.acs.org/content/dam/acsorg/policy/acsonthehill/briefings/lasers/nas-report-summary.pdf.

trial they testified in for a two-decade period prior to 2000. Of twenty-eight FBI examiners studied, twenty-six overstated forensic "matches" in ways that supported the prosecution 95 percent of the time in a sample of 268 cases studied.* Shockingly, thirty-two of those defendants were sentenced to death and fourteen have already been executed. To its credit, the FBI has teamed with the Innocence Project and NACDL to review cases that may warrant motions for a new trial. But the vast majority of criminal prosecutions are at the state level, which utilize local and state crime lab analysts to present similar opinion testimony at trial. This federal level review highlights a strong likelihood that many more state prisoners may be wrongly convicted on the basis of such unreliable testimony.

What reforms would ensure fairer trials?

In the landmark 1963 *Brady v. Maryland* case, the United States Supreme Court ruled that prosecutors are required to share any exculpatory information they have. But the court also gave prosecutors a big loophole: They only have to disclose evidence that is "material" to the person's guilt or innocence. Because John Norsetter did not believe Fawn Cave and Debbie Holsomback when they called him to relate Stephen Armstrong's confession in New Mexico, he therefore could claim that he did not have to share that with me or with Ralph Armstrong, who was sitting in prison; he could argue that the new information was immaterial. After Steven Avery's first wrongful conviction in 1985, it turned out that the prosecutor had all along withheld information about another suspect, Gregory Allen, the very man who would be implicated eighteen years later through DNA testing. Leaving it to the prosecution to make such crucial decisions is like asking tennis

---

* Spencer S. Hsu, "FBI Admits Flaws in Hair Analysis over Decades," *Washington Post*, April 18, 2015. https://www.washingtonpost.com/local/crime/fbi-overstated forensic-hair-matches-in-nearly-all-criminal-trials-for-decades/2015/04/18/39c8d8c6-e515–11e4-b510–962fcfabc310_story.html.

players at Wimbledon to call their own foot faults. The criminal justice system encourages prosecutors to win at all costs. Many prosecutors resist those pressures, but some don't, and often they never get caught.

If prosecutors and law enforcement officials *do* get caught violating requirements, they should face appropriate consequences. A Texas prosecutor deliberately hid information about another suspect when he sent a man named Michael Morton to prison for killing his wife. Years later, Morton was cleared and the prosecutor's secret file was uncovered, showing that his young son had told the police his father wasn't home, that his wife's credit card was being used in another city soon after the killing, and that neighbors had seen a strange van parked repeatedly on the street. By then, the prosecutor was a sitting judge. This violation was so egregious that a legal team, led by Barry Scheck, successfully sought the prosecution and disbarment of the former prosecutor. Not only did he have to step down from the bench, he actually was forced to serve five days in jail. The notorious case of the Duke University Lacrosse team sexual assault prosecution involved a prosecutor's suppression of exonerating DNA results. The prosecutor, Mike Nifong, was forced to resign, but he had to serve only twenty-four hours in jail for his misconduct, and then only because the judge found him in contempt of court for misrepresentation to the judge. And these examples are extraordinarily rare reckonings.

The pendulum may finally be swinging in favor of the protection of a criminal defendant's due process rights. A huge scandal in Orange County, California, erupted after it became known that local prosecutors for decades were using jail informants to produce incriminating evidence against defendants in return for secret promises of privileges and leniency. In some instances prosecutors allegedly had jailhouse snitches secretly record defendants who were represented by attorneys, in gross violation of the right to counsel.[*] As a result of such episodes,

* Matt Ferner, "Orange County DA's Office Finally Acknowledges Jailhouse Informant Program Exists," *Huffington Post*, June 10, 2016. http://www.huffingtonpost.com/entry/orange-county-jailhouse-informant-program_us_575b236be4b0ced23ca81b2c.

a law was recently enacted in California making it a felony, punishable by up to three years in prison, for a prosecutor to alter or intentionally withhold evidence. But the potential for criminal punishment may be a weak deterrent if it is never enforced. Who will prosecute the prosecutors?

Civil liability may prove to be a better deterrent. Private attorneys could be encouraged to act as private attorneys general, ensuring that defendants' rights are not violated by overzealous prosecutors. Courts have held that prosecutors have broad immunity from civil lawsuits for things they did when carrying out their duties. While there are sound underlying reasons for this basic principle, so that prosecutors are not chilled from fulfilling the responsibilities of their office, that does not mean it should apply absolutely. But this immunity is pretty much ironclad with only one minor exception: If a case has not yet been charged, but a prosecutor is advising or directing law enforcement, he or she is therefore acting in more of an investigative role than in a prosecutorial capacity. In that case, the prosecutor has only "qualified immunity," which will not protect her from deliberate law violations.

In Ralph Armstrong's case, Norsetter "advised" a cop in 2006 to remove Charise Kamps's bathrobe belt from the clerk's office for testing, in violation of a standing court order. But because the case had already been charged—twenty-five years earlier—and was pending in the appeals system, the court ruled that Norsetter was functioning as a prosecutor and so was entitled to absolute immunity. Surely an exception is warranted when a court finds that a district attorney has acted in bad faith and destroyed exculpatory evidence. Change will only come about if prosecutors know that there are serious—and very likely to be enforced—consequences to their misconduct. Unfortunately, history shows that some prosecutors will continue to take risks if they know they can't be held civilly liable.

In civil cases, each side has the right to take statements from witnesses under oath. These are called depositions. In criminal cases, the prosecution often can compel witnesses before the trial to testify in front of a grand jury, yet the defense has no similar power in most states. Witnesses are under no obligation to speak with investigators or lawyers for the defense. Prosecutors point out that defendants cannot be compelled to testify at any time because of their Fifth Amendment rights, and for that reason, their lawyers should not be able to force witnesses to provide pretrial statements. Yet, in a civil case, only money or property is at stake; defense lawyers in criminal cases, when life and liberty are on the line, ought to be able to require, within reasonable limits, witnesses to testify before trial under oath. And if witnesses are "jailhouse snitches"—inmates who claim to have heard another prisoner make incriminating remarks—the favors they receive for their testimony should be disclosed at least to the defense, and to the jury if they testify at trial. History has shown them to be a perniciously unreliable source of evidence.

The defense should also have more freedom to introduce third-party liability—that's legalspeak for "other suspects." As things now stand in Wisconsin and a number of other states, the defense cannot adduce evidence that someone else may have committed the crime unless it can prove that said person had a direct connection to the offense, such as means and opportunity, and also that the person had a specific motive. This is bizarrely unbalanced, because the prosecution never *has* to show that a defendant had a specific motive to commit a crime, only that he or she did it. The state proved no reason whatsoever for Steven Avery to kill Teresa Halbach. Neither did anyone else have a reason to kill her, as far as we could tell. But that is beside the point. She could have been killed by someone else at the scrap yard—a family member, a customer, a delivery person—or one of the many other people who had the means and opportunity. Few of them had as many reasons *not* to commit the crime as Steven Avery. Despite this, Judge Willis ruled (and the Wisconsin court of appeals agreed) that we could not introduce any evidence that suggested someone else could have killed Teresa Halbach because we could not prove a motive.

That rule needs to be fixed. A person accused of a crime has a constitutional right to present a meaningful defense. That right is not absolute, however, and courts can exclude defense evidence that distracts the jury from its central focus by pointing the finger at another suspect who had no legitimate connection to the crime. But the rule in Wisconsin that precluded Avery from presenting other suspects goes too far. It arbitrarily denies the defense based on the victim's character in a given case. If the victim in a homicide was especially disliked or had many enemies, a number of suspects could have equal motives to kill. But a victim not known to have any real enemies would have few, if any, people with a motive to kill her. A person wrongly accused of a crime obviously did not choose the victim. If no one in the world had a motive to commit the murder, why should the defendant be blocked from telling the jurors that it is realistic for them to consider other suspects?

Perhaps one of the most urgent reforms is the reduction of sentences that are excessively punitive. We should change laws that impose mandatory minimums and allow judges and lawyers to use their discretion to fashion more sensible outcomes. Harshly punitive or minimum sentencing laws often arise as part of an effort to solve social problems, and this approach simply doesn't work. For instance, studies have found that most mental health care in the country is being provided by penal institutions. Mandatory minimums also provide the prosecution with too much leverage in the plea-bargain process; a defendant may not be guilty of the lesser crime offered, but he or she will accept a plea to avoid a worse outcome.

In a few places around the country, new courts are being established that take a problem-solving approach when cases are brought before them. One effort is the Red Hook Community Justice Center in Brooklyn, New York. The judge, defense lawyers, and prosecutors try to reach agreement on ways to handle the low-grade social problems of defendants who might otherwise keep getting arrested. Clinics in the courthouse can link them with social services on the spot. A study by the National Center for State Courts in 2013 found that a person sent to the regular criminal courts in downtown Brooklyn was fifteen times more likely to receive jail than a person who appeared in Red Hook. As for recidivism, adults sent to the regular court were 10 percent more likely to be arrested within two years, and juveniles 20 percent.

There are variations on this approach in other jurisdictions, and some in the defense bar are rightly concerned that these new courts may coercively require guilty pleas as the price of admission before services like drug treatment are offered.* These courts should allow defendants to obtain services before a guilty plea is entered, with the incentive that successful completion of programs will result in dismissal or significant reduction of the charges. These courts bear careful monitoring to ensure that the constitutional right to a trial is not denied, but it is good to see that we are beginning to break our dependence on incarceration. Such projects deserve public support.

So, too, do issues of policing reform. The videotaped shootings of unarmed black men and others have brought the question into sharp relief in the United States. Most of the injuries of poor police practice are not fatal or even physical: A study of police practices in Ferguson, Missouri, by the United States Department of Justice found that enforcement practices were not based on public safety concerns but on raising revenue for the municipality. Blacks were disproportionately fined, arrested, or subject to the use of force based on unlawful bias, not because they were committing more crime.† The conversation about policing cannot begin and end with lethal shootings.

---

* National Association of Criminal Defense Lawyers, "America's Problem-Solving Courts: The Criminal Costs of Treatment and the Case for Reform," September 2009. https://www.nacdl.org/criminaldefense.aspx?id=20191&libID=20161.

† M. Berman and W. Lowery, "The 12 Key Highlights from the DOJ's Scathing Ferguson Report," *Washington Post*, March 4, 2015. https://www.washingtonpost.com/news/post-nation/wp/2015/03/04/the-12-key-highlights-from-the-dojs-scathing ferguson-report/?utm_term=.a77625aff579.

How can we ensure everyone has access to quality legal assistance, regardless of their ability to pay?

People of all economic ranks break the law, but getting in trouble for it is primarily an affliction of poor people. A vast majority of defendants must rely on the right to lawyers provided "without cost." Fundamental as it is, this right is met on grudging terms by our society. States have contracts with public defenders' offices, and also a schedule of fees they can pay to the private lawyers who handle cases that cannot be taken by the public defenders. When I started practicing law in 1981, the private lawyers in Wisconsin were paid $35 an hour for time spent outside of court and $45 for time in court. It climbed to $50 an hour in the early 1990s. Then, astoundingly, in 1995, the rate was reduced to $40 an hour for time in court or out. And this is where the rate remains more than two decades later. It is the lowest hourly rate in the country, but rates are not much better elsewhere. Wisconsin is at the bottom of a shameful barrel; this is how much Len Kachinsky was paid for defending Brendan Dassey. However, money alone is not sufficient. Bar associations must provide training and set mandatory minimum standards before any lawyer can qualify to be on the indigent defense panels.

Governments must provide adequate pay and training for competent defense lawyers for the indigent. The modest taxpayer savings gained by chronic underfunding of indigent defense are far outweighed by the costs of this shortsightedness: wrongful conviction of the innocent, actual perpetrators remaining at large, and millions of dollars in civil lawsuit judgments.

CLOSING
STATEMENT

A question I get asked repeatedly, goes: Do you really think Steven Avery is innocent?

Yes, I believe Avery is innocent. This is my opinion, which I know is not worth very much, but my opinion is based on an assessment of the evidence. More important to me is one of the *real* questions posed by *Making a Murderer*. Could anyone have come away from that trial *without* reasonable doubt about Avery's involvement? If the answer is no, the jury should have found him not guilty. We don't have a verdict of innocent. It's guilty or not guilty. The state's burden is to present proof of guilty beyond a reasonable doubt. If the jurors had such doubts, they should have found him not guilty.

I see three significant pieces of incriminating evidence in the Avery case. One: His blood was found in her RAV4. Two: Her cremains were found in a burn pit in his backyard. Three: Her vehicle was found in the scrap yard where he worked.

On the other hand, he truly had no reason to kill Teresa Halbach. His life was on the verge of changing, and he was about to receive hundreds of thousands dollars in compensation from the legislature, a payment that was separate from any he might be awarded after the civil rights lawsuit that appeared to be going very well. It is true that the prosecutor does not have to establish a motive, but without one, the legitimate, unanswered questions about each piece of physical evidence make the absence of a motive all the more glaring.

The discovery of Teresa's vehicle by two women only twenty or thirty minutes after they walked onto the Avery property was peculiar, especially in the context of the phone call made by then sergeant Colborn a day or two before. Rather than the radio, which he knew was being recorded, he used a private cell phone to call in the license plate of the Halbach vehicle. Confronted with his own voice in court, and perhaps surprised that this call *had* been recorded, Colborn had no reasonable explanation, though he insisted that he was not looking at the vehicle.

If Steven Avery *had* committed the crime, why would he park Teresa's RAV4 so it was jutting into a lane instead of putting it within a row of cars where it would have been less obvious? And why was this vehicle still there, days later, less than one hundred yards or so from the car crusher? Evidence showed that Avery had been crushing other cars. Why not this one, too? Getting rid of it this way would surely have been more effective than an effort at camouflaging it with branches and boards, which was so poor it was, in effect, an invitation to look closer.

Like the car, when you look closely at the presence of the bones, you find details that suggest this was not what it seemed. Only about 40 percent of the victim's cremains were recovered, and not all of that from Steven Avery's backyard. Some cremains were about 150 yards away in a barrel in the backyard of a neighboring home. Also, in a quarry not far from the Avery property, what appeared to be bones from a female human were discovered, though they were unsuitable for testing and so could not be definitively identified.

And where were all of these bones burned? If the original burn site was *not* Steven Avery's burn pit, then it was clear to me that Avery was innocent, because no one would go to the trouble of destroying a body successfully elsewhere and then carrying part of it home. The state claimed that the majority of the recovered cremains were in Steven Avery's burn pit and argued that this showed the burning had taken place there. But their investigators, by taking no pictures of the bones as initially discovered, then shoveling them into boxes, destroyed a great deal of evidence that might have provided clues about which of the locations was the original site. They also barred the county coroner from the scene and only alerted the state's forensic anthropologist—an expert in investigating burn sites—after the bones were in a box and on their way to her office. The Canadian expert we called, a witness who previously had only ever testified for the Crown, raised serious doubts about the state's theory. In cases where burned bones were found in more than one site, he said, the place with the greatest quantity of cremains was the secondary location—that is, the bones had been moved there from the original burn location. That also is common sense. If someone was going to move the bones to obscure the original site, it would make no sense for them to leave the majority in place and move only a few elsewhere. Why, then, were some of Teresa Halbach's bones in the burn barrel? The state never answered this question.

I've already discussed the availability of Steven Avery's blood vial as a source of the stains in the RAV4, explained why Ken Kratz's claim of "sweat DNA" is scientifically impossible, and shared the very innocent and plausible explanation for the discovery of Avery's DNA on the hood latch—that is, if it wasn't planted like the blood seems to have been. The remarkable discovery of the ignition key for the RAV4 in Avery's bedroom was also very odd. It was not found until the *seventh* search, and it was found by one of the officers who had been deposed just a few weeks earlier in the civil rights lawsuit. And there was no trace whatsoever of Teresa Halbach's DNA on the key, even though she presumably handled it many times a day for six years. Only a *tiny* quantity of Steven Avery's DNA was present, consistent with someone planting it by rubbing a toothbrush, or any number of other DNA-laden personal items, that could easily have been found in his residence.

Steven Avery's new attorney, Kathleen Zellner, has filed a motion asking for a range of biological tests unavailable at the time we tried his case. Many of them have to do with advances in blood test science, such as ways to calculate or estimate the age of DNA. Throughout our representation of Steven Avery, we were fastidious about ensuring that evidence was not consumed by existing testing methods, in anticipation of newer, better ones that might come along that might not only exclude him but also shed some light on the identity of the real culprit or culprits. Because if Steven Avery didn't kill Teresa Halbach, and I believe he did not, then who did?

That's a reasonable question, and one we gave a great deal of thought to. In a motion we made before Avery's trial, we listed others who had ample opportunity to kill Teresa Halbach, but we did not specifically accuse anyone. However, as you'll remember, Judge Willis did not permit us to explore those possibilities at trial. I've never believed that Teresa Halbach's body was burned in Steven Avery's burn pit. My theory is that she was burned elsewhere, and the cremains were gathered up in a burn barrel—a dime a dozen out in the country—and then dumped into Steven Avery's burn pit, most likely at night. Because it was dark, the culprit or culprits didn't realize there were still bones in the bottom of the barrel, which they put on the neighboring property next to three barrels that are normally there.

Many intriguing alternative theories have been discussed, and continue to be, in great detail on social media and websites such as Reddit. Other individuals who were not named in court documents warrant close scrutiny, but it would be unfair to accuse or implicate people in a one-sided forum. We have already seen far too much of that from the sheriff and prosecutor in the Avery case.

Speaking of which: What about the claims that Ken Kratz has made in various forums about all of the "incriminating" evidence either not covered in the documentary or not allowed at the trial? My reading of the record shows Mr. Kratz is neither careful about the facts nor prudent about what he says. For example, Teresa Halbach was a professional photographer whose assignments for *Auto Trader* magazine had brought her to the Avery scrap yard on several occasions to take pictures of cars that were being offered for sale. Kratz has claimed that on one of these occasions, Steven Avery greeted Halbach at his door wearing only a towel, and this frightened her so much that he thereafter had to "lure" her to his property by hiding his identity—such as by giving the *Auto Trader* office a fake name instead of his own when he called to make an appointment. The underlying assumption, that the towel incident made Teresa Halbach fearful of Avery, was belied by the testimony of the *Auto Trader* receptionist, Dawn Pliszka, called by Kratz to support his argument. Judge Willis first heard Pliszka's testimony outside the presence of the jury, and he found that it did not support Kratz's claim and that it was irrelevant and inadmissible. Pliszka said that in the course of a routine brief call with Teresa Halbach, somewhere around October 10, the two of them had been talking about "different things that had happened during our day that were unusual, or funny, or different customers and things like that."

She testified Teresa said that once she had a customer who came out in a towel.

A. The only—I just said, really, and she said, yeah, and she said, yeah, and she laughed and just said kind of, ewww, you know.

Q. Okay. You said kind of what?

A. Ewww.

Q. Ewww.

A. Yeah, just that.

Dawn agreed that Teresa just laughed it off as something she thought funny. She never complained that it made her fearful or intimidated in any way. Moreover, she said that although this conversation had taken place around October 10, it was very brief and came up in regular chit-chat about business. She did not know how long prior to that date the towel incident really occurred. Judge Willis found that it could have been weeks or months earlier, as far back as June, and thus it had little relevance to Kratz's argument. Teresa Halbach had been to the Avery yard many times during that interval, so there was no indication that the towel incident made her fearful or otherwise drove her to avoid it.

Pliszka also explained why Avery had left his sister's name, not his own, when he called *Auto Trader* for the appointment—the vehicle was Barb's van, titled in her name, "B. Janda." He'd asked the receptionist to send "'that photographer who had been out there before. He was selling a minivan and needed her to take photos,'" and he gave the address, which was on "Avery Road." When she spoke with Teresa Halbach later, Pliszka testified, Halbach had said, "'Yeah I'm able to get that photo. And by the way it's the Avery brothers and I'm on my way'"—so Teresa clearly knew where she was going. Pliszka confirmed that the phone number was in that area of the state to which Teresa Halbach was assigned, so she was always the photographer who went to the Avery yard.

Finally, as Dawn Pliszka testified, *Auto Trader* records also showed that on October 10, Steven Avery had made a private arrangement with Teresa Halbach to take a photo of a vehicle he had for sale. This was so standard a practice that the magazine categorized them as "hustle shots," which paid more than an assignment she received from the office. It seemed to indicate that Steven Avery had Teresa's cell phone number (as records later proved), which meant he could just have called her directly on October 31. Pliszka even agreed that, if he had wanted to kill Teresa Halbach that day, Steven Avery could have reached her directly for a private appointment instead of calling the *Auto Trader* office and leaving an easy trail to his address.

So, while it's true that none of this testimony was included in *Making a Murderer*, it is not true that this testimony was powerful evidence for the prosecution. On the contrary, the evidence concerning the towel incident failed to support Kratz's argument to the judge for relevance, and it fails to support his post-documentary claims that the filmmaker's omission of it proves their bias against the state.

The same is true of Kratz's claim that the bullet found in Steven Avery's garage, with Teresa Halbach's DNA on it, was conclusively proven to have been fired from the gun found in Avery's bedroom. William Newhouse, the Wisconsin State Crime Laboratory analyst who conducted the tool-mark comparison examination, did express the opinion that the bullet was fired from that particular rifle, but his opinion is far from conclusive.

Tool marks are generated when a hard object (the tool) comes into contact with a relatively softer object, and the basic premise of so-called ballistics theory is that certain "tool marks" found on fired bullets or casings—the striae, or scratches, that a gun barrel can score on bullets, or the mark that the breech face of a gun can leave on fired casings—can be linked to particular types of guns and compared to one specific gun through class, subclass, and individual characteristics.[*] However, a 2008 National Academy of Sciences report concluded that this premise of uniqueness has not been scientifically established. "A significant amount of research would be needed to scientifically determine the degree to which firearms-related toolmarks are unique or even to quantitatively characterize the probability of uniqueness,"[†] it cautions, declaring that "the validity of the fundamental assumptions of uniqueness and reproducibility of firearms-related toolmarks has not yet been fully demonstrated." Like hair, handwriting, and bite-mark comparisons—and *unlike* fingerprint and DNA evidence—there is no rule by which an examiner can declare an exclusion if there is a single difference between two samples. Studies have shown only 21–38 percent of the marks will match up on bullets fired *from the very same gun*,[‡] yet when an analyst like Newhouse compares a bullet and rifle, he may declare it a "match" when only 21 percent of the markings on the bullet match the gun.[§] In other words, almost 80 percent of the marks *do not* have to match.

On cross-examination of Newhouse, the jury was shown photographs that Newhouse took through a comparison microscope with a test-fired bullet from Steven Avery's rifle on one side and the bullet found in Avery's garage on the other. Newhouse was forced to admit

---

[*] A. Schwartz, "A Systemic Challenge to the Reliability and Admissibility of Firearms and Toolmark Identification," *Columbia Science and Technology Law Review* 6 (2005). http://www.stlr.org/cite.cgi?volume=6&article=2.

[†] National Resource Council/National Academy of Sciences, *Ballistics Report*, National Academies Press, 2008. https://www.nap.edu/read/12162/chapter/2#3.

[‡] Newhouse testimony, Avery Trial Day 14 at 125. [Full cite TK]

[§] Ibid.

that the bullet he claimed matched Steven Avery's rifle showed "a great deal of differences" from the bullet he test-fired from that rifle.[*] Newhouse also testified that his lab protocol required two analysts to examine a bullet comparison, but as to the critical bullet found in Avery's garage he had no written documentation to prove that anyone else reviewed his subjective conclusions.[†]

Finally, the rifle found in Steven Avery's bedroom, a Marlin Glenfield Model 60 .22 caliber rifle, is among the most common in the world. Tens of thousands have been manufactured over several decades.[‡] The very same model .22 caliber rifle was also found in the house where Bobby Dassey lived, but that gun was not even compared by the state's analyst to any of the bullets or casings found in Steven Avery's garage.[§]

Newhouse's testimony was not included in *Making a Murderer*, but if it had been, it would have shown that the tool-mark evidence was far from the powerful conclusive evidence Kratz claimed it was.

However, there aren't always as many indicators of a client's innocence as there were—at least to me—in the Steven Avery case. At cocktail parties, people often ask me how I can defend people who I know are guilty. In truth, at a personal level it is easier to defend someone I know is guilty than someone who I believe is innocent. I could screw up. I could make a mistake. And because of me, an innocent person could end up in prison. The pressure of representing an innocent person is grindingly intense.

In movies or TV shows, it's common to see a defendant walk in, throw money on the table, and say something like, "I'm guilty, but you're going to get me off, and I'm going to lie in court and get away with it." But real life as a criminal defense lawyer isn't remotely like this. The vast majority of people who are guilty admit their guilt. In

---

[*] Ibid. at 155.

[†] Ibid. at 170.

[‡] Ibid. at 147.

[§] Ibid. at 146.

fact, they've often admitted it before coming to me. The more important questions for me as their lawyer are: What are they guilty of? Are
they overcharged? What is the appropriate punishment or resolution?
A big part of my job is to understand why they need a lawyer in the
first place. Some courts are so busy, they run one case after the other
and defendants become nameless. The defense lawyer's job is to make
the human case, as much as or more than the legal case, in court. A
person with an addiction needs treatment, not jail. If you deal with the
root cause of the problem, they won't reoffend and may instead become
contributing members of society. Even people who have done things
that are wrong, or hurtful to others, still deserve to be treated as human
beings. They can still be redeemed.

During my first year in Milwaukee at the public defender's office,
after handling an endless stream of misdemeanor cases, I finally got to
represent a client on a felony charge—the big time. He was out on bail,
but one day he did not show up to court. I called and called, and got
no answer.

Finally, I heard a groggy voice on the line.

"Oh?" said the defendant. "I had court today? I overslept."

I thought, *How can you sleep? How could you not remember that this
was your day in court on a serious felony?*

Gradually, it dawned on me. This court date may have been the
most important event in my young professional life, but my client had
other things going on. He did not have a job, and he had a family to
support.

As a public defender, a lot of what you do is social work, connecting
people to the right resources to help them get ahead. You do what you
can to try to pull people out of bad situations, but sometimes it doesn't
work. There are times when all you can do is put a Band-Aid on the
problem and hope. In Victor Frankl's famous memoir, *Man's Search for
Meaning*, he describes how he survived in a Nazi concentration camp
by refusing to let his captors take away his spirit and faith. That's what
pulled him through. I kind of approach my job that way. I've shared
that book with clients.

If defendants have some sort of faith in their lives, in my experience they are much more likely to weather the difficult times than if they don't. This is true with the families of defendants, too. Even people sentenced to life without parole can contribute to the world if they have some belief in something bigger than themselves. Faith is often central to rehabilitation. I try to encourage people to open up to the possibilities of faith. They don't always take my advice. That's fine. They have to do it for themselves. I had to find my way back to my own faith. Having cancer and surviving it sharpened my focus on my job as my vocation in life; it was, even before I got sick, but I just didn't appreciate it as much.

I've always been drawn to the underdog. The defense of citizens accused of crimes, some of them very serious, is intertwined with my faith and with my belief that every human being matters. Life is sacred. We can't just throw out the bad or ignore the poor or the people who are disliked or the people who live on the wrong side of the tracks. Even in towns where the trains never run.

In the summer of 2016, a tall, broad-shouldered man with silver hair stood outside a Morton's Steakhouse in Chicago, leaning against the wall as he smoked a cigarette. The man wore a light summer suit and sunglasses. His name was Ralph Armstrong.

The state of New Mexico had finally agreed to release him from prison, although he remains on parole indefinitely from his conviction there in 1972, eight years before the murder of Charise Kamps, and even now wears a GPS ankle bracelet. He was in Chicago for a deposition in his lawsuit—he was suing officials in Madison for keeping him in prison nearly three full decades for a crime he had not committed and covering up evidence that showed his innocence. He would not be recognized as the man with the long, flowing hair arrested for the murder of Charise Kamps thirty-six years ago. Ralph Armstrong had been my client for fifteen years, about half the time he was in prison, and almost from the outset we had evidence that pointed to his innocence. Again and again, the courts slammed the door on him. We pushed back. Finally, that incredible e-mail arrived just as I was beginning the Steven Avery trial.

Like modern-day Rip Van Winkles, people released after decades in prison find a very different world. When Ralph Armstrong was arrested in 1980, almost no one could have had a computer at home or on a desktop; there were no cell phones, no World Wide Web, and no streaming movies. But Armstrong figured it out, became a successful car salesman, and built a new life for himself. Most sixty-four-year-old men are thinking about retirement after a long working career. Denied that career, Ralph is just getting started. My work with him is finished, but I was delighted to get a photograph of him outside that steakhouse in Chicago.

Ralph also sued John Norsetter and the Madison Police Department detective and Wisconsin State Crime Laboratory analyst who violated the court's order and destroyed the exculpatory semen stain. As I mentioned earlier, under a legal rule that gives prosecutors absolute immunity from a civil rights case for conduct they commit in the capacity of their official duties, Norsetter managed to get most of the claims against him dismissed. Even though the judge found that Norsetter deliberately violated the court's order in bad faith and destroyed the evidence that may have proven Ralph not guilty, American law protects him from being sued. Other claims remain and the civil rights lawsuit is still pending as I write.

Nearly three centuries ago, Alexander Hamilton said that habeas corpus—a power granted to federal judges to decide if a prisoner is being unlawfully held—was a "bulwark" of the United States Constitution because it gave the judiciary the ability to thwart the illegal use of power by other branches of government. Throughout American history, the writ has protected people from government abuses: After the Civil War, it was used to stop Southern states from jailing freed slaves on trumped-up charges, and during World War II writs of habeas corpus freed people who were illegally interned. Clarence Earl Gideon, a drifter in Florida with only an eighth-grade education, was charged with burglarizing a pool hall. He asked the judge to appoint a lawyer for him but was turned down and then found guilty. Gideon asked the Florida appellate courts to overturn his conviction but lost there, too. Finally, he made a handwritten plea to the United States Supreme Court for a writ of habeas corpus. The court granted him the writ, declaring that poor people had the right to counsel in criminal cases.

However, in the first decades of the twenty-first century, such writs are rarely granted: Fewer than one-half of one percent of the prisoners who apply for them are successful. All the way through the Wisconsin appellate court system, Brendan Dassey's lawyers pleaded for judges to overturn his conviction, which was based entirely on the statements that were extracted from him without a parent or lawyer present. The Wisconsin courts excused the behavior of the investigators, going item by item through the interrogations and finding no fault with any individual statement or promise they made.

The memo Dean and I had written in 2007 showed how these threats, claims, promises, and lies were all connected and how they led to the incriminating statements Brendan had made. It was disappointing that no Wisconsin state court had the guts to use the facts we showed, or those presented by Brendan's attorneys in post-conviction motions, to apply the law in Brendan's case and find the interrogation of him on March 1, 2006, to have been unconstitutionally coercive and therefore unreliable. But Wisconsin state court judges are elected, and apparently none wanted to take an unpopular stand in a case of this magnitude.

Federal judges are appointed, not elected, and history—most vividly in recent times, during the civil rights battles of the 1960s—shows that federal courts are often the last bastion of protection for individual rights. Almost a decade after our memo exposed the hollow, illicit core of Brendan's interrogation, Steven A. Drizin and Laura Nirider, lawyers from the Center on Wrongful Convictions of Youth at Northwestern University, took the Brendan Dassey case into the federal courts. Magistrate William E. Duffin issued a ninety-one-page decision granting a writ of habeas corpus to Brendan. His reasoning was that the coercive part of the interrogation should not be looked at in isolation but as part of a relentless tide that carried Dassey far from reality as he understood it.

Duffin wrote:

> Especially when the investigators' promises, assurances, and threats of negative consequences are assessed in conjunction with Dassey's age, intellectual deficits, lack of experience in dealing with the police, the absence of a parent, and other relevant personal characteristics, the free will of a reasonable person in Dassey's position would have been overborne. . . .
>
> No single statement by the investigators, if viewed in isolation, rendered Dassey's statement involuntary. But when assessed collectively and cumulatively . . . it is clear how the investigators' actions amounted to deceptive interrogation tactics that overbore Dassey's free will.

Duffin did not reverse the conviction on the grounds of Len Kachinsky's ineffective assistance of counsel, but he did make these observations: "Although it probably does not need to be stated, it will be: Kachinsky's conduct was inexcusable both tactically and ethically. It is one thing for an attorney to point out to a client how deep of a hole the client is in. But to assist the prosecution in digging that hole deeper is an affront to the principles of justice that underlie a defense attorney's vital role in the adversarial system."[*]

The magistrate ordered the state to release Brendan or retry him within ninety days. Just as the state did in Ralph Armstrong's case, the prosecution in Brendan's case refuses to admit the mistakes in the interrogation. As I write, the state has appealed the federal judge's ruling to the Seventh Circuit Court of Appeals in Chicago. Meanwhile,

---

[*] *Dassey v. Dittmann*, No. 14-CV-1310, 2016 WL 4257386, at *20 (E.D. Wis. Aug. 12, 2016).

Brendan's lawyers are trying to get him released pending that appellate court's decision.

Unfortunately, Steven Avery's appellate lawyers did not seek habeas corpus relief, so the objective review of federal judges was never applied in his case. But his new lawyer, Kathleen Zellner, who took on his case in early 2016, has asked permission to deploy an array of new tests on the case evidence. We told Judge Willis in 2007 that we wanted that evidence to be available when testing technology had advanced. That day may be coming.

You sometimes hear when an innocent person is freed, a wrongful conviction recognized, that these reversals of history show that "the system is working." It took twenty-nine years for that day to come for Ralph Armstrong, eighteen years for Steven Avery after his first wrongful conviction, and ten years for Brendan Dassey—now more because of the state's appeal. I don't know if that day will come again for Steven Avery, or when. So many courts and officials ducked their duties and kept these men incarcerated that we are only kidding ourselves if we say that these cases prove the system fixes its own mistakes. That is the illusion of justice. I confess to feeling a sense of vindication from the federal court's recognition of what we argued about Brendan's interrogation so many years ago, but this should not be mistaken for satisfaction. It has been a day too long in coming, a run too far to make.

But there is no choice other than to keep going.

Acknowledgments

The idea for this book has been simmering for several years, but it got off the ground through the efforts of my literary agent, Flip Brophy at Sterling Lord Literistic, Inc. She provided sage advice and opened doors for me I could not have opened on my own. At Harper, my editor, Hannah Wood, worked tirelessly and had an unerring eye for the vision and structure of this book. She clearly understands the importance of the work of defense lawyers in our dysfunctional justice system, which is to demand that all individuals be treated with fairness and humanity. Special thank also to Harper's Heather Drucker, and I'm grateful to David Hirshey, formerly at Harper, for his help in the early stages of this process. Jim Dwyer's advice and assistance were also priceless.

I'm especially grateful to my trusted friend and colleague in criminal defense Dean Strang. His call to me in February 2016 set in motion all the incredible experiences that grew out of my representation of Steven Avery and the Making a Murderer documentary and its aftermath. Film makers Laura Ricciardi and Moira Demos richly deserve the Emmy awards their groundbreaking documentary received. They started a phenomenal international conversation about justice like no one who has come before them.

I'm very lucky that Dudley Williams is both my very good friend and law partner. For twenty-three years, we've had the pleasure of sharing a law practice dedicated to the best representation possible for clients of all walks of life who come to us in times of need. Dudley is atop a long list of associates, colleagues, and mentors in my work and professional associations deserving of my thanks. My assistant, Barbara Steffel, deserves special acknowledgment for the many ways she has supported me and my work. Her keen attention to detail and infallible instincts have rescued me more than once.

Barry Scheck has been a good friend and colleague for many years, though I never thought when I said yes to his request for assistance I would be signing on for fifteen years in the Ralph Armstrong case. I had great support from his Innocence Project lawyers David Menschel, Colin Starger, and Ezekial Edwards, and many bright law students. Also, the keen eyes of my student intern Kenzie Kilb helped find crucial facts in Armstrong's twenty-year-old case record. Another student intern of mine, Maria Lyon, provided critical support and organization of hundreds of tips from viewers of Making a Murderer when I was in danger of drowning from thousands of contacts.

My speaking agent, Zach Mullinax of Creative Speakers Worldwide in Minneapolis, helped me and Dean reach thousands of members of the public this past year in more than forty cities in the United States and around the world who thirst for fair justice for Steven Avery, Brendan Dassey, and thousands of others like them in their own communities. They provided many thought-provoking questions, which helped shape parts of this book.

Ralph Armstrong and many more of my clients put their faith in me, and I hope they feel I gave it my all, no matter the outcome. Steven Avery and his family, including Delores and Allan Avery, also put their faith and hopes in me and Dean, and despite the outcome of the trials, both of us remain dedicated to see the unjust convictions of Steven and Brendan overturned.

My parents, Walter and Margaret Buting, gave me the education and foundation of Catholic faith that sustains me in this challenging but rewarding career as a criminal defense lawyer. My siblings, Tom, John, Marianne, Mike, and Rosemary; their spouses, Terry, Bjorn, and Rina; and my deceased brother, Joe, taught me the importance of strong family support in all the challenges of life. They have always been there for me.

My children are a constant source of joy and pride as they grow into their own adult lives: Stephen, in a seminary in Rome discerning the call to Catholic priesthood, and Grace, embarking on a career in the entertainment industry in Los Angeles.

Finally, my wife, Kathy Stilling, is my muse in so much of my life and the real force behind my writing this book, including her countless manuscript reviews. I count myself lucky to work with Kathy every day as my law partner where we can seamlessly blend both our family and work lives. Her constant love and encouragement are the primary reason for my success.

About the Author

Jerome F. Buting is a shareholder in the Brookfield, Wisconsin, law firm of Buting, Williams & Stilling, S.C. He received his undergraduate degree in forensic studies from Indiana University and his law degree from the University of North Carolina at Chapel Hill. He was board director of the National Association of Criminal Defense Lawyers, past president of the Wisconsin Association of Criminal Defense Lawyers, and chair of the Wisconsin State Bar Criminal Law Section. He lectures worldwide and is frequently sought for his legal expertise. He is also the recipient of the Fierce Advocate Award from the John Jay College of Criminal Justice, the James Joyce Award from University College Dublin, and the Trinity College Dublin Praeses Elit Award.